Crimes of Dissent

ALTERNATIVE CRIMINOLOGY SERIES
General Editor: Jeff Ferrell

Pissing on Demand:
Workplace Drug Testing and the Rise of the Detox Industry
Ken Tunnell

Empire of Scrounge:
Inside the Urban Underground of Dumpster Diving,
Trash Picking, and Street Scavenging
Jeff Ferrell

Prison, Inc.:
A Convict Exposes Life inside a Private Prison
by K.C. Carceral, edited by Thomas J. Bernard

The Terrorist Identity:
Explaining the Terrorist Threat
Michael P. Arena and Bruce A. Arrigo

Terrorism as Crime:
From Oklahoma City to Al-Qaeda and Beyond
Mark S. Hamm

Our Bodies, Our Crimes:
The Policing of Women's Reproduction in America
Jeanne Flavin

Graffiti Lives:
Beyond the Tag in New York's Urban Underground
Gregory J. Snyder

Crimes of Dissent:
Civil Disobedience, Criminal Justice, and the Politics of Conscience
Jarret S. Lovell

Crimes of Dissent

*Civil Disobedience, Criminal Justice,
and the Politics of Conscience*

Jarret S. Lovell

NEW YORK UNIVERSITY PRESS
New York and London

NEW YORK UNIVERSITY PRESS
New York and London
www.nyupress.org

Library of Congress Cataloging-in-Publication Data
Lovell, Jarret S.
Crimes of dissent : civil disobedience, criminal justice, and
the politics of conscience / Jarret S. Lovell.
p. cm. — (Alternative criminology series)
Includes bibliographical references and index.
ISBN-13: 978-0-8147-5226-5 (cl : alk. paper)
ISBN-10: 0-8147-5226-8 (cl : alk. paper)
ISBN-13: 978-0-8147-5227-2 (pb : alk. paper)
ISBN-10: 0-8147-5249-7 (pb : alk. paper)
1. Civil disobedience—United States. 2. Social movements—
United States. 3. Crime—United States. I. Title.
JC328.3.L68   2009
303.6'2—dc22   2009005919

New York University Press books are printed on acid-free paper, and
their binding materials are chosen for strength and durability. We
strive to use environmentally responsible suppliers and materials to
the greatest extent possible in publishing our books.

Manufactured in the United States of America

c 10 9 8 7 6 5 4 3 2 1
p 10 9 8 7 6 5 4 3 2 1

Contents

Preface   vii

Acknowledgments   xiii

1   Crime and Dissent   1

2   Society and Its Discontents   31

3   Dissent as "Pure" Crime   65

4   Policing Dissent   103

5   Working the System   139

6   The Impact of Dissent   175

Appendix: Activist Profiles   207

Notes   215

Index   231

About the Author   239

Preface

Most of the time, though, we're bored to tears by eggheads with no
criminal practice of their own.
                              —Alain Mabanckou, *African Psycho* (2003)

Alain Mabanckou's novel *African Psycho* tells the story of Gregoire, a
would-be serial killer who not only is consumed by an unhealthy fascina-
tion with crime but who also is filled with an overpowering rage toward
experts who purport to understand the mind of a criminal. Amid countless literary jabs that critique everything from a crime-obsessed media
to the failings of the police, this protagonist of sorts saves his harshest
lashings for the most loathsome of all crime watchers: the criminologist.
"They claim to be analyzing crimes, but have they committed even one?
What kind of nonsense is that?" Declaring the writings put forth by academics to be nothing but "a lot of nonsense," he vows to ignore criminology outright until the day when "criminals, real ones, start teaching their
subject themselves."[1]

Should the fictional Gregoire be given the chance to hold these pages
in his hands, he probably would be satisfied with its approach to the study
of crime. There are no accounts of murder, bloodlust, or dismemberment,
to be sure. There are, however, plenty of passages detailing the actions of
persons—criminals if you will—who deliberately and publicly violate the
law as expressions of protest against perceived racial, economic, or other
social injustices. Moreover, these accounts are provided not by second-
party observers but by the very persons who perform these transgressions.
Indeed, both as a criminologist and as this book's author, I have been neither a dispassionate observer nor a detached bystander of the phenomena
at hand. Instead, I have been an active participant in some of the very
transgressions detailed throughout the chapters that follow.

And I am not alone in my dissent. In recent years, concern over such issues as corporate globalization, third-world debt, environmental degradation, and the rise of militarism has been manifested in large-scale public demonstrations unseen since the civil-rights and anti-Vietnam movements. In Seattle 1999, thousands of activists comprising environmental, labor, and human rights organizations took to the streets in opposition of policies set in motion by the World Trade Organization (WTO). On February 15, 2003, millions of people in over one hundred cities worldwide protested against an impending war in Iraq. And in November of each year, activists from both secular and religious peace networks trespass onto the military base in Fort Benning, Georgia, calling for the U.S. government to shut down the training school formerly known as School of the Americas (SOA). These are but a few of the displays of dissent staged by activists around the world who find themselves increasingly dissatisfied with politics as usual.

Among the tactics used by more seasoned activists organizing for social change are those of civil disobedience, nonviolent resistance, and direct action. Requiring the deliberate and public violation of established law, these strategies of dissent pose numerous risks to the participants including arrest, criminal prosecution, and the stigmatizing effects of being labeled a social deviant. The staging of civil disobedience also creates numerous challenges to law-enforcement personnel, who often find themselves unprepared or unaccustomed to managing these forms of protests, especially when they involve a large number of people. Judges, too, must decide whether, or how, to impose punishments on protesters who clearly violated the law but who do not pose a risk to the public and who are not likely to be amenable to rehabilitation by any means of incarceration.

Clearly, the study of dissent has relevance to people concerned with the politics of crime and the curtailment of deviance. Yet despite the apparent importance of social protest to the study of crime and law enforcement, research into this important topic within the disciplines of criminology and criminal justice is neglectfully scarce. To address the paucity of scholarship examining the intersection of crime and dissent, this book adopts a multidisciplinary and multimethodological approach to aid in an understanding of the violation of law as a means of attaining justice. First, it draws on lessons from history, social and political theory, literature, and religious studies to present an overview of the longstanding motivations and rationalizations for civil disobedience. It also culls information from activist training manuals, anarchist publications, mainstream news outlets, and alternative media to place dissent in a contemporary political context.

Second, this book makes use of my own experiences as someone "guilty" of committing various crimes of dissent. Indeed, as an activist, I have been arrested for my involvement in a sit-in at the district office of a Southern California congressperson who would not pledge to end funding for the war in Iraq; I was arrested in Minneapolis while attempting to serve a mock arrest warrant to the chairman of a munitions firm whose company manufactures landmines and cluster bombs, allegedly in violation of international humanitarian law; on the sixtieth anniversary of the bombing of Hiroshima, I was one of approximately two hundred activists arrested for trespassing onto the grounds of the Nevada Nuclear Test Site—a location that has been dubbed the most bombed place on the planet. And on the dawn of the 2004 Republican National Convention (RNC) in New York City, I was arrested and detained for thirty-six hours after failing to disperse from what police deemed to be an unlawful assembly on a sidewalk. Of course, I have also engaged in various acts of dissent that have not resulted in my arrest. I have used my body to block the entrance to military recruitment centers in protest of the wars in Afghanistan and Iraq; I have protested the (ab)use of animals in the circus; under an enormous police presence, I have rallied against the policies of the World Economic Forum and corporate globalization; and I have marched to defend the content of a progressive, listener-supported radio station. These and other protests I have performed were done as acts of conscience rather than for research purposes. That my research reflects my preexisting commitment to social change is a benefit for which I am grateful.

Third, this book complements the discussion of political theory and my own dissent with a chronicle of the experiences of twenty-one activists from across the political spectrum who have transgressed the law as a means of attaining justice. Throughout the book, these activists provide the reader with insight into the short-term and long-term personal and social consequences that may result from the public display of dissent. They also shed light on their views regarding how justice "works" (or does not work) in our political and judicial system. Finally, they document their interactions with police, with the courts, and with corrections systems while detailing the various strategies they employ as they traverse the criminal justice system.

The activist interviews were conducted between the spring of 2005 and the winter of 2007. I used a snowball sampling method to identify individuals working within activist communities who were actively engaged in illegal dissent. This sampling method ensured that interviewees represented a range of issues from across the political spectrum.[2] To initiate the snowball referral chain, I contacted three seasoned protesters who are familiar to me; each was actively engaged in civil disobedience, nonviolent resistance, and direct action. These initial contacts were persons respected by various groups involved in social protest; indeed, two of the three initial contacts have published articles and guidebooks of sorts on how to carry out activism. Each of these participants provided me with referrals to additional individuals. To ensure representation from across issues and ideologies, I then contacted a fourth individual by phone who is well-known in pro-life/anti-abortion activism and who not only agreed to an interview but also provided me with additional referrals. All interviews followed a rough template that was updated as data collection progressed.[3] Roughly half the interviews were conducted face-to-face, often at the site of community organizing or organizational meetings or at the participant's home. All other interviews were conducted by telephone. Interviews ranged in length from one to two hours and were recorded for future transcription using a digital voice recorder.

Because many of the activists interviewed for this book have been arrested in excess of fifty times during their careers, it was hard for me to get a precise estimate of the number of crimes represented in the interview pool. For example, one activist told me, "I *think* I've been arrested fifty-nine times for nuclear weapons issues," and an opponent of abortion responded to my question about the number of times he had been arrested by saying, "I don't have any idea. I've spent days, weeks, and months in jail . . . fifty to sixty times, all over the country." The best answer that an animal rights activist could give me was that he had been arrested "*at least*" a dozen times that he could recall. Suffice it to say that collectively the information presented in the pages that follow is based on *hundreds* of actions stemming from acts of dissent ranging from the blocking of medical centers where abortions are performed to the blocking of a department store that sells fur. My best guess is that the interviewees are responsible for over 450 arrestable acts of dissent and for countless other acts of dissent that do not result in an arrest.

Still, the voices featured in this book do not reflect a random or even a representative sample of activist communities or of protest actions.

Indeed, as has been the case with other studies on social movements within the United States, the activists who agreed to recorded interviews represent a racially homogeneous sample, with all but one activist being white.[4] Moreover, most of them can be considered middle class, though an assessment of income was somewhat harder to measure because many participants worked for nonprofit, religious, or activist organizations and individually did not earn middle-class incomes. Instead, they relied on the goodwill of spouses, family, and friends whose donations allowed them to live somewhat comfortably. Finally, most of the participants were highly educated. Two held doctorates and several held master's degrees. A discussion of whether activists as a population represent a demographically diverse constituency appears later in the text. For now, the reader is cautioned not to generalize from the narratives contained in the chapters that follow.

A final word about the activists featured in this text is in order. Although civil disobedience signifies a public display of dissent, for various personal reasons, some of the participants in this study have requested that I conceal their identities within this publication. To oblige them, I refer to them by pseudonyms, indicated by the use of only first names, which appear in quotation marks when they are introduced. Also, when necessary, quotations from recorded interviews have been edited for clarity. Finally, the appendix to this text provides brief biographical sketches of some of the activists interviewed for this book. What follows is my best attempt to document the patterns and perspectives of seasoned activists who are willing to transgress the law in the pursuit of social justice. It is my hope that the reader will gain a better understanding of (and sympathy for) those who are committed to social justice—however individually defined. Political opinions aside, I dedicate this work to them.

Acknowledgments

In the vernacular of activism, an affinity group is a social network that serves as a protester's primary source of support, encouragement, and solidarity. As both an author and activist, I have been fortunate to have had the support of my own ever-expanding affinity group. I would like to acknowledge these important members whose support has made this book possible.

The idea to convert my activism into a uniquely criminological academic endeavor stemmed primarily from a series of conversations with Dr. Shelly Arsneault, who is not only my colleague at California State University, Fullerton, but who is also a close friend. If this book could be said to have a coauthor, it is undoubtedly she who is responsible for the best these pages have to offer, while I am to blame for its limitations. I also thank all my other Fullerton colleagues, who have provided me with much guidance. And Jeff Ferrell has for me become a mentor of sorts by allowing for the possibility of such a thing as "alternative" criminology and by supporting the idea for this book. Thank you.

Outside academia, I am privileged with a close circle of friends who support my efforts. It was many years ago (over a vegan lunch) that I first confided in my friend Lynda Hernandez about my frustration over the limitations of legal dissent and about my desire to go to jail for justice. Rather than try to dissuade me, she joined me on a road trip to the Nevada Nuclear Test Site along with my friends Todd Van Eaton, Joshua Boyle, and Melissa Armstrong. That trip was truly one of the most meaningful moments of my life, and I thank them for making it possible. Since then, I have had many amazing protest and life adventures with them, for which I am grateful. Thanks also to Pat Alviso and Jeff Merrick, Beverly "Lanie" Anderson, Diane Fishel, Desiree Funsch, Eddie Garza, Gordon Johnson, Tom Lash, Abraham Ramirez, Mike Ryan, Ruth and Ted Shapin, Thu-Trang Tran, Al White, and the entire Orange County peace community.

I would like to acknowledge the activists whose perspectives and experiences helped to shape this book—only some of whom are mentioned
here by name. Jeff Dietrich, an amazing friend; Catherine Morris, Martha Lewis, David Gardner, Mike Wisniewski, and the entire Los Angeles
Catholic Worker community; James Tracy, Sharon Lungo, Ben Shepard,
and Sanderson Beck, my teachers; Steve Clemens (he let me crash at his
home); Marv Davidov; Flip Benham; Ellen Barfield; Buddy Guy; Ed Hedemann; Freeman Wicklund; and everyone else who asked to remain
nameless.

Finally, I thank the following people for bailing me out (often literally)
and for believing in me when it mattered most: Alan Saltzstein, Zemin
Zhang, Anne Mabry, Bill and Judy Karp, my mother, and my entire
family.

You are all to blame . . .

1

Crime and Dissent

We feed the hungry, clothe the naked, shelter the homeless and protest the war. Sometimes we get arrested for it. That in a nutshell describes what we do.

—Jeff Dietrich, Los Angeles Catholic Worker

This book is about political dissent that tiptoes gingerly over the demarcation between legality and criminality. It tells the story of the homeless who staged a sit-in at the Department of Housing and Urban Development (HUD) and converted the headquarters into their home until they were carried away in handcuffs by police. It highlights the war tax resister who has withheld some seventy thousand dollars in federal taxes in opposition to the military budget. Although this man has never been arrested on charges of tax evasion, he has been arrested for advocating tax resistance in the lobby of the Internal Revenue Service (IRS). And this book introduces the reader to the Raging Grannies, an organization of women who ironically maintain that if people must die in a war, then it may as well be the elderly. Thus, they routinely visit military recruitment centers across the country and demand that they be allowed to enlist. Not willing to accept no for an answer, they refuse to budge and are arrested for their act of patriotism.

Each day independent media are filled with headlines detailing the stories of political actors who engage in open and direct challenges to the dominant political climate as a means of communicating dissent. Sometimes these challenges are playful, such as when a group of activists concerned about corporate takeover of public space hold a sit-in at a downtown Disney Store and chant, "It's my right not to live in a shopping mall!" or when activists working to protect a community garden dress up as tomatoes and stand in front of the demolition bulldozer to ensure the spectacle on the evening news of local police arresting vegetables. Other times, the challenges are somber or even harshly confrontational, such as when a woman pours her own blood on the walls of the Pentagon in protest of war or when activists block access to a medical clinic where abortions are performed or when animal-rights activists chain themselves to the entrance of a national department store that trades in fur, while carrying a blood-red banner that reads "Fur Is Murder," or when a man places his body on railroad tracks to prevent the delivery of weapons to a military base.

Call these actions by their traditional nomenclature of civil disobedience, nonviolent resistance, and direct action, or refer to them as those who actually perform these actions do by using such labels as public-space activism, creative action, carnival, divine obedience, street theater, and even taking theology to the streets. In truth there are as many names for these acts of dissent as there are strategies, and there are as many strategies as there are actors. And although each strategy differs in its level of confrontation, risk, and playfulness, they all share one unifying component: each requires a modicum of criminality in its staging and execution, rendering these protest strategies what I refer to collectively as *crimes of dissent*.

When confronted with a policy or practice that is found to be morally objectionable, many individuals feel that they have little choice but to choose a path of resistance over the politically accepted (and expected) course of unwavering obedience to established law or social practice. For choosing this path, dissenters run the risk of being branded dangerous, irrational, destructive, subversive, and, of course, criminal. Yet these crimes are not behaviors common to hardened criminals. Instead, they are protests staged by conscientious individuals committed to a given ideology or to a particular way of life.[1] Whether these individuals are antiwar or environmental activists, whether advocates for AIDS research dollars or pro-life "rescuers," or whether they are religiously inspired or firmly rooted in secular politics, all have chosen to place themselves in direct conflict with the very laws—not to mention with the very law enforcers—that maintain the prevailing social structure, triggering what is sometimes a rather sizeable response from the criminal justice system.

But why do activists need to break the law? When confronted with an offending law or practice, why not simply use the democratic structures and procedures already in place to address these grievances? What motivates an individual openly and deliberately to disobey a law as an act of dissent? What are the hopes and goals of people willing to step outside legal boundaries in the pursuit of their vision of social justice? What personal or professional risks, if any, do these activists face? How are these political and social agitators handled by members of law enforcement, by the courts, and by people working within correctional facilities? Given the potential costs of working for justice outside conventional means, how do those who engage in these strategies of dissent define and measure whether their efforts have proven "successful" in the short term or in the long run? An attempt to answer these questions is the purpose and subject of this book.

For now, suffice it to say that for the individual determined to reverse perceived ongoing and institutionalized injustices, nothing is more anathema to the prospect of social change than the very notion of *law and order*—a notion that merely sustains the status quo.[2] This association of law and order with the status quo is the reason why individuals choose to violate the law to initiate a social disruption despite the possibility of punishment. It is hoped that the visible staging of a legal transgression will open the eyes of a populace that for too long has remained dormant in the face of injustice and oppression. The goal of the dissenter, then, is to spark the imagination of the politically, economically, and socially disenfranchised and to reveal possibilities that exist outside the legal boundaries of our current culture, so long as one is willing to venture beyond these boundaries. In short, through such strategies as civil disobedience, nonviolent resistance, and direct action, the act of committing a "crime" is transformed into a voice of dissent.

Conscientious Objections

By now it should be apparent that this book is about people who conscientiously object to what passes for justice in the U.S. political system. Of course, I suspect that already some readers themselves may object to the suggestion that the deliberate violation of law can constitute anything other than what it is—a crime—let alone something noble like a protest against a social injustice. After all, if one is unhappy with a law, one is free to change it through currently available mechanisms such as the legislative process and the ballot box. Further, people should not be free to pick and choose which laws to obey and which to violate. Not only will allowing that kind of freedom serve as an invitation for others to join in such violations, but it will also contribute to disrespect for *all* laws. As one critic put it, "Disobedience to law is bad enough when done secretly, but it is far worse when done openly, especially when accompanied by clothing such acts in the mantle of virtue."[3] If we allow people to take the law into their own hands, it will only be a matter of time before we have violence, riots, vigilantism, and even terrorism. These are all valid concerns. Therefore, let me briefly address them point by point. A more comprehensive examination of some of these commonly raised objections is found throughout the pages of this book.

It is certainly true that free and democratic societies provide citizens with the legal means to address (or redress) policies or practices of concern. In fact, the ability to seek redress of grievances represents a cornerstone of democratic governance. It naturally follows, then, that political dissenters are less justified in their use of unconventional methods of redress until all timely legal means have first been exhausted. In fact, it is this exhaustion of all legal means that helps to strengthen the moral justification for an open violation of law since dissenters then can draw attention both to the existence of a grave injustice and to an inability or refusal on the part of the courts or policymakers to correct it. In short, a violation of law *before* all conventional means of redress have been exhausted undermines the rationale for protesters' actions, and it therefore fails to add credence to protesters' legitimacy or broader concerns. Therefore, for crimes of dissent to earn public support and to approach moral legitimacy, activists typically adopt the rule that all available conventional means of redress must first be pursued.

At the same time, one must acknowledge that strict proponents of law and order (herein referred to as legal *absolutists*) overstate the extent to which conventional channels are amenable to fostering meaningful social change. For example, legal absolutists contend that one can turn to the ballot box and simply vote injustice out. Yet even though the United States prides itself on its access to the vote, for much of its history the most oppressed citizens did not have access to the ballot box—rendering them hardly "citizens" at all. American slaves did not have the luxury of voting themselves out of bondage, nor did women have the option of voting themselves the right of suffrage. Without those legal options, oppressed people in the United States engaged in rebellions, underground railroads, illegal sit-ins, marches, blockades, and other acts of social agitation. Although at the time such acts were treated as crimes in the eyes of the law, today these minor disruptions to law and order serve as hallmarks in the pursuit of justice and democracy.

Yet even access to the vote cannot address myriad structural injustices that are embedded within the system, such as those of racism and poverty. A critic of the electoral process, historian Howard Zinn put it rather bluntly when he argued that those who espouse the "power and vitality" of the vote as a means to eradicate deep-rooted social injustices are "living in an antiquated romantic dream very far from political reality."[4] Consider, argues Zinn, that minorities in U.S. ghettos have been participating in electoral politics for years and have repeatedly elected black leadership, but representative leadership has simply not been enough to remove the chains of injustice stemming from hunger, poor housing, and discrimination. In addition to these matters of race and class, the ballot box also fails to bring voters close to matters of foreign policy. It remains one of the flaws of our democratic system that "the closer we get to matters of life and death—that is, to questions of war and peace—the less does democracy function." Thus, Zinn continues by noting that the 1964 presidential vote "went decisively to that candidate who rejected the idea of escalating the war in Southeast Asia. He won, and then escalated the war."[5] More recently, exit polls from the 2006 midterm elections indicated that Democrats were swept into Congress largely out of frustration over the Iraq War. With the election over, the Republican president called for an escalation of troops in the Middle East and for increased funding for the war; many Democrats, who constituted the "opposition" party, pledged not to stand in the way. It would seem, then, that people opposed to poverty, racism, and militarism are left with little choice but to seek alternatives to the ballot in voicing their dissent.

Of course, there is always a concern among legal absolutists that the open violation of one law by activists will lead to a much broader disregard for *all* laws among the general public. Fortunately, history does not bear out this concern; the limited staging of civil disobedience throughout history simply has not led to broad-based and indiscriminate crime. In fact and upon closer examination, it appears that the opposite is true: that the strict adherence to the law despite evidence of injustice can itself lead to broad-based social unrest, for why should anyone respect a legal system that ultimately sustains a wrong?[6] Indeed, urban riots and rebellions are often expressions of outrage performed by people suffering longstanding and unaddressed injustices. These uprisings serve as messages directed at a political system that for too long has been unwilling or incapable of reversing harms through more formal and conventional means.[7]

As a final objection to the staging of crimes of dissent, legal absolutists frequently raise the specter of violence whenever discussions of dissent arise. Specifically, they compare people who publicly and nonviolently break a law and accept their punishment with those who commit violence and evade responsibility for their deeds. The conflation of those who perform civil disobedience with the common violent offender is curious, for whether positioned on the left or right of the political spectrum, those who engage in strategies of civil disobedience, nonviolent resistance, and direct action voice a strong aversion to violence. For some of them, theirs is an aversion to the raw violence of war or to the structural violence of poverty and inequality. For others, it is an aversion to the clinical violence of abortion or to the retributive violence of the death penalty. Regardless of political persuasion, the history of civil disobedience is a history that is largely rooted in a tradition of nonviolence and in the teachings of such pacifists as Jesus, Mohandas Gandhi, Dorothy Day, and Martin Luther King, Jr. All these strategists shared a common belief that nonviolence is the most effective and morally sound means of achieving widespread social change, and following this tradition, all the activists interviewed for this book adhere to the tenets of nonviolence.

When the history is examined closely, it is clear that, in one of the ironies of history, significant advances in social justice are often brought about largely through the deliberate and publicly staged violation of laws. And it is an irony that is frequently acknowledged by historians and social movement scholars. For example, political scientist Gene Sharp has documented considerable historical evidence that what he calls political "noncooperation" in the form of civil disobedience and nonviolent resistance has been an effective means of bringing about significant political or social change when other avenues were unavailable.[8] In a historical account of nonviolent conflict throughout the twentieth century, Peter Ackerman and Jack Duvall demonstrate how "entire societies were transformed" through strategies of civil disobedience and noncooperation, strategies that helped subvert the operations of governments.[9] And Donatella Della Porta and Mario Diani note that sit-ins, blocking traffic, tax resistance, and other unconventional and illegal strategies of political persuasion have ironically enough become "increasingly legitimized" as effective means of promoting social change.[10]

With acknowledgment of the potential for progressive if not revolutionary change through noncooperation with the law, it is important to note that those who partake in these strategies need not be revolutionaries driven by a radical or progressive desire to bring about a wholesale change of government. In *The True Believer: A Study on the Nature of Mass Movements,* Eric Hoffer notes that quite a bit of conservatism runs throughout the history of social movements. After all, "To change things is to ask for trouble." Therefore, "the difference between the conservative and the radical seems to spring mainly from their attitude toward the future." Fear of the future causes some people to cling to the past, whereas faith in the future renders others "receptive to change."[11] Civil disobedience, passive resistance (i.e., noncooperation), and direct action have therefore been used in many attempts at policy change that are both conservative and progressive. And just like efforts within the ballot box and the court of law, those efforts that take place in the streets sometimes prove immensely successful, and sometimes they fail.

But although historians and political theorists grant the transformative power of illegal dissent, the idea that the breaking of laws might sometimes be warranted as a precursor to the attainment of social justice is one that too often is overlooked by scholars within the fields of criminology, criminal justice, and justice studies. The reasons for this oversight are understandable, though by no means excusable. As Matthew Robinson points out in an insightful analysis of the discipline of criminal justice, as a whole the criminal justice system does not have among its objectives the goal of attaining a much broader *social* justice, which can be defined here as the eradication of discrepancies in political power and access to public services that occur along racial, ethnic, gender, sexual orientation, religious, and economic demographics. In fact, the case could easily be made that with the poor and racial/ethnic minorities disproportionately involved at every stage of the criminal "justice" process, the criminal justice system today is organized in a way that actually contributes to social *in*justice.[12]

One objective of this book, then, is to merge the disciplines of criminology, criminal justice, and justice studies more broadly with those of political theory and social movement studies by exploring the possibility that a modicum of domestic unrest and even "crime" may serve as necessary antecedents to significant social change and the attainment of social justice. For decades, social movement scholars have been researching the extent to which illegal, disruptive, and even violent protest tactics can prove influential in expediting social change when conventional political processes fail. Notable among these scholars has been Charles Tilly, who has examined rebellions and social dissent throughout history and has concluded that the use of "disruptive political tactics" by the politically disenfranchised often improves their chances of success. These tactics can include tax rebellions, machine breaking, food riots, and the occupation of city hall, to name a few.[13] Frances Fox Piven and Richard Cloward have reached a similar conclusion. In their 1979 study *Poor People's Movements: Why They Succeed and Why They Fail*, they argue that strategies of economic disruption (including but not limited to industrial strikes, the mass withholding of rent, and machine breaking) are the most powerful political tools among groups that lack such conventional (i.e., institutional) resources as lobbyists, political parties, and access to the ballot box.[14] And William Gamson argues in his provocative book *The Strategy of Social Protest* (1991) that disruptive and illegal tactics by challenging groups are more often met with what he calls "political acceptance" by the establishment, resulting in new policy "advantages." He concludes that those disenfranchised groups that throughout history have been unruly and that have been willing to transgress the law in pursuit of social justice have experienced the most notable successes.[15]

What has emerged from all this scholarship is a growing body of resistance theory that has as its objective an understanding of the processes, circumstances, and historical contexts under which social protest fosters meaningful and lasting political change. Though the literature on the successes (and failures) of political resistance is far too broad for present purposes, one thing that appears certain is that when the course of history has met with significant political, social, or economic gains, there have almost invariably been legal transgressions and strategies of social unrest at play. For example, all the following achievements in social justice have emerged only after a series of struggles that included the use illegal strategies of political communication:

- *The abolition of slavery* in the United States was accomplished in part through a series of illegal actions, some open, some concealed. These include Harriet Tubman's Underground Railroad, the willingness of abolitionists to give sanctuary to runaway slaves, and of course, slave revolts. Although these actions alone were not enough to end slavery outright, these illegal acts nevertheless brought about freedom to many slaves individually and helped place the issue of slavery onto the national agenda.
- *The introduction of labor laws and unions* within the United States was possible only through such actions as "illegal" strikes organized by the Industrial Workers of the World ("Wobblies") and other actions that eventually

led to the eradication of child labor, improved working conditions, minimum wages, benefits, and the establishment of the forty-hour work week. Notable among these actions was the first nationwide railroad strike in 1877 that shut down lines across the eastern United States in protest of the poor wages paid to workers. This action caused law enforcement to fire on the poor and hungry strikers, many of whom opened the freight cars where food was stored.

- *Women's suffrage* within the United States was accomplished only after thousands of women marched in the streets, endured hunger strikes, and submitted to arrest and jail for their illegal appeals to gain the right to vote. One of the more noteworthy events was the decision of the National Women's Party to establish "Sentinels of Liberty" posts in front of the White House beginning in January 1917. Essentially, women kept vigil outside President Wilson's White House to point out the contradiction of fighting for freedom abroad in World War I while oppression continued at home. Picketing in front of the White House during wartime became an illegal act, and in June 1917, the arrests began. Nearly 500 women were arrested, and 168 women served jail time, with some brutalized by their jailers. By 1918 President Wilson declared his support for suffrage, and in 1920 the Twentieth Amendment to the U.S. Constitution was ratified.

- *India's independence from Britain* was accomplished through a strict adherence to a strategy of *ahimsa,* or nonviolence, led by Mahatma Gandhi. After a lengthy campaign that included Indian noncooperation with British rule, a boycott of all British materials and goods, civil disobedience in the form of the great Salt March, and Gandhi's willingness to endure a lengthy hunger strike, India won independence from Britain in 1947.

- *Civil rights legislation* was secured because of a willingness of activists such as John Lewis to defy Jim Crow legislation deliberately and openly, even at the risk of police batons, water cannons, arrest, and jail. An African American male, John Lewis helped set the civil rights movement into full motion when he and other activists who were trained in the tactics of nonviolence sat down at lunch counters designated for whites only. The willingness to disobey Jim Crow laws quickly became contagious, and it was not long before the laws were eliminated outright.[16]

These are just some of the widely acknowledged historical contributions of illegal actions to the struggle and ultimate attainment of social justice along various political axes. Today, activists working on a host of other issues from across the political spectrum continue to employ these strategies of dissent in the pursuit of social justice, however it is individually defined. And although the verdict on the success of current campaigns is still in question, historically at least, these strategies can and often do work.

Despite the effectiveness of these strategies, it is still common for well-intentioned individuals to "recoil from the very concept of disobedience," even in the presence of a gross injustice, and even when the disobedience in question is passive and nonviolent.[17] It seems, as Zinn has argued, that we in the United States have become "so far removed from our own revolutionary tradition . . . that we consider as unpardonable transgressions of law and order what are really mild acts, measured against the existing evils."[18] Consider the news coverage of the millennial negotiations of the World Trade Organization (WTO) that took place in Seattle 1999. While many observers of the massive protests were quick to criticize the handful of masked protesters constituting the anarchist Black Bloc who damaged the storefront plate glass of a Starbucks franchise in protest of the below-poverty wages it paid to growers, few commentators drew parallels between *these* masked protesters destroying *coffee* and those more celebrated protesters who in 1773 similarly wore masks and climbed aboard three ships owned by the East India Company and engaged in the destruction of *tea* in one of the most famous acts of patriotism: the Boston Tea Party. This comparison of the Black Bloc anarchists in the streets of Seattle with those who staged the Boston Tea Party is not meant to suggest that every strategy of dissent is necessarily noble or that all forms of social agitation are equally noteworthy or effective. Instead, it is merely cited here as illustrative of how obedient we as a culture have become, even in the face of widespread injustices, so long as we can guarantee that law and order will prevail.

A Little Bit of Anarchy

It is the dogged commitment to law and order—rather than to justice— that many contemporary activists find problematic. When pinned down, people will acknowledge that the law sometimes fails to deliver justice. Yet they are quick to add that the law is all that stands in the way of anarchy. But when the alternative is institutionalized injustice protected by the rule of law, why not tolerate a little bit of anarchy? After all, anarchy is not about chaos or about throwing bricks and bombs or even about breaking windows, though this is the image of anarchy made popular in news

Image courtesy of Crimethinc.

accounts of popular protest. Rather, anarchy among other things is merely the notion that one has the right to reject any authority whose moral code is beyond the dictates of personal conscience. In this regard, anarchy begins by refusing to be represented by, or to represent, others. It posits that people ought to be obligated to obey only decisions that they themselves recognize as just. Quite simply, anarchists believe that there should be no moral obligation to a law merely because it can be imposed on the masses (often with force) by some political authority.[19]

But anarchy is not a form of vulgar individualism, although there are some anarchists who identify themselves as individualists. Anarchism really is a wholesale repudiation of the individualistic tendencies of our electoral system, which reduces voters into the categories of "winners" and "losers"; it is a repudiation of the individualistic tendencies of ownership culture, in which resources are increasingly monopolized; and it is a repudiation of the individualistic tendencies of a wage system that finds wealth concentrated into the hands of a few despite the fact that wealth is created through the labor of many. In place of individualism, many anarchists prefer a system marked by "a continual exchange of mutual, temporary and, above all, voluntary authority and subordination."[20] The Russian anarchist Peter Kropotkin has referred to this type of social arrangement as "mutual aid." He argues that mutual aid is essential to human evolution and to the health of society.[21] Indeed, one need only look toward the deleterious effect on society of the individual pursuit of profit and power to see the wisdom in Kropotkin's words.

Aside from the myth of blanket individualism, another misconception about anarchism is that it is a rejection of *all* authority in *all* circumstances and at *all* times. In reality, what many anarchists oppose is the imposition of authority on a population. They reject any expectation of complete and absolute deference to any institution, especially when they have not been persuaded that doing so is personally or collectively prudent. Such unyielding deference, the anarchist Mikhail Bakunin has argued, is "fatal to my reason, to my liberty, and [it will] transform me into a stupid slave, an instrument of the will and interests of others." Instead, anarchists may accept "all natural authorities" that emerge after "all influences of fact" become persuasive to the individual.[22] Under anarchy, then, it is the self that is the ultimate moral authority, not the State. Emma Goldman, one of the most recognizable anarchist figures, therefore concludes that anarchism "is the only philosophy which brings to man the consciousness of himself."[23]

Unfortunately, and often against our better judgment, when it comes to matters of morality we find ourselves increasingly deferring to power. To understand this tendency, consider the influence of the State on our personal morality. Under the guise of a social contract, or for the purpose of maintaining law and order, we as individuals are often forced to repress our own sense of morality and justice for the sake of interests of State. As citizens of State, we allow war, hunger, homelessness, and lack of access to health care to remain everyday facts of life. Yet as individuals, most of us would never take up arms against another person or let our friends and neighbors or even strangers go without food or medicine when these are clearly in abundance or deny them housing or clothing when collectively we have the resources to provide them with these essentials. This explains why Peter Kropotkin argues passionately against individuals deferring to the State to eradicate injustice. It is the State after all that is responsible for these injustices and for the creation of new Statist immorality that sustains these ills. Instead, Kropotkin argues that the individual should act for him- or herself and according to individual morality to get rid of oppression, without an expectation that someone (e.g., a politician) or something (e.g., the political or legal process) will automatically accomplish this on his or her behalf.[24]

This do-it-yourself approach to eradicating injustice is one shared by contemporaries of Kropotkin. Consider the story of Keith McHenry and the activist group Food Not Bombs. Cofounded by McHenry in Boston during the early 1980s, Food Not Bombs is an informal network of anarchist activists that sets up food lines in public parks and on city streets.

This service is certainly laudable and charitable. Yet Food Not Bombs is hardly a charity at all, at least not in the conventional sense, because more often than not, charities are large corporate-like entities whose hierarchical structures and bureaucratic organization often prevent aid from reaching its target in a timely or efficient manner.

As an alternative, Food Not Bombs operates in the belief that if people really want to help the homeless, they may as well feed them directly. And why not make it easy for homeless people to get the services they need by setting up food lines in the very parks and on the very streets where they live? To achieve this end, activists take it upon themselves to visit neighborhood bakeries, produce stands, and grocery stores at the close of business to recover day-old breads, fruits, and vegetables that would otherwise be discarded. With these in hand, they cook up vegan soups and dishes that they serve directly to the hungry. At the same time, they distribute literature that draws a link between such domestic problems as hunger and military spending. And they do these things not in a shelter but in plain view of city officials, who would prefer that the homeless become less visible.

Unfortunately, while antiwar activists within Food Not Bombs were drawing a connection between hunger and military spending, during the 1980s academics were attempting to draw a connection between social "disorder" (what became known as the "broken windows theory") and crime. So even though newspapers reported that city shelters were unable to fully accommodate swelling homeless populations,[25] simply for setting up street-level soup kitchens, members of Food Not Bombs were repeatedly arrested for violating various public nuisance and so-called quality-of-life ordinances that prohibited such activities as loitering, panhandling, and serving food without a permit. Explaining the law-enforcement crackdown, McHenry recalled to me, "overall, we'd been arrested in San Francisco over one thousand times during the 1980s and 1990s," simply because Food Not Bombs continued to feed the homeless in violation of city ordinances. As he explained, "When we were first arrested, churches and charities like the Salvation Army worked in opposition of our efforts and made statements against us. They said that we were the leadership necessary for the insurrection of the poor." In reality, the biggest focus of Food Not Bombs was to cut out the middle man and simply do something themselves by collecting food and serving it to the needy while handing out literature on peace. "For us, it's more about 'doing' and 'taking action' than it is about spending so much time at meetings as it tends to be with so many other organizations."

The logo for Food Not Bombs.

Whether the do-it-yourself attitude of anarchism is manifested through the feeding of the homeless in violation of city ordinances or through some other "illegal" action, the point here is rather simple, as has been made clear by a leading journal of contemporary anarchist thought: "it doesn't matter what a person believes 'should' be the case. . . . it only matters what one *does*."[26] In this regard, whenever people take initiative and address social problems directly, that is a form of anarchism. Whenever people act out of conscience rather than convention, that is a form anarchism. Whenever people place their bodies on the line and perform a crime of dissent in an attempt to renegotiate laws "both written and unwritten," it is a form of anarchy in both theory and practice.[27] It follows, then, that crimes of dissent constitute individual acts of anarchy. And although the activists interviewed for this book do not necessarily identify themselves as anarchists either ideologically or socially, they are nevertheless engaging in little acts of anarchy (in the best sense of the word) each and every time they challenge the State and act for themselves.

Sadly, though, as we have seen, when forced to choose between law and order on the one hand and social justice on the other, there is a tendency for people to opt for the former rather than the latter. The American writer Henry David Thoreau, who was himself jailed for refusing to pay taxes in protest of war and the institution of slavery, questioned this cultural practice of strict obedience to a legal code when presented with a gross injustice. If the collective adherence to law must always supersede individual acts of conscience, Thoreau asked, "Why has every man a conscience then?" In fact, Thoreau argued that laws "never made men a whit more just" and often have been the source of injustice. He concluded that we should all strive to be persons of conscience first and citizens of the State second.[28] Similarly, the late anarchist Ammon Hennacy once quipped that laws are wholly unnecessary since the good people do not need them and the bad people do not obey them, so what use are they? In that respect, how many students are taught that Martin Luther King, Jr., argued *against* having too much respect for the law? Writing from a jail cell in Birmingham, King cautioned those who championed civil rights but were opposed to breaking any law—even Jim Crow laws—never to forget that everything Hitler did in Germany was "legal," while those who disobeyed Hitler's orders were criminals.[29] Even today, activists continue to point to the segregated South as illustrative of the perils of mistaking order for justice, as expressed to me by an activist in the following statement: "Jim Crow laws were horrible. How could you live in the South (especially if

Food Not Bombs cofounder Keith McHenry arrested in 1988. This was the first of over one thousand arrests of Food Not Bombs volunteers for sharing free food in San Francisco.

you were Black) and just obey those laws every time? It must have been galling for [them] . . . but they weren't going to break the law."

Ultimately, then, the purpose of this book is to argue for a new approach to the concept of law and order, one that allows for a little bit of anarchy. Although the rule of law is certainly something to be respected, we must never forget that laws are of little value when they fail to promote ideals of justice and fairness and instead serve to sanction and institutionalize daily injustice. This book therefore serves as a plea for the disciplines of criminal justice, criminology, and justice studies to become less disciplined in their approach to the rule of law and to refamiliarize students with the possibility that nonviolent crimes of dissent staged publicly as expressions of protest often constitute meaningful forms of political expression that can serve as progenitors of lasting social justice.

The Great Moral Innovators

Criminology was not always so disconnected from the transformative aspects of dissent. In an important lecture delivered at the Sorbonne in January 1903, Émile Durkheim—who is considered one of the fathers of criminology—actually referred to people who openly challenge legal boundaries as "the great moral innovators" of society. Granted, he also referred to social dissenters as persons who were "morally incomplete." Still, Durkheim conceded that disobedience is an essential element to the overall health of a social unit. Praising the political agitator, he wrote,

> Was not Christ such a deviant, as well as Socrates? And is it not thus with all historical figures whose names we associate with the great moral revolutions through which humanity has passed? Had their feeling of respect for the moral rules characteristic of their day been too lively, they would not have undertaken to alter them. To dare to shake off the yoke of traditional discipline, one should not feel authority too strongly. Nothing could be clearer.[30]

Thus, although Durkheim is most frequently credited with having argued at length that legal transgressions are functional in the sense that they strengthen the established moral code, he also was persuasive in highlighting the relativity of morality itself. Nevertheless, the point should not be oversold, for Durkheim was careful to caution his readers not to confuse two very different feelings: "The need to substitute a new regulation for an old one; and the impatience with all rules, the abhorrence with all discipline."[31]

Critically based criminological theories have explored the possibility that various crimes and illegal actions serve as expressions of dissent. Under radical theory, crime results from class struggle and from the subsequent economic inequalities produced as a result of the mass accumulation of wealth. Therefore, whether subconsciously chosen or by design, crime is ultimately a reaction—a protest if you will—against class-based social conditions. Although Karl Marx and Friedrich Engels dismissed the notion of a revolutionary criminal class per se, writers operating from within the New Left have suggested that crime and social conflict may at times prove to be a progressive force in that the occurrence of crime reveals cracks in the foundations of society.[32] Thus, banditry reveals itself as a potential force for change in society, white-collar crime exposes the exploits and excesses of capitalism, and shoplifting and other forms of theft serve as strategies of income or property redistribution.[33]

Many conflict criminological theories explore crime and dissent from a purely political perspective, rather than from a behavioral perspective. In the political perspective, the dissent lies not within the manner in which criminality becomes manifest (i.e., banditry, shoplifting, or rioting); instead, it exists in the very fact that each crime committed serves as a reminder to the ruling power that the political center simply cannot hold. For conflict theorists, the whole process of drafting and enforcing laws exposes a social structure rooted in power in which a political majority imposes its values on a political minority that itself is positioning to be the next ruling power. Therefore, crime is best understood as behavior of the powerless against the powerful, in that people who do not maintain an ideological orientation in sympathy with a political majority are likely to have their dissent defined as "criminal" by the State.

For present purposes, the strength of conflict theory is most readily found in its recognition of the political nature of much criminal behavior. Simply put, that which is criminal is always political. (That the reverse is also true is the subject for yet another book). Indeed, George Vold's discussion of group conflict theory explicitly argued that behavior commonly treated as crime is really an attempt at political reform. Labor strikes, lockouts, draft dodging, and even property destruction are best seen as political actions, even though such actions may lead to direct physical clashes between police and protesters. Vold contended that the best case for treating these crimes as mere acts of dissent lies in the fact that there are relatively few instances of successful prosecution of such lawlessness.[34] This is the case presumably because most observers recognize these actions as incidental to the larger power plays directed at the level of legislative, executive, and judicial government. As is shown in chapter 5, the activists interviewed for this book who have been arrested for crimes of dissent similarly encountered few prosecutions.

Although there is no denying the relevance of critically based criminological perspectives to an understanding of the subject at hand, these theories are not without their limitations. Radical criminology's assertion that crime functions as a progressive and transformative act suffers from the paradox that the typical victims of crime are the people most in need of a socioeconomic revolution, such as women, racial and ethnic minorities, and the working class. It is hard to imagine how the racially or economically disenfranchised benefit from crime. Moreover, with regard to group conflict theory, many of the activists interviewed for this book reject the notion that their actions represent a means to "power." Instead, many of them characterize their acts of dissent as designed to *reduce* and ultimately destroy the manifestation of political or economic power within society. They therefore do not ascribe to conflict theory's assertion that theirs is a struggle for the control of the police power of the State. Indeed, many of the voices quoted throughout this book reject wholeheartedly the very idea of "the State."

The limitations of radical and conflict theories notwithstanding, crimes of dissent are certainly behaviors that are ideologically driven, and they may even serve as longstanding strategies of cultural "self-help" and social control. Legal scholar Donald Black has observed that what is widely regarded by contemporary standards as forms of criminal behavior has often been described by anthropologists as moralistic conduct staged to express grievances and possibly even to resolve interpersonal disputes. For example, in regions of East Africa the seizure or destruction of property by one individual against another "might at first appear to a modern observer as unprovoked theft" when in fact it is intended as "a response to the misconduct of the victim." In some other cultures, violence and even homicide is "rarely predatory." Instead, it is largely retaliatory, with "capital punishment administered on a private basis." This last point is essential, for it touches the center of Black's theory. In cultures in which formal law is weak or nonexistent, crime itself becomes both a form of punishment and a reprimand—that is, it serves as a form of social control that communicates a cultural value. The crime also becomes a mechanism of self-help in that the people themselves become responsible for conflict resolution.[35]

There are many areas of convergence between what are deemed crimes of dissent and those staged as self-help. With each, the behavior in question is staged to communicate some cultural grievance. Moreover, both crimes of dissent and crime as self-help are prevalent when law is absent or when it fails to provide for the aggrieved party. And in both categories it is the people who act for themselves to redress (or address) a perceived injustice. Like Howard Zinn, then, Donald Black recognizes that the law is unavailable not only in many historically distant or geographically remote contexts but also in many contemporary scenarios and especially among "lower-status people of all kinds—blacks and other minorities, the poor, the homeless." At the same time, one must recognize that it is only in a contemporary and "civilized" context that the behaviors of self-help have come to be viewed legalistically as "crimes." At least in some contexts, "rather than being proscribed, violent self-help is prescribed as a method of social control."[36] This attitude toward self-help is quite different from the one toward crimes of dissent, which are almost invariably behaviors that—when performed in the intended context—are in fact legally proscribed. Finally, crimes of self-help largely take place in the absence of formal law or centralized democratic governance, whereas crimes of dissent are staged to communicate a failure of law and of the State.

If any lesson can be drawn from the discussion of crime as self-help, it is that what is considered a crime in some cultural contexts may be viewed as moralistic behavior in others. Following this lesson, this book applies a cultural-criminological perspective to the examination and understanding of various crimes of dissent. Cultural criminology explores "the many ways in which cultural and criminal processes come together,"[37] thus highlighting the fact that many cultural practices have come to be defined as criminal in certain political circles. In *Cultural Criminology*, Jeff Ferrell and Clinton Sanders characterize cultural criminology rather simply as the study of "crime as culture" and "culture as crime" by noting that everyday popular undertakings are regularly recast as crime, and vice versa.[38] They argue that it is the illegal status of many of these practices that gives birth to criminal subcultures, which are formed to carry out collectively the prohibited activity while often challenging its illegal status publicly.

One objective of cultural criminology that is particularly relevant to the present study of dissent is its attempt to "reinterpret criminal behaviour (in terms of meaning) as a technique for resolving certain *psychic con- flicts*—conflicts that in many instances are indelibly linked with various features of contemporary life/culture."[39] Among the "psychic conflicts" that plague the contemporary cultural landscape are the competing forces of *personal* or *cultural* morality on the one hand and *political* or *legal* responsibility on the other. Fortunately, implicit in cultural criminology is a recognition of the need to reconsider the false dichotomy distinguishing cultural values and criminal practices. The truth is that that which is criminal is in many instances also cultural. It is also the case that many cultural conditions (e.g., war, racism, underfunded AIDS research) serve as precursors to what are deemed "criminal" actions carried out as acts of dissent to communicate opposition to politics as usual.

Yet contrary to existing definitions of cultural criminology that tend to hint that a spillover of crime results primarily from the encroachment of conservative values on the cultural landscape, as demonstrated throughout this book, many of the so-called crimes of dissent are in actuality cultural reactions to liberal or progressive political agendas. This book therefore attempts to move cultural criminology beyond a purely "leftist" understanding of the crime-making process. The fact remains that if cultural criminology is to move beyond progressive or leftist circles to become a fruitful methodology for understanding deviant behavior and the construction of meaning, it must be willing to acknowledge the parallels between liberal and conservative cultural movements as reactions to changing cultural norms.

Cultural Criminology and the Pleasure of Resistance

Without diminishing the very real pain and suffering stemming from the policies to which the activists detailed in this book are opposed, and without dismissing the very real sacrifices and consequences that result from this opposition, one theme that periodically emerged from my interviews with activists is that there is much pleasure to be derived from openly fighting the system. Take for example this description of euphoria or of an almost religious-like sensation experienced by "Veronica," an antinuclear activist: "I always feel the best in my whole life when I'm doing an action and going to jail. . . . That's why I've done it so many times. I feel good. And I feel spiritually connected. I feel really good!" At the age of sixty, Veronica has devoted some twenty-five years of her life to fighting the threat of nuclear warfare. Her longevity within the antinuclear movement serves as a testimony to the pleasure derived from resistance, since one suspects that many activists would otherwise experience burnout from facing what often appears to be an insurmountable challenge. Similarly, Sharon Lungo is an activist who has spent years organizing for the rights of indigenous people. She described feeling "exhilarated" when engaging in legal resistance. Having been raised as a Catholic Latina, at twenty-seven years old Sharon recalled having "a lot of fear" driven into her heart during her childhood. "I was taught to be very conformist, and I had to struggle with myself at this idea of being confrontational." Ultimately, she found her activism to be personally "very liberating."

This pleasure of resistance is a feeling that I too have experienced firsthand through the performance of my own acts of dissent. It was a pleasure of resistance that I have experienced when I took to the streets of New York City to protest the agenda of the 2004 Republican National Convention and cheered on the people arrested for reclaiming the streets in a Critical Mass bicycle ride. Days later, I too landed in jail for failing to disperse from an unpermitted protest in Times Square. It was a (solemn) pleasure of resistance that I experienced when I was one among hundreds who trespassed onto the grounds of the Nevada Nuclear Test Site (widely regarded as the most bombed place on the planet) on the sixtieth anniversary of the bombing of Hiroshima. It was an exhilarating pleasure that I experienced when I used my body to block the entrance to a military recruitment office in Hollywood, California, and helped to shut it down—if only for just one day. It was a pleasure of resistance that I experienced when I was one of seventy-eight activists arrested in Minneapolis for attempting to serve the CEO of a large munitions company with a mock notice to appear in court to testify to his company's alleged violation of international humanitarian law. After being cited and released, all seventy-eight of us (and several dozen organizers) headed to the local diner for pancakes and a postaction party. And it was a pleasure of resistance that I experienced when I was one of six protesters arrested for occupying the office of a U.S. congresswoman. When she refused to commit to voting against funding the continued occupation of Iraq, we made our intentions clear. As long as she was committed to the occupation of Iraq, we were committed to the occupation of her office. During our fourteen-hour sit-in, our supporters delivered to us (care of the congresswoman) homemade food, wine, and blankets. Proving that we had love in our hearts, from the inside we managed to use our cell phones to order pizzas for the congressional staff.

RE: State of Minnesota (City of Edina)
Plaintiffs

vs

AlliantACTION 42 et al
Defendants

The People, On Behalf of the
Hennepin County District Court
Division IV - Southdale
7009 York Avenue South, Edina, MN 55435

ORDER TO APPEAR

DA: November 30, 2006

Subpoena ad testificandum

TO: Daniel J. Murphy, CEO, Alliant Techsystems, Inc.

You are ordered to appear on November 30, 2006 and testify as to:
• your knowledge of International Law and its application to Alliant Techsystems decisions to design and produce, when contracted to: cluster munitions; landmine systems; nuclear missile rocket motors; depleted uranium munitions; etcetera.
• your understanding of the term "indiscriminate".

The Defendants have included the document "Employee Liabilities of Weapons Manufacturers Under International Law" to assist in your preparations for testimony.

SO ORDERED OCTOBER 2, 2006

HAND DELIVERED BY

ACCEPTED BY

AlliantACTION.org

FRONT ▲ BACK ▼

ATK CORPORATE HEADQUARTERS

PARKING LOT

POINT of CONVERGENCE

DRIVEWAY

LINCOLN DRIVE

PARKING RAMP

POND

HIGHWAY 169

5th STREET

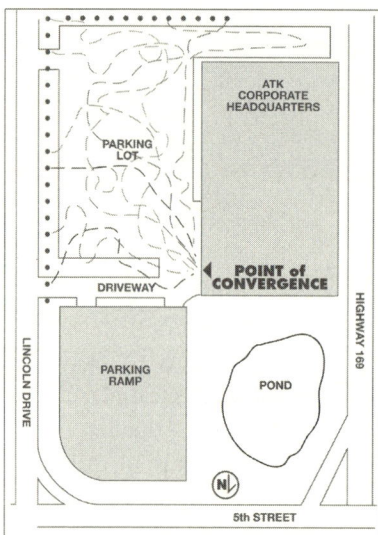

NOTE: If inadvertently arrested, these are the possible legal consequences. It is offered only as a guide and should not be considered legal advice.

• Edina Trespass ordinance: petty misdemeanor
• Minnesota Trespass ordinance: misdemeanor
• Giving False Name to Police - gross misdemeanor
• Obstruction of Justice / Resisting Arrest: Misdemeanor or Gross Misdemeanor

• **Petty Misdemeanor:** maximum penalty is $300 fine - bench trial - 2 court appearances
• **Misdemeanor:** maximum penalty is $1000 and/or 90 days in jail - jury trial - 3 court appearances
• **Gross Misdemeanor:** maximum penalty is $3,000 and/or one year jail - jury trial - 3 court app.

The court will impose a $75 surcharge in addition to any fines levied.

In an act of nonviolent direct action, seventy-eight activists were arrested on Mahatma Gandhi's birthday while attempting to deliver a subpoena to the CEO of Alliant Techsystems, a munitions supplier that manufactures landmines and cluster bombs.

All of this brings us back to cultural criminology, for one of its strengths as an area of inquiry is its recognition of the pleasures that are often derived from the transgression of legal norms. It is a recognition first made popular in academic circles upon the publication of early-twentieth-century scholar Mikhail Bakhtin's insightful study *Rabelais and His World*. In this study, Bakhtin argued that the carnival of the Middle Ages and the Renaissance allowed for a temporary suspension of social hierarchy and sparked a "second life" for peasants and commoners. Specifically, the carnival's emphasis on scatology, the excesses of its "Feast of Fools," and the crowning of a fool as king created a "world upside down," where forbidden pleasures were brought to the surface, often with an underlying air of protest. Yet although Bakhtin's study sparked an array of academic investigations into the pleasures to be derived from resistance, his emphasis on folk culture suggested to many of his contemporaries that in our mediated world these subversive pleasures were only possible when filtered through some cultural medium, such as art or film.[40] But that is not the case. Resistance need not be merely vicarious.

Activists stage an "occupation" of a congressional office after the congresswoman refused to pledge no more funding for the U.S. occupation of Iraq. The author reads aloud the names of war casualties. (Photo by Mike Wisniewski)

Within activist circles, it was Emma Goldman who insisted that revelry and revolution were not only agreeable forces but also potentially synonymous experiences. Aside from being an anarchist, Goldman was a devoted dancer. According to popular accounts, one day she was talking about her dancing when a male anarchist said to her that dancing was much too frivolous an activity for an anarchist and that she would be better off devoting her attention to more serious affairs. Goldman replied, "If I can not dance, I want no part in your revolution."[41] As the movement for racial equality evolved into one pushing for economic justice, activists both in Europe and the United States emphasized the pleasures to be derived from legal transgressions. In the late 1950s and throughout the 1960s, a group of French avant-garde artists and intellectuals founded the publication known as the *Situationist International,* through which they called on their readers to spark a cultural revolution to "bring to light forgotten desires."[42] Meanwhile, in the United States, Abbie Hoffman founded the Youth International Party (Yippies) with the goal not only of transforming the whole of society but of having fun while doing it. Likening the subversion of authority to an LSD trip, his writings on revolution alluded to Antonin Artaud's dramaturgical theories, in which the separation between participant and observer is—ideally at least—nonexistent. For Hoffman, revolution was all about the shock and pleasure inherent in bucking the system.[43]

In the post-9/11 political climate, activism responded to the establishment's carefully orchestrated campaign of fear with protest strategies marked by the pleasure of the absurd and of the spectacle. Writing in the *Journal of Aesthetics and Protest,* activist Benjamin Shepard explained that with promises of permanent war in the offing, "the time seemed right for a shift in movement direction."[44] Instead of adopting protest strategies bogged down by policy-driven slogans, tiresome marches, and trite rallies, grassroots organizers seized the opportunity to transform the politics of gloom-and-doom into a party atmosphere. The goal was to subvert the climate of suspicion and apprehension with one that encouraged political participation. To that end, protesters adopted strategies designed to "create a brand of protest which merged the joyous ecstatic spirit of exhilarating entertainment with a political agenda" aimed at preventing war.[45]

Very quickly, then, the streets became stages for Guerilla Theater. On one corner, activists donning varsity apparel became the Radical Cheerleaders and shouted clever social commentary in a playful and participatory manner to passersby: "Solar and wind are safe and clean / Let's shut down the oil machine! / We are here to let you know / The time has come for oil to go!"[46] On another corner, a satirical protest troupe known as the Billionaires for Bush carried absurdist placards announcing their demands: "Widen the Income Gap" and "Free the Enron 7!"[47] All this theater was designed to render political opposition both welcoming and immensely pleasurable at a time when the thought of dissent seemed rather foreboding. Yet these strategies merely reconnected activism with the age-old pleasures to be derived from subverting authority.

With the recognition of the pleasure in resistance, there is always the risk of downplaying the very real sacrifices that are made in the pursuit of justice. Doing so is particularly problematic when examining resistance movements in developing nations and in nondemocracies, where the stakes of dissent are high. Even within advanced democracies, it is likely that experiencing the pleasures of resistance is a privilege of the already privileged. The theme of privileged protesters is one that is explored later in the book. For now, it is important to acknowledge that with many acts of resistance, one would be hard-pressed to identify the pleasure to be derived from water cannons, attack dogs, bomb threats, and police repression. Moreover, even when pleasure is derived, activists try not to let it interfere with the ultimate objective. Simply put, the pleasures of resistance are secondary to their primary goal, which is the attainment of justice.

At the same time, it is only recently that criminology has even come to explore the possibility that pleasure could be derived from stepping outside moral or legal boundaries. In the book *Seductions of Crime*, sociologist Jack Katz acknowledges the "delight in deviance," at least from the vantage of the deviant. For Katz, "Somehow in the psychological and sociological disciplines, the lived mysticism and magic in the foreground of criminal experience became unseeable." Yet those who commit crimes often lay claim to a "moral status of transcendent significance."[48] Thus, the performance of crime becomes a performance of pleasure. For cultural criminology, crimes of dissent can deliver the actor a pleasure of resistance. They constitute a return to the carnival, where the disregard for social norms and political hierarchies becomes socially liberating and personally meaningful. Indeed, in a series of pioneering studies, Jeff Ferrell has described illegal street protests, billboard and hip-hop graffiti, and squatting as acts that "detonate the festival of the oppressed."[49] For Ferrell, mainstream criminology has suffered from a lack of insight into the meaning of crime for the people who commit it, and it suffers from a lack of recognition that the public display of criminal behavior, especially behavior that inconveniences the powerful, can evoke feelings of liberation and empowerment among society's disenfranchised. Cultural criminology addresses this oversight by noting that in many instances the performance of crime is also the play of carnival, and vice versa—a point that has been cleverly elucidated in Mike Presdee's book *Cultural Criminology and the Carnival of Crime.*[50]

The Reconstruction of Cultural Meaning

Cultural criminology acknowledges that the pleasures derived from resistance almost invariably occur in the context of a "subculture." Sociologist Albert Cohen has noted that the pressures of conformity that dominate society are also the very forces that serve as the precondition to the emergence of subcultures. These subcultures are composed of individuals sharing "*similar problems of adjustment*" to the mainstream. It is within these subcultures that individuals learn the rationalizations, motives, and techniques of delinquency, thereby allowing for the legal transgressions to occur. It follows that what is commonly referred to as "delinquency" by the dominant culture is a means by which individuals collectively deal with these problems of adjustment. Thus, delinquent behavior is also the expression of "common understandings, common sentiments, and common loyalties."[51]

For cultural criminologists, subcultures are not merely groups whose behaviors signify an unwillingness to conform or adjust to a mainstream. Rather, their behaviors (or "crimes") are often attempts to redefine the very moral boundaries of what passes as acceptable for the mainstream political establishment. Thus, dumpster diving or "scrounging" is not merely a means of survival for the downtrodden; it is also a strategy used by outsiders intent on reversing the cultural tide of capitalist over-consumption, as Jeff Ferrell explains in his book about dumpster diving, *Empire of Scrounge.* "Many in the empire of scrounge [i.e., dumpster diving] work to promote a similar political dynamic, to invent oppositional readings as they go about salvaging, reconstructing, and repositioning the commodity waste of consumer culture."[52] Similarly, the illegal street bicycle rides that form the Critical Mass movement not only have the goal of reclaiming the streets for equal use by cyclists; they also seek a veritable revolution in transportation in which mass transit and bicycles surpass automobiles in both use and popularity. The extent to which dumpster diving and reclaim-the-streets activities have evolved from local activities performed by various groups to international networks of committed activists illustrates the extent to which subcultures are far from merely malcontents but are instead groups whose opposition is designed to spark a revolution of everyday life.

The crimes of dissent discussed in this book are designed to trigger a cultural revolution, and they likewise are rarely carried out by lone individuals. They are carried out by subcultures that plan and perform the protest, negotiate with police, and address the legal aftermath of the protest. "Affinity groups" represent the primary social or subcultural networks for individuals planning to do civil disobedience. Sometimes, affinity groups are an informal and even ad hoc association of like-minded activists who meet only days or even hours before an action. Other times, affinity groups are more formal and require much deliberation. The benefit of working in an affinity group, as one civil disobedience training manual notes, is that "feelings of being isolated or alienated from the movement, the crowd, or the world in general can be alleviated through the familiarity and trust which develops when an affinity group works and acts together."[53] Affinity groups therefore form the basic cultures of illegal dissent. They provide a sense of solidarity, friendship, and protection for a core group of activists willing to plan, stage, and participate in a particular protest action. Although this book contains interviews with individuals, the reader must bear in mind that each activist is part of a larger culture of dissent.

Beyond affinity groups is a much broader social network of individuals and organizations that provides social support for people willing to risk arrest for a given cause. Although not everyone is personally positioned to risk arrest, many people nevertheless act in solidarity with affinity groups by providing such services as day care for the children of participants, free legal service for arrestees, transportation to and from court, and donations to legal defense funds. Other people simply show their support by agreeing to feed pets while their fellow activists are incarcerated, to pay predated bills if jail time appears certain, and to provide much needed moral support for those facing arrest and imprisonment.

It should now be apparent that these crimes of dissent signify collective behavior organized within, and instigated by, cultural networks. Today, it is not uncommon to speak of activist "communities" or collectives, let alone "schools" of activism where individuals learn the skills, methods, and techniques of nonviolent resistance and direct action. All the protesters profiled in this book can be said to operate within a larger culture of activism—however loosely organized—and it is through the support and friendship provided by this culture of activism that these various acts of dissent are able to occur.

Crime and Dissent in the New Millennium

Nowhere was the culture of activism more on display than when an estimated thirty to fifty thousand protesters converged in Seattle in 1999 to protest the millennial negotiations of the World Trade Organization (WTO). International concern over such issues as corporate globalization, "third-world" debt, environmental degradation, and free-trade policies was manifested in what became one of the largest demonstrations since the civil rights and anti-Vietnam movements. "Teamsters and Turtles . . . Together at Last!" became the battle cry of the new solidarity that sprang forth amid the shattered plate glass, the overturned newspaper-dispenser bins, and the clouds of pepper spray that dissipated in the moist Northwest air. Steelworkers and longshoremen in union-patched jackets marched shoulder to shoulder with environmentalists donning sea turtle costumes in homage to the aquatic species—after a previous decision by the WTO ruled that certain endangered-species laws posed a barrier to free trade. What was once a seldom-understood hodgepodge of international trade agreements that fell under the oversimplified tagline of "globalization" had emerged as a visible threat to economic, environmental, and social justice, and it was not just anarchists and tree huggers who were now concerned.

As documented in the book *Five Days That Shook the World*, which offers a day-to-day retelling of the protest events, between November 28 and December 3, 1999, protesters from around the world converged in Seattle not only determined to voice their opposition to the neoliberal agenda of "free" trade—an agenda that opponents see as one that favors industrialized nations at the expense of developing nations—but determined to bring the negotiations to a standstill. On Tuesday, November 30, activists formed human chains outside hotels and in front of the convention center, preventing delegates' access to the trade negotiations taking place. Elsewhere, protesters from such groups as Earth First!, Global Exchange, Jobs with Justice, the Rainforest Action Network, and the Alliance for Sustainable Jobs and the Environment participated in large-scale sit-ins and occupied important downtown intersections, further obstructing delegates' access to the trade negotiations. So effective were the human blockades, sit-ins, and the like that no less a figure than U.S. Secretary of State Madeleine Albright was locked down in her Seattle hotel. By the end of the day, two thousand or so protesters (only a fraction of the total estimated protest attendees) engaged in civil disobedience and helped to bring about a cancellation of the opening ceremonies for the WTO ministerial. Three days and countless acts of dissent later, delegates left Seattle without agreeing on an agenda for future trade talks.[54]

In the wake of Seattle, much has been written about the successes of the illegal street actions and protests that ultimately proved effective in shutting down the WTO. The *Oregonian* declared the WTO protests a success and noted that the human blockades, protest circles in downtown intersections, and other strategies of civil disobedience "turned back dozens of delegates and proved far more disruptive" than anything dished out by the people bent on rioting or property destruction.[55] Meanwhile, the *Seattle Post-Intelligencer* reported the protests to be "the first intense show of activism in the country since the 1960s," one that "united a cross-section" of people from laborers to students.[56] And journalists Alexander Cockburn, Jeffrey St. Clair, and Allan Sekula referred to the protests in Seattle as "shining hours" in the history of popular protest that were marked by successes achieved through strategies conducted "entirely outside the conventional arena of orderly [i.e., "legal"] protest, white paper activism and the timid bleats of . . . professional leadership."[57]

Seattle was clearly the beginning of *something*, perhaps of a new social movement marked by recognition of a shared struggle. The enactment of the North American Free Trade Agreement (NAFTA) in 1994, which was championed by the ostensibly liberal Clinton-Gore administration, inevitably brought about awareness among labor that the same political and corporate entities that exploit natural resources without compunction likewise do not hesitate to exploit human resources. Yet Seattle was also a testimony to the power of civil disobedience, nonviolent direct action, and other crimes of dissent, since it was the illegal sit-ins and human blockades outside the convention center that ultimately proved successful in causing a collapse of the WTO negotiations. Although it cannot be denied that the widely reported property destruction initiated by a handful of anarchists also helped bring the negotiations to an abrupt end, this form of direct action did not occur in exclusion. Instead, it was merely a small component of what was a much larger and fully orchestrated campaign of protest that used unconventional and nonviolent means to achieve the desired ends. And it was a campaign whose success is still being measured. As Cockburn et al. concluded about Seattle,

If the direct action protesters had not put their bodies on the line throughout that entire week, if the only protest had been that under the official AFL-CIO banners, then there would have been a 15-second image of a parade on the national news headlines that Tuesday evening and that would have been it. The WTO would have gone forward with barely a ripple of discord except for what the African and Caribbean nations had managed to foment from the inside.[58]

Meanwhile, and discussed in chapter 4, for law enforcement the crimes of dissent staged in the streets of Seattle signaled a new, if not renewed, phase in crowd control—one marked by so-called free-speech and no-protest zones as well as the use of chemical weapons to attack nonviolent protesters and an increased militarization of policing tactics. Despite the political fallout and resignation of the Seattle police chief in response to what many people perceived as overly aggressive police tactics, these are policing strategies that have continued to evolve as anti-corporate-globalization demonstrations haven given way to antiwar demonstrations and to crimes of dissent directed against the politicians, government agencies, and corporate entities responsible for perpetuating the war in Iraq as well as the many dubious facets of the so-called war on terror. Today, with such legislation as the USA PATRIOT Act now in effect, freedom of expression through the deliberate violation of law becomes even more problematic, as provisions in these laws attempt to label acts of dissent forms of "domestic" terrorism. This development should be of concern to individuals operating from both the political Left and Right.[59] Whatever it is that Seattle truly signified, one thing for certain is that the realignment of political and economic power at the dawn of the twenty-first century has sparked an increase of, and a focus on, new forms of political resistance and new crimes of dissent that will continue to evolve with the ever-changing political climate.

2

Society and Its Discontents

Societies have the criminals they deserve.
—Alexandre Lacassagne (1885)

That the tens of thousands of people who protested the WTO in Seattle comprised a mix of anarchists, machinists, environmentalists, and steelworkers was inevitable. By the end of the millennium, the totality of effects wrought by globalization was felt by a wide swath of the public. People upset about the outsourcing of jobs and environmental degradation now had a common enemy, and they were vocal about the lack of generic pharmaceuticals on the international market or the privatization of water and other natural resources. The problem, as many people saw it, was that corporations were expanding their influence into virtually every aspect our lives. Whether through financial campaign contributions, through the consolidation of the mass media, or through the manufacturing and mass marketing of consumer culture, citizens from across the political spectrum (and from across the globe) felt that the private sector had overextended its role in economic, political, and social activities both domestically and abroad, and people were determined to do something about it.

The Seattle protests against the WTO therefore constituted a new tenor of growing social discontent, especially within open and free democracies such as the United States. But although the movement against corporate governance truly became manifest at the end of the twentieth century, for many academics recognition of the problem was not new. In 1959 sociologist C. Wright Mills identified the existence of a small "power elite" composed of political, corporate, and military figures positioned to draft policy directly or at a minimum positioned to shape the decisions that affect the lives of the masses. Mills even went so far as to suggest that because of corporations' political and financial connections to heads of State, for all practical purposes they have "actually occupied many positions of power within the formal political system."[1] Of course, with access to political figures come legal privilege and the differential implementation of law, especially when corporate campaign contributions are at stake. As Edwin Sutherland noted in 1949, people responsible for implementing justice "are afraid to antagonize businessmen," for among other consequences, "such antagonism may result in a reduction in contributions to the campaign funds needed to win the next election."[2] More recently, in *Culture, Inc.,* Herbert Schiller documented the drive to bring under corporate management "as many elements of economic and social activity as possible," including myriad mechanisms of public expression. Writing a decade before the events in Seattle unfolded, he called on readers to create "a new political movement" specifically organized to challenge the corporate takeover of contemporary governance.[3]

In assessing the rise of corporate dominance, many observers identify the aftermath of the Second World War as the era when corporate power became most pronounced. Indeed, the roots of contemporary discontent over corporate globalization can be found within the international trade institutions and policies that emerged at the end of the Second World War. Specifically, after the war ended, the United Nations Monetary and Financial Conference was assembled at Bretton Woods, New Hampshire, where the International Monetary Fund (IMF) was created to finance the reconstruction of Europe and to prevent international economic crises. To be sure, the IMF is a public institution. It is financed by taxes provided by citizens from contributor nations. It was established to allow countries experiencing financial problems to continue with global trade uninterrupted. The IMF initially recognized that even so-called free markets require regulation to prevent economic and social catastrophe. By the 1980s, however, the IMF operated according to an ideology that viewed any regulation as a barrier to capital. Under a new doctrine of neoliberalism, officials from the IMF encouraged countries to "liberalize" their economies, that is, to reduce or do away with such barriers as tariffs and humanitarian or environmental regulations.[4]

Soon, multinational corporations based in the United States and in Europe began outsourcing jobs and purchasing goods from foreign manufacturers. American and European citizens whose governments had been among the biggest promoters of neoliberalism began to feel the impact of what has come to be known as corporate globalization. While champions of free trade lauded it as a means to create more jobs for Americans, the increased use of cheap foreign labor coupled with an increase in imports often resulted in job losses. Those manufacturing jobs that remained intact were nevertheless quite unstable since employees were (and continue to be) always under the threat that companies would relocate abroad when requests for improvements in wages and working conditions were sought. By and large, globalization also failed to benefit the consumer, as was widely promised, since corporate savings were seldom reflected in the cost of goods. Thus, *The Field Guide to the Global Economy* reported that in 1994 "General Motors built a new factory in Silano, Mexico to produce Suburbans for the U.S. market. GM paid $18.96 per hour for U.S. labor but only $1.54 for labor in Mexico. And yet, the price of Suburbans continued to go up."[5] Even big-box retailers such as Wal-Mart that offered consumers low prices in the short term cost them in the long term, because the store's dependency on cheap foreign labor reduced U.S. manufacturing jobs, thereby driving down domestic wages among competing manufacturers.[6]

In time, the negative impacts of corporate globalization were felt by many, thereby changing the political spectrum from one that throughout the 1980s had been a left-of-center/right-of-center dichotomy into one that by the century's end was a top/bottom or even private/public dichotomy.[7] Then, in 1995 the WTO was established to monitor and govern the policies of international trade. Ideally the WTO could have functioned to protect the interests of global citizens, but as it stood it did not constitute a democratic institution, even though its policies affected citizens of the world. Instead, its rules were written by and for corporations. Moreover, its proceedings and trade negotiations were conducted in secret, and it ignored any attempt at input from citizens', labor, environmental, and consumer groups affected by its rulings.

When the WTO decided to hold its closed-door millennial trade negotiations in the U.S. Pacific Northwest, it attracted interest groups and activists who converged on Seattle to voice their dissent. One such activist was Sharon Delgado. A pastor of a church, Delgado also held two master's degrees: a Master of Divinity degree and a Master of Arts degree that focused on what she called "environmental theology." As she explained it to me, "Christianity had focused attention on human relationships with God, but not on human relationships with the natural world." Environmental theology recognizes the destruction of the environment as synonymous with the destruction of God's domain. So although Delgado had been a longtime environmental activist prior to Seattle, she admitted to having never really thought too much about corporate globalization before the WTO. On sabbatical from her church in the months prior to the millennial negotiations of the WTO, she immersed herself in reading and reflecting on the underlying economic problems that tied many issues of concern together.

The more that Delgado read about the negative environmental and social impacts of economic globalization, the more she realized that the underlying causes of the harm were interconnected. "Whenever we get something really going and rolling, oftentimes the big interests will apply so much pressure that it ends up not going anywhere. The ones who make the rules and benefit from the current system make change very difficult." Thus, in 1993 the WTO declared a regulation of the U.S. Clean Air Act to be illegal because a requirement that called for the production of cleaner gasoline constituted a barrier to the corporate world's "right" to free trade. Years later, the WTO again declared as an illegal trade barrier a provision of the Endangered Species Act. The provision in question called for shrimp sold in the United States to be caught with gear that protected endangered sea turtles from accidental capture. At the end of the twentieth century, the WTO continued to declare as trade barriers tariffs on wood and lumber products, thereby increasing the demand for timber and furthering the practice of deforestation.[8]

So when Delgado learned that the WTO was holding its millennial trade negotiations in the United States, she realized she had enough. She was tired of corporate control of government. More broadly, she was concerned about citizens' loss of control over the machinations of governance. She decided to do something about it. "I did some nonviolence training and did a huge amount of work and helped to shut down the meetings of the WTO. . . . I was part of the group that was planning to do direct action, and we did." With a caravan of about 125 people from her community, Delgado made the trip to Seattle, formed a human chain with other protesters, and shut down the trade negotiations. Here is how she explained her experience in Seattle:

> I was at Union St. and J. There were probably about seventy-five to a hundred of us actually blocking the intersection, but there were hundreds of supporters. We divided up in our affinity groups . . . and some of us formed affinity groups on the spot, and then we decided that our group would help take that intersection.

When asked about her goal in going to Seattle, Delgado was rather direct:

> My goal was to make a point and to be part of a large protest so that the world would know about the WTO and people in the world would know that there's a huge amount of opposition in the United States to this institution. . . . Our political process has been co-opted by transnational corporations that basically buy the politicians. So it's really not a democracy. It's a corporatocracy or plutocracy or whatever. And the majority of people feel so powerless. We're told it's a democracy, and it's not, and people don't understand why they're feeling so powerless.

A Glimpse into the System

Years after Seattle, globalization still fails to fulfill its promise of an economically equitable and socially just marketplace. International trade policies overwhelmingly benefit Western and industrial economies, while the economies of developing nations ("developing" serving as a euphemism for "struggling") become increasingly mired in debt. All the while, workers' rights and environmental standards are deemed barriers to trade under international agreements. Moreover, the closer integration of the world's civilizations wrought by globalization has also failed to bring an end to, or even a diminution of, military conflagrations, as was hoped. Genocide and ethnic cleansing are as present as ever. Military spending by the world's leading superpower continues to outpace spending on social programs. Even before the U.S.-led war in Iraq, the Pentagon's funding for war preparation was greater than $310 billion. That averaged to military expenses of about $700 million a day—enough to feed the hungry in the most impoverished of nations.[9]

But corporate globalization alone cannot account for the myriad flaws in our system. Consider the following: in the United States today, worker productivity is up, but wages are down. At one time, the minimum wage was able to sustain a family of three. Today, it fails to keep a working parent with a child above the poverty line.[10] Poverty is increasing, and real earnings are declining.[11] Women continue to earn less than what men earn. A CEO working today on average earns more than twelve hundred minimum-wage workers. This figure is up from ninety-seven minimum-wage workers just twenty years ago.[12] Clearly, as the rich continue to get richer, the poor are becoming poorer. Racially, black household incomes average 62 percent of those for whites. Nearly one-quarter of all African Americans live in poverty, a figure that compares to less than one in ten for non-Hispanic Whites. Moreover, the life expectancy for whites continues to exceed that of blacks due in part to the deadly combination of poverty and a lack of access to preventive health care. Meanwhile, with poverty comes street crime. Today there are over two million people locked up in U.S. jails and prisons, the majority being poor minorities. According to The Sentencing Project, one in every eight black men in their twenties is in prison or jail on any given day. At current rates of incarceration, one of every three black males born today can expect to be imprisoned at some point in his life.[13]

Despite the promise of globalization and the promise of a new century, our system is broken. Worse, it is not easily fixed through conventional means. Take elections, which U.S. citizens are taught are the most precious means to exact social change. It turns out that one of the biggest predictors of success at the ballot box is not ideology or policy agenda but rather the amount of money raised by a political campaign. In fact, the Center for Public Integrity reports that "in *every* U.S. presidential election since 1976, the candidate who has raised the most money at the end of the year preceding the election" became his party's nominee for the general election. Moreover, the Alliance for Better Campaigns estimates the amount that candidates, parties, and issue groups spent on political campaigns to be "slightly more than $150 million in 1980 and more than $1 billion in 2002." Also in 2002, incumbent U.S. senators seeking reelection raised an average of over $5.5 million, while incumbent congresspersons on average raised nearly $1 million to maintain their seats in the House. It is no wonder that roughly 40 percent of the U.S. Senate is composed of millionaires, since it appears that only people with deep pockets (or with friends having deep pockets) can get elected. By comparison, less than 1 percent of Americans are within the millionaire class. Economically, then, the United States is home to a government that is hardly representative of the constituency it serves, especially when the constituency under consideration is the nation's abjectly poor.[14]

It is interesting to note that the biggest donors to these costly political campaigns year in and year out tend to be large multinational corporations with deep pockets and an army of lobbyists working at their behest, thereby rendering the concept of "one person, one vote" somewhat laughable. But it is not only an issue of *who* is financing elections; it is also an issue of what these financiers expect in return. Citing voting records that clearly benefit the special interests of the largest campaign contributors rather than the general interests of the constituency as a whole, The Center for Public Integrity has referred to large corporate donations as "buying influence." Apparently, voters agree. When surveyed, 84 percent of citizens said that members of Congress will be more likely to "listen to those who give money," and only 24 percent believed that their representatives are likely to give the opinion "of someone like them" special consideration.[15] It would seem that from the vantage of the average citizen, electoral politics is hardly an avenue for bringing about substantive social change. Perhaps this fact helps to explain why so few Americans actually turn out to vote.

The influence of money also helps to explain why one is not likely to find a sympathetic voice for social change in the pages of U.S. newspapers, since the interests that maintain the prevailing political structure also own the media charged with reporting on it. Today a handful of multinational corporations—the very same corporations that rank among the top contributors to the Democratic and Republican parties—control the bulk of global media outlets. This trend of media consolidation is actually part of a development in market capitalism that has involved the consolidation of banks, oil companies, and other industries into the hands of the power elite.[16] And as media consolidation increases, the willingness of news outlets to hold power accountable to the public naturally decreases, since corporate media require politically neutral or "objective" content in order for parent companies to market their fare to the widest possible audience—a fact not lost on paying advertisers.[17] What we are left with, then, is news media that are more concerned with celebrity gossip than with issues of social or economic justice.

This dumbing down of the media and—by extension—of the electorate helps to explain the superficiality of headlines printed in daily newspapers. Indeed, as planes were hitting the Twin Towers and the Pentagon on the morning of September 11, 2001, Chicago residents awoke to a story in the *Chicago Sun Times* that reported that 70 percent of its polled readers were "more reluctant" to go swimming following a series of highly publicized Florida shark attacks. (Never mind that Chicago is nowhere near Florida and does not border the Atlantic Ocean.) The *New York Times* ran a seventeen-hundred-word feature that morning questioning whether a ban on the fishing of sharks was leaving bathers more vulnerable to attack. Meanwhile, the *San Francisco Chronicle* focused its coverage on an alleged predator of another type—Democratic congressman Gary Condit—whose future remained uncertain while an investigation into missing intern Chandra Levy (with whom he allegedly had an affair) was under way.[18]

After the 9/11 attacks, the largest radio broadcaster in the United States, Clear Channel, issued a list of songs deemed inappropriate for radio play (a list that included John Lennon's "Imagine" and Edwin Starr's "War," as well as all songs by Rage Against the Machine) because their lyrics may be viewed as critical of the government's rush to war, possibly offending some listeners and diminishing the size of its audience.[19] When the United States did indeed go to war, CNN president Walter Isaacson authorized his cable news service to provide two different versions of war coverage: "a critical one for global audiences and a sugarcoated one for Americans."[20] At that point, any testimonial to free speech in the United States could no longer be taken seriously.

Even art museums, which have traditionally served as arenas for the creative expression of dissent, no longer allow for cutting-edge political or social critique. Beginning in the 1980s, cultural critics began to denounce corporate sponsorship of art museums as an encroachment on the freedom of expression, arguing that "the corporate outreach to museums is obviously not intended to induce social instability in the political realm. Its objective is quite the opposite."[21] Today, the line between art and advertising is one that is becoming increasingly blurry. Thus, the Guggenheim's 1998 homage to the "art" of the motorcycle featured a BMW R1200C, which was described as "the soul of American motorcycling." The fact that BMW is not an American-owned motorcycle manufacturer was one that the Guggenheim simply chose to disregard. After all, the exhibition's sponsor was—of course—BMW. And if tests for general standards of decency for all National Endowment for the Arts (NEA) recipients was not cause for concern enough, in January 2004 the Bush White House announced a proposed $18 million increase to the NEA to be used almost exclusively for works that First Lady Laura Bush announced were designed to remind Americans of their cultural legacy.[22] One can never be sure, but it is doubtful that art that provided a negative interpretation of the U.S. legacy qualified for government funding.

Finally, what were once basic government entities such as the military and the criminal justice system have become increasingly privatized, thereby moving more of our governance outside the direct reach of public accountability. By summer 2007, the number of U.S.-funded private contractors in Iraq exceeded that of U.S. combat troops, with the contractors performing duties previously the domain of soldiers. Moreover, at least 150 private correctional facilities house over one hundred thousand inmates throughout the United States.[23] Even education and other social services are increasingly being relegated to the private sector through voucher programs and legislation allowing for the federal funding of private "faith-based" charitable organizations. High school civics lessons aside, it seems that a government that is both directly accountable to its constituency and easily amenable to change is rapidly disappearing, as the private sector continues to exert its influence on political campaigns, the freedom of expression, and basic social services. These factors help to explain why today "Johnny can't dissent"—as Thomas Frank put it[24]—at least not in a meaningful sense, not without kicking up some dust, and not without the risk of legal recrimination.

The Problem with Civilization

"How has it happened," wrote Sigmund Freud in the aftermath of the First World War, "that so many people have come to take up this strange attitude of hostility to civilization?" It is a question worth asking. For even when big-money and corporate influence can be kept out of political processes, society and its governance can still prove to be a source of widespread discontent, because far from rendering humans happier, civilization simply replaces the power of the individual with the power of the State. It follows, then, that much of what social theorists refer to as conflict and discontent, and even what law enforcement refers to as crime, may in fact be humankind's struggle to accommodate what Freud called the moral "claim of the individual" in light of the "cultural claims of the group."[25]

Absent the trappings of much of Freud's psychoanalytic theory, *Civilization and Its Discontents* finds Freud directing his inquiry outward toward culture itself; as such, his essay reads more like a diagnosis of the modern State than one of the modern mind. For Freud, civilization begins with the imposition of restrictions on human nature. "[M]embers of the community restrict themselves in their possibilities of satisfaction, whereas the individual knew no such restrictions." Certainly, unrestrained freedom "is no gift" of civilization and modern society; to the contrary, liberty is greatest absent the restrictions of civilization. Unfortunately, human nature often calls for collective living, yet human nature and civilization often have competing interests. The civilizing process therefore is the process of placing restrictions on humans in their natural state of affairs.

And therein lies the problem, for although Freud noted that the "first requisite of civilization" is the assurance that laws will be adhered to by the collective, the civilizing process "implies nothing as to the ethical value of such a law."[26]

In any given civilization or social system, then, there is an inherent tension between personal morality on the one hand and collective responsibility on the other. The fact is that in modern times, it is the collective (i.e., the State) that has become the highest authority governing people's lives. Its influence over our decisions has surpassed that of the Church, the family, and even individual conscience. The State provides us with our sense of safety, it allocates our natural resources, and it even educates our children. And whether a totalitarian regime or an open and participatory democracy, it is the State that shapes the daily routines of our lives. So ubiquitous is the presence of the State that most of us simply cannot imagine an existence apart from it.

Of course, there is nothing inherently problematic with the State playing such a central role in our lives so long as its authority emanates from the people through some sort of social contract in which we agree to live collectively under a set of shared rules, norms, values, and beliefs that in turn become manifest through the State. But what happens when an individual no longer finds his or her values or morals adequately represented by the social contract? Does the State still maintain its legitimacy? Why should the State, and not the individual, be the supreme source of authority? If individuals must always cede their conscience to some higher political entity, why has everyone a conscience, as Henry David Thoreau famously asked? Are we only truly free to act on our will within the confines of the ballot box while keeping our morals in check between elections? What happens if an election fails to yield the policies (and personalities) that represent our beliefs? At what point does the social contract break down, rendering the State a source of coercion in which compliance to the law becomes forced?

These are the very questions that confronted Ed Hedemann. Today a war tax resister, during the Vietnam War, Hedemann discovered that his allegiance to the social contract breaks at the very point when war (and its preparation) begins. A self-described anarchist and pacifist, Hedemann is of the mindset that one cannot simultaneously organize for peace while paying for war. Unfortunately, the collective conscience is of a completely different mindset than Hedemann's, and federal law leaves him with little choice: either he can pay for war, or he can risk going to jail. Hedemann has opted for the latter; as a result, he has not paid his federal income taxes (some seventy thousand dollars' worth by his account) in thirty years, and he is always facing the possibility of jail time. How he has managed to avoid jail for tax resistance while remaining public about his dissent is discussed in the next chapter. For now, it is the tension between his personal and collective conscience that is of immediate relevance. "I don't want to go along with something that I think is wrong, like raising money for the military. To me, that's horrifying! It's against everything I believe in. I'm not going to willingly pay the government so they can kill." As he explained, no one and nothing should ever be able to compel him to do that which is against his conscience.

Interestingly, like so many other activists I have met during my research, Hedemann was raised in a conservative family that he described as being "very much into obeying the law and doing as you're told by the government." Relatively apolitical during the early years of Vietnam, as an undergraduate at Berkeley, Hedemann's opposition to the war slowly began to grow. Then, in January 1969, his life changed when he received an induction notice from the government. "I was forced to make a decision. . . . immediately I had to think about, well, how against [the war] was I? Was it just *this* war? *All* wars? Was I willing to go to jail in opposition?" Ultimately, Hedemann reported to the induction center and refused to serve. "It was a really touchy decision, and I talked with a lot of people and did a lot of reading very quickly. . . . I decided . . . I just could not go in. . . . I'd be willing to go to jail." Luckily, after refusing service and being told that he would be hearing from the government, he never did hear back. Years later, he obtained his FBI files and discovered that the draft board had made an error that might have been reversible in court.

But whereas Hedemann became a tax resister and refused to cede to government authority without having to go to war, "Bob" became a tax resister only *after* serving time in the military. A soldier in Vietnam, Bob was stationed in what he told me was "the war room" where many of the combat plans for his unit were devised. Appalled at what he saw, when he got out of the service, he immediately declared himself a conscientious objector. But it was not until a few years after his military service that his girlfriend, pregnant at the time and considering an abortion, brought him to consider tax resistance. "I found out that abortions [at the time] were being funded through the tax system. My son was almost one of those; he almost became an abortion." Suddenly, Bob's opposition to the violence

WHERE YOUR INCOME TAX MONEY REALLY GOES

U.S. FEDERAL BUDGET **2009** FISCAL YEAR

TOTAL OUTLAYS (FEDERAL FUNDS) $2,659 BILLION

Non-MILITARY: 46% AND $1,210 BILLION

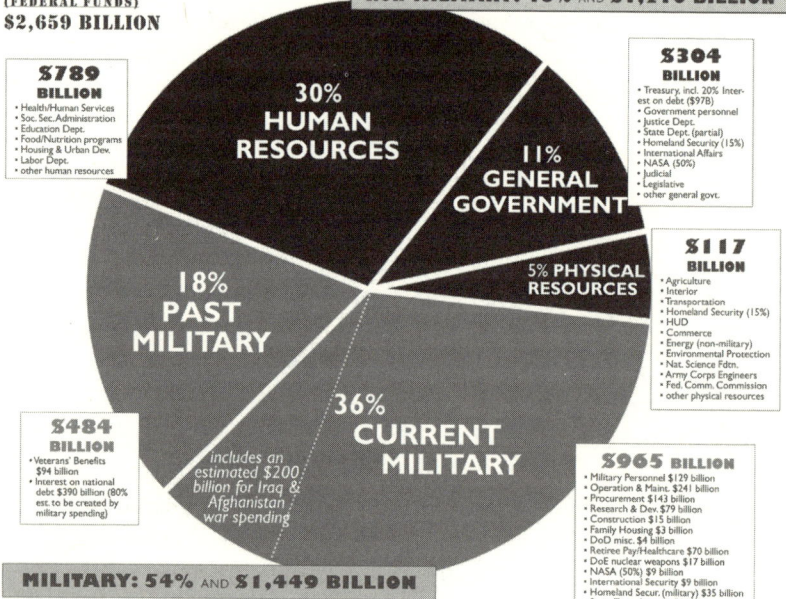

$789 BILLION
- Health/Human Services
- Soc. Sec. Administration
- Education Dept.
- Food/Nutrition programs
- Housing & Urban Dev.
- Labor Dept.
- other human resources

30% HUMAN RESOURCES

11% GENERAL GOVERNMENT

$304 BILLION
- Treasury, incl. 20% Interest on debt ($97B)
- Government personnel
- Justice Dept.
- State Dept. (partial)
- Homeland Security (15%)
- International Affairs
- NASA (50%)
- Judicial
- Legislative
- other general govt.

5% PHYSICAL RESOURCES

$117 BILLION
- Agriculture
- Interior
- Transportation
- Homeland Security (15%)
- HUD
- Commerce
- Energy (non-military)
- Environmental Protection
- Nat. Science Fdn.
- Army Corps Engineers
- Fed. Comm. Commission
- other physical resources

18% PAST MILITARY

$484 BILLION
- Veterans' Benefits $94 billion
- Interest on national debt $390 billion (80% est. to be created by military spending)

includes an estimated $200 billion for Iraq & Afghanistan war spending

36% CURRENT MILITARY

$965 BILLION
- Military Personnel $129 billion
- Operation & Maint. $241 billion
- Procurement $143 billion
- Research & Dev. $79 billion
- Construction $15 billion
- Family Housing $3 billion
- DoD misc. $4 billion
- Retiree Pay/Healthcare $70 billion
- DoE nuclear weapons $17 billion
- NASA (50%) $9 billion
- International Security $9 billion
- Homeland Secur. (military) $35 billion
- State Dept. (partial) $6 billion
- other military (non-DoD) $5 billion
- "Global War on Terror" $200 billion

We added $162 billion to the last item to supplement the Budget's grossly underestimated $38 billion in "allowances" for the "War on Terror," which includes the wars in Iraq and Afghanistan

MILITARY: 54% AND $1,449 BILLION

HOW THESE FIGURES WERE DETERMINED

"Current military" includes Dept. of Defense ($653 billion), the military portion from other departments ($150 billion), and an additional $162 billion to supplement the Budget's misleading and vast underestimate of only $38 billion for the "war on terror." "Past military" represents veterans' benefits plus 80% of the interest on the debt.* For further explanation, please go to www.warresisters.org/piechart.htm.

These figures are from an analysis of detailed tables in the "Analytical Perspectives" book of the *Budget of the United States Government, Fiscal Year 2009.* The figures are federal funds, which do not include trust funds — such as Social Security — that are raised and spent separately from income taxes. What you pay (or don't pay) by April 15, 2008, goes to the federal funds portion of the budget. The government practice of combining trust and federal funds began during the Vietnam War, thus making the human needs portion of the budget seem larger and the military portion smaller.

*Analysis differ on how much of the debt stems from the military; other groups estimate 50% to 60%. We use 80% because we believe if there had been no military spending most (if not all) of the national debt would have been eliminated.

Government Deception

The pie chart (right) is the government view of the budget. This is a distortion of how our income tax dollars are spent because it includes Trust Funds (e.g., Social Security), and the expenses of past military spending are not distinguished from nonmilitary spending. For a more accurate representation of how your Federal income tax dollar is really spent, see the large graph.

Source: Congressional Budget Office for FY2008

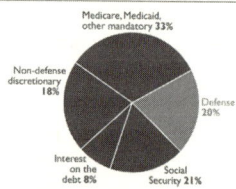

- Medicare, Medicaid, other mandatory 33%
- Non-defense discretionary 18%
- Defense 20%
- Interest on the debt 8%
- Social Security 21%

WAR RESISTERS LEAGUE 339 Lafayette Street • NY, NY 10012 • 212-228-0450 • www.warresisters.org

Updated annually, this pie chart published by the War Resisters League serves as a powerful recruiting tool for the war-tax-resistance movement.

of war gelled with his views on abortion. "I'm a pro-life person. I don't believe in abortion, murder, war. I don't believe in capital punishment. . . . I don't kill anybody for nothing. That's God's job, not mine."

Describing his soul and spirit as "grieving over my participation in paying for murder," whether through war, abortion, or even capital punishment, Bob began researching tax resistance. At the same time, he admitted to having had problems contemplating this strategy of resistance, because he "believed in the legal system." Indeed, speaking to Bob, I got the sense of a true patriot, someone who believed in the "idea" of the United States of America but who simultaneously believed that his country either had lost its way or had never really lived up to its promise. And that is why he engaged in the politics of conscience; after all, "if you want to have clean hands, you cannot participate in any way, shape, or form" with that which violates one's sense of morality.

The "Psychic Conflicts" of Governance

This discussion of the politics of conscience brings us back to Freud, to the problems of society, and to the social conflict that the problems of civilization can produce. Once we begin to understand the centrality of the State in our daily lives, we can begin to recognize the inherent tension or psychic conflict—as cultural criminologists call it—between the competing concepts of *autonomy* and *authority*.[27] In the widely read (and much debated) treatise *In Defense of Anarchism*, political philosopher Robert Paul Wolff defines autonomy as a state of complete freedom. Autonomy is marked by obedience only to laws or policies that one has personally enacted; it is to be completely free from any values and morals that have been imposed rather than chosen. It follows that the only restraints on individual autonomy are those that are naturally self-imposed. But since we must all live collectively and cooperatively if we are to survive as a species, we recognize that we must forsake some autonomy. So we do so for the good of the collective. When we do so, though, the collective quickly becomes a source of authority, but—and this is crucial—it is an authority to which we have willingly given our consent. Authority, then, is best understood as "the right to command . . . and the right to be obeyed."[28] It is, however, a concept that is wholly distinct from *power*, since power—like violence—is the ability to compel compliance. A clever example from Wolff illustrates the difference:

When I turn over my wallet to a thief who is holding me at gunpoint, I do so because the fate with which he threatens me is worse than the loss of money which I am made to suffer. I grant that he has power over me, but I would hardly suppose that he has authority, that is, that he has a right to demand my money.[29]

Civilization therefore requires autonomy to yield to authority for the sake of harmony and collective living. But this requirement presents the fundamental shortcoming of governance: if freedom is synonymous with autonomy, then how can a society that restrains autonomy still claim to be free?

One solution proffered by political philosophers is to ensure that the newly entered-into social contract adheres to the tenets of democracy so that the authority always represents the will of the people. But when political philosophers speak of democracy, what they have in mind hardly resembles contemporary forms of democracy. Instead, theirs is a model of democracy that exists in its most pure and idyllic form: unanimous direct democracy. Wolff refers to unanimous direct democracy as "classical democracy" because when practiced, "every person votes on every issue" until a consensus is reached. This characteristic is crucial, since individuals need only consent to laws that they themselves have created, ensuring that *no one* forfeits any autonomy.[30]

Already, the reader is likely to dismiss unanimous direct democracy as both hopelessly quixotic and as an exercise in futility since consensus is such a high threshold for which to strive. Yet there are many settings that almost always operate according to this consensus process; most notably for criminal justice students is the jury system. But consensus is also used in friendship and/or family networks in which the goal is not to secure a "winning" vote but rather to ensure that every member of the group is satisfied or can live with the outcome of a decision. Thus, unanimous direct democracy, or consensus decision-making, as it is more commonly known, can work well when there is already a high level of agreement among members of a group. Indeed, many activist groups operate almost exclusively according to the consensus process, because "consensus is a decision-making process that reflects commitment to the right of every person to influence decisions that affect them," as one activist training manual explains.[31] Through consensus, then, activists avoid replicating the very flaws of contemporary governance in which authority impinges on autonomy. Unfortunately, the practice of consensus decision-making becomes problematic when group settings become too large and ideologically diverse. With the complexity of daily life, it simply becomes too difficult for each member of society to be able to attend each vote. Moreover, as groups become larger, they become more diverse in opinion, making unanimity all but impossible. Even if citizens could somehow render an opinion for every vote, there is simply no way to ensure that each voter can be fully informed about each potential act of governance. For all practical purposes, then, consensus decision-making cannot work in large nation-state settings and must be limited to what many political philosophers call natural or intentional communities.

A way around the difficulties of consensus decision-making, for which every voter must agree with every decision, is the compromise of majority rule. Since a vote of unanimity is nearly impossible in ideologically diverse political settings, constituents allow for decisions that garner more than half the vote to become law. The argument for majority rule is utilitarian in nature as it ostensibly produces the greatest good for the greatest number of people. But how are we to characterize voters who find themselves within the political minority? Must they be bound to rule of law decided for them (rather than *by* them) by a political majority? Once again, we are confronted with a political system in which individuals such as Hedemann and Bob find themselves obligated to live under a law unreflective of their conscience. Granted, a popular counterargument points out that members of the political minority *agreed* to be governed by the laws of the majority. Perhaps, but so what? They still must live under the rule of law chosen by others. When this situation occurs, one simply cannot claim to be free. As Wolff points out, to agree to live by the rules of others' choosing is merely to agree to a condition of "voluntary slavery,"[32] and who wants that?

But the problems of majority rule do not end there. Even if we accept that we may periodically have to be governed by policies not of our choosing, we cannot overcome the very real existence of permanent political minorities. If individuals know they will repeatedly end up in the political minority, they quickly realize that there is little chance of effecting their will by voting their conscience, and they naturally gravitate toward the political majority. This factor, what social-contract theorist Jean-Jacques Rousseau termed a "tyranny of a majority," helps to explain the dominance of the two-party system in the United States, where voters who may otherwise vote for a third-party candidate choose not to vote their conscience for fear of ending up in the permanent political minority.

Instead, they opt to vote for what they call the lesser of two evils. That they at least had an opportunity to participate in the great democratic tradition is probably of little comfort to those feeling consistently disenfranchised and disempowered. Citizens want more than an opportunity to participate in the democratic process; they also want real choices as well as the real potential for outcomes that are reflective of their values. Unfortunately, majority rule cannot guarantee this possibility.

Another resolution to the problem of unanimous direct democracy is for populations to appoint representatives charged with the task of voting on behalf of the public. This system overcomes the requirement that every citizen vote on every issue. Ideally, representatives vote solely on the basis of the instructions received from their constituency. But doing so would require the representatives constantly to poll their constituency, which may not have the time to be as informed as a full-time politician. Often, then, the practicalities of democracy require representatives to vote according to their own sense of what is best for their constituency. That is, representative democracy is more often a process of governance that is "for the people" and not "by the people," and when that is the case, democracy is hard to distinguish from, say, a monarchy, since the outcome calls for a constituency to be subject to the decisions of others. They have simply been given a chance to elect their masters.

Clearly autonomy is threatened by the practicalities of majority rule and representative democracy since individuals are legally obligated to obey laws not directly of their choosing. To be fair, proponents of representative democracy correctly point out that citizens always have an opportunity to freely choose their representatives during elections, but doing so is often of little consequence, since no voter can accurately predict what issues are going to arise while representatives are in office, let alone how they will vote. "Even when we have a seat at the table" of government, one activist told me, "it doesn't do anything a lot of the time." Another activist told me that his experience working on the 1988 Michael Dukakis presidential campaign made him realize that merely a change in political representation was not "going to be the way out of the Reagan years" since there was no guarantee that the Democrats were going to mitigate any of the conditions of the poor, which was the topic most of concern to him.

This uncertainty in a decision-making process by way of representation explains why critics characterize the practice of selecting political representation as being little more than a voter's compiling a wish list. Even Rousseau wrote that citizens in representative democracies who consider themselves to be free are "gravely mistaken"; instead, they are "free only during the election." In fact, he argued that as soon as the election is over, the people are once again "enslaved."[33] These issues explain why activists opt for less conventional means of political expression, such as civil disobedience, direct action, and other crimes of dissent. Without these means, "you're just waiting for the next election," as one activist put it, "and there's at least 365 days from one November to the next. Direct action really allows us to vote every day."

Finally, we must confront the topic of the rule of law and the maintenance of order, which is of the most immediate relevance to the subject of this book. If democracy through representative and majority rule cannot rectify the autonomy/authority conflict, then even within open democracies, citizens are forced to live according to laws not always of their choosing. When that happens, the law fails to resemble a neutral or even a benign entity. In fact, when laws are not morally reflective of the consciences they guide, they represent a source of power, if not of political violence, since one is never really free to dissent without consequence. In a seminal article addressing this point, the late Yale Law School professor Robert Cover argued that the law is inextricably linked to violence through the practice of judicial interpretation, through prosecutorial application, and of course, through law's enforcement by police, incarceration, and even death. This "violence" of the law begins with a legal interpretation in which a judge articulates an understanding of a legal text, "and as a result, somebody loses his freedom, his property, his children, even his life." For Cover, a focus on legal interpretation is essential because in a very real sense the law only exists through interpretation. Legal interpretation, Cover argued, "may be the act of judges or citizens, legislators or presidents, draft resisters or right-to-life protesters," which means that each interpretation is rooted in the perspective of the interpreter, who "speaks from a distinct institutional location."[34] Even proponents of a particular legal clause cannot guarantee how any given judge will interpret the legal text. Thus, free-speech advocates may have cheered when Justice Potter Stewart ruled against a legal claim of obscenity; yet his famous quip "I know it when I see it" simply illustrates the extent to which the law cannot stand on the merits of the written word alone. In an instant, then, legal rulings in even the most open and free democracies can resemble monarchical orders and decrees.

Practically speaking, it is not through interpretation but through tangible legal processes that the violence of law becomes manifest. Consider what happens when people dissent. Equipped with guns, clubs, and other accoutrements of violence, police are called in to force compliance. The law, therefore, is really akin to an iron fist in a velvet glove. Granted, many citizens will earnestly claim to agree with most of the laws composing the legal system, but that is merely a fortunate convenience. Freedom, after all, is about choice. Therefore, freedom is not measured by what people can do when they agree with government; rather, it is measured by what people can do when they disagree. It is not about acceptance but about the ability to enact change when desired. Yet the law is inextricably linked to the concept of order, with violence as a means of protecting the prevailing status quo.

When individuals choose to ignore a law and opt for the politics of conscience, the violence of the law ultimately reveals itself in the flesh. Cover argued that martyrdom represents a proper starting place to understand truly the violence inherent in legal interpretation and, by extension, in government. It is the martyr, after all, who chooses autonomy over State. As a result, he or she suffers the violence of punishment. As such, it is the martyr who helps us see what is present whenever interpretation of the law takes place. It is when everyday citizens begin to resemble prisoners chained to laws and policies not of their choosing and it is when people from all walks of life begin to feel powerless to break free from these very chains that bind them that anarchy becomes a necessity to resolve the psychic conflicts that plague life in contemporary civilization.

An Autonomous Approach to Life

The preceding primer on the psychic conflicts of governance reveals what has been ever present in the annals of history: that "law without violence is unthinkable."[35] Even democratic systems (en)force the rule of law through their maintenance of a monopoly on the legitimate use of violence. But although most citizens willingly surrender their own personal beliefs for those of the collective, in any given State one can find a sometimes small, sometimes sizeable population unwilling to surrender to the violence of law. By failing to give in, these unwavering individuals become criminals by sheer act of dissent. In so doing, they behave in a manner that adheres to the principles of anarchism.

Despite what most people think, anarchism does not have to be thought of as "another world order" or an entire social system that stands in for the current political order. Anarchism can be conceptualized (as it is here) as merely "an individual orientation toward oneself and others, as a personal approach to life."[36] It is an orientation wherein people refuse to forfeit their conscience to anyone or anything that attempts to micromanage their lives. Anarchism, therefore, is simply a firm position against the surrender of conscience to anyone or anything. It is neither toward the left or the right on the ideological spectrum. In fact, the historian of anarchism Paul Avrich identifies myriad ideological strains of anarchism including Anarchist-Communists, who organized in communal settings of mutual benefit; Anarcho-Syndicalists, who sought worker control over factories and industry; and to a lesser extent Individualist Anarchists, who reject any formal social organization. Today, there are people who claim to be Libertarian Anarchists, such as culture critic Richard Kostelanetz.[37]

With a recognition that discussions of anarchism need not always provide a complete and detailed social arrangement, it is important to note that the characterization of anarchism outlined here is not without its detractors, for the very reason that it fails to propose a comprehensive and workable social system that would replace the State. In a book-length response to Wolff's treatise *In Defense of Anarchism*, Jeffrey Reiman criticizes Wolff's vision of anarchism on the grounds that its near complete focus on *moral* autonomy renders it *politically* "neutral."[38] Looking at Wolff's argument, political scientist Robert Dahl has argued that the mere opposition to laws is not a sufficient demarcation of anarchism; one must also be opposed to the very concept of the State that imposes these laws. He thus criticizes Wolff for failing to provide a complete political defense of anarchism, as the title of his treatise promises.[39] Dahl's is a valid criticism, though not necessarily a fair one. Writing for fellow anarchists, anthropology professor David Graeber has argued that when it comes to debating the viability of anarchism in contemporary society, "The dice are loaded. You can't win," because "when the skeptic says 'society,' what he really means is 'state,' even 'nation-state.'" For Graeber, when anarchists are asked to explain anarchism, "what we're really being asked for is an example of a modern nation-state with the government somehow plucked away."[40] Further, anarchist attempts to influence public policy that fall short of outright revolution always seem to be interpreted as an acceptance of the State. Yet in a much-debated article on anarchist strategizing, Chris Crass rejects the notion that short-term efforts to influence policy are antithetical to anarchist principles. Acknowledging that anarchists today exist in "societies of millions," he advocates an anarchism

Flip Benham, director of Operation
Save America.

that incorporates a multitude of tactics—including those that in the present appear only geared at reform.[41]

Whether we choose to call it anarchism or not, we can say for certain
that people on both sides of the ideological spectrum refuse to compromise conscience. Consider Flip Benham of Operation Save America, who
has been arrested over fifty times during his life for blocking access to
clinics where abortions are performed. He identified himself to me as a
Free Methodist who is aligned with the tenets of the Constitution Party,
which is somewhere on the far right of the political spectrum. Although
by no means an anarchist, Benham summed up the problem of democratic practice quite nicely: "politics . . . is the art of compromise, compromising principle in order to come to some solution where both sides
can agree." Yet there are many issues over which many people feel one
should never compromise. For Benham, abortion is not "a political issue," although he admits that "it certainly manifests itself in the political
realm." As he sees it, there simply is no "political" solution to the issue

of abortion, by which he means that there is no room for compromise of conscience. Recognizing that law is merely a question of interpretation, he claims that it is irrelevant "who George W. Bush [or any other president] really puts on the Supreme Court," since for him, abortion falls outside of law's domain. Since he feels that it is an issue that should be won morally rather than politically, he has chosen to take his theology to the streets through direct action.

Benham's approach to the law is not unlike that of antiwar activists, who have placed their bodies in front of military recruiting centers in the belief that they, too, are protecting innocent life. One war resister I met identified herself as a firm supporter of a woman's right to choose. At the same time, she acknowledged being able to identify with the motivation of pro-lifers. She even agreed that "they have every right to express their political opinions." In her mind, however, the distinction is one between preventing personal actions on the one hand and political actions on the other. That is, for her, people who prevent access to family planning centers impinge on one's private sphere and thereby impinge on her autonomy, whereas people (such as herself) who blockade in front of a military center are preventing acts carried out on behalf of an illegitimate power: the State. Of course, abortion protesters could counter that people who block recruiting centers likewise impinge on one's private sphere and thereby impinge on the autonomy of the person seeking to serve in the military.

Members of Operation Save America share a sidewalk with pro-choice advocates outside a women's health clinic. (Operation Save America)

Whatever one's personal beliefs, the point here must not be lost. Cultural criminology teaches us that values and norms are a terrain of ideological struggle. As such, conservative values sometimes impinge on liberal or progressive lifestyles. In other instances, progressive lifestyles encroach on conservative lifestyles. In both cases, cultures define dissent as criminal when people insist that "these are my morals, this is what I believe in, and this is who I am," as the woman countering military recruitment put it. And whether people are positioned on the left or right of the ideological spectrum, this approach to law underlies crimes of dissent. Thus, as another progressive activist opined, "I don't agree with them, but just like me, [with] people who block abortion clinics, it's because it's what's inside of them." It is this refusal to concede one's conscience that is the anarchist ideal.

If these tenets of anarchism sound idealistic, that is because they are idealistic, but it is an idealism that is also infused with realism. People who adhere to the principles of anarchism behave as realists when they reject the idealism that war, capitalism, and conspicuous consumption can somehow bring about peace, freedom, equality, and prosperity for all. Those who adhere to the principles of anarchism behave as realists when the espouse Thoreau's perspective that "Law never made men a whit more just."[42] Those who adhere to the principles of anarchism behave as realists when they adopt a healthy level of skepticism toward bosses, politicians, and corporations that profit off us while claiming to have our personal interests in mind.

But anarchism is more than merely a personal philosophy; it is also a praxis—which really just means that it is the practice of converting one's conscience into meaningful action. For most citizens in our politics as usual, political "action" is little more than strategizing on how to replace one government official with another through elections. Yet this conventional political action does little to preserve one's autonomy. Whether our political activism is measured by voting, by working for a political candidate, or even by gathering petitions for a ballot measure, most of us intuitively know that regardless of our efforts, the day-to-day content of our lives will remain unchanged. And why should we expect our lives to change when the outcome of our political action will still be completely removed from our everyday, lived experience? Moreover, elections fail to build any lasting or perpetual momentum. Why waste time on an endeavor that has no guarantee of longevity or success when the alternative has no such limitations? Instead of expending all our energy, creativity, and resources to help elect *others* who assure us they will act on our behalf, why not simply heed the anarchist ideal and act for ourselves instead? By acting for ourselves there are no term limits on our autonomy. By acting for ourselves we are limited only to the extent of our imaginations.

When thinking about politics as usual, it is important to recognize that most of us blame "those in power" for perpetuating existing injustices. Power, though, is not a singular entity or character trait. Rather, it is a relationship—a tacit agreement really—between those who govern and those who are governed or, more accurately, between the oppressor and the oppressed. It requires the complicity (or simply the passivity) of the masses. Rarely, though, do we ever acknowledge the role that each of us plays in perpetuating these injustices by limiting our politics and activism to elections and campaigns wherein we once again pass the responsibility onto those in power. Power, then, is always fragile, since its locus is always with the people. But once the oppressed masses refuse to be complicit in the rule of the oppressor, the power dynamic between the two players is threatened.[43] The longer one remains complicit in the injustices of the powerful, the longer one remains both an oppressor and the oppressed. Anarchy, therefore, refuses to separate politics from the immediate, everyday experiences of individual men and women. It calls on individuals to take direct action by asserting their autonomy and by acting for themselves. Of course, individuals need not consider themselves anarchists to be driven toward dissent. Nor do dissenters need to possess special or unique personalities that allow them the freedom of conscience to act separately from the masses. They need only a vision of a better world and a willingness to work toward its realization.

Profiles of Discontent

Now that I have outlined some of the problems of civilization and the limitations of democracy to redress them, what can be said about the discontented within society who choose to transgress law in protest once democracy has failed? Why do they dissent through illegal means? Do they embody selfish personas whose desire for individual gain trumps their commitment to collective convention? Do they possess a total disregard for the rights of others? Do they signify a class of people—nihilists perhaps—who reject all doctrines other than one that promotes disruption toward the status quo? In this final section of the chapter, I attempt to answer some general questions about the characteristics of people who dissent.

It is seductive to think of criminal acts as purely selfish behaviors. The murder committed by a jilted lover acting out of jealously, the con performed by a businessman driven by greed, the drug hit taken to feed a physiological need—these are common narratives within crime fictions and daily news headlines. In each account, the gains of the crime are solely personal, while the costs of the transgressions are passed onto the law-abiding public. Yet that is not the case for crimes of dissent, which are often acts of selflessness and altruism. To be sure, it is not unreasonable for crimes of conscience to begin with egoistic motives. Humans, after all, are driven by self-preservation, and they go to great lengths to protect their interests, whether personal or political. At the same time, one must recognize that people who dissent tend not to be egoists. This observation has been addressed rather pointedly in Albert Camus's book *The Rebel.* "It is for the sake of everyone in the world," wrote Camus, "that the slave asserts himself."[44] Indeed, although the slave may be motivated by a desire for personal liberation, the revolt of the slave is always an assertion of universal humanity. His rebellion does not belong to him alone; it belongs to all who are in chains.

Similarly, people who participated in the marches, sit-ins, and even the riots that occurred during the civil rights movement were not merely asserting their personal equality; they organized collectively under the banner of race, and in so doing they asserted the rights of all persons who have a racial minority status. During Vietnam, people who refused the military draft were certainly out to protect themselves; at the same time, their act of egoism necessarily united them in solidarity with the innocent victims of the war. In fact, one Vietnam draft dodger I interviewed admitted that what began for him as an act of self-protection quickly evolved into a career of activism. As he explained it, he was "conscripted into resistance." Decades later, and now years beyond draft age, this activist continues to protest war through his involvement in the peace community.

The rebel, therefore, begins a campaign seeking personal fulfillment but cannot do so without naturally raising issues that necessarily align him or her with a broader community. In this way, dissent sparks the formation of collective identities, or shared definitions of social or cultural status. Whatever individual motivations bring a rebel to action, the person is always guided by broader cultural forces that situate him or her within a unique social context marked by such distinguishing factors as race, class, gender, and sexual orientation. It is for this reason that Alain Touraine has argued against social movements scholarship marked by "the reduction of the system to the actor, the actor to the system, and the division of one from the other."[45] Instead, it is helpful to think of the protester as one among many individuals similarly situated within a social hierarchy. This discussion brings us back to the concept of community and *affinity groups*, for contemporary activism is rarely manifested through a lone individual. Instead, society's discontented coalesce in groups marked by a common social, political, economic, or spiritual identity such that an action by one member of the community attempts to advance the interests of all members of that community.

Even if we allow for a measure of egoism in rebellion, many times activism is guided solely by altruism. As Camus noted, rebellion often begins simply because humans are unwilling to witness suffering or injustice, even when there is an unlikelihood of being personally or directly affected by that injustice. For Benjamin Shepard, an activist I met in the spring of 2005, simply witnessing the smoke-filled sky in the aftermath of the Los Angeles/Rodney King riots was enough to push him to his first protest. A student at a private university at the time of the riots, here is how he described his entry into activism:

> I had driven through South-Central a few times in my four years in and around Los Angeles. But when the riots broke out, that was very much a sense of "Man, I've heard about Watts, I've heard about Detroit." But like, I just had a sense that this can't keep on going on. You ignore a cancer in a part of the city that is hardened by poverty—it's not a way a city can live. I remember playing Frisbee and watching smoke go up in the air through the clouds in the distance. And we were not supposed to leave the campus for a few days before graduation. And that was to me, Wow! So history to me felt very alive at the moment. And it was the first protest that I participated in on the campus. [It was] in response or solidarity to the L.A. riots.

Today, Shepard is active in an array of social causes with the goal of improving conditions in U.S. inner cities, anything from needle-exchange programs to inner-city community gardens to fighting the corporate takeover of public space. All this activism resulted not from having been oppressed himself but from having witnessed the oppression of others.

In the same way, activism within the animal-rights movement is predominantly an altruistic endeavor, stemming as it does not from the suffering of the self but from an awareness of the suffering of other living things. Freeman Wicklund, a thirty-eight-year-old animal-rights activist when I met him, was in the sixth grade when he first began to learn about the suffering of animals, and this awareness changed his life forever.

> In my sixth-grade Spanish class we had a bull-fighting unit where I learned what happened during a bullfight. I always thought it was against the law to harm animals. I assumed there were laws in place and that everything was humane. . . . But then when I saw the bullfighting unit I was totally freaked out, and I started to spar with my Spanish teacher over it. She was like, "Well, this is a cultural thing," and I'm like, "Yeah, but cultures can change. We used to have slavery in this culture, and we realized it was wrong and we got rid of it." She's like, "Yeah, but animals are going to be killed for food anyway." And I said, "Yeah, but that doesn't give you a license to torture them." And that was the first thing that jarred me, and after that conversation I realized I was going to become a vegetarian at some point. It really didn't sit well with me. Later on, in the ninth grade, I did a persuasive speech on vegetarianism. I thought, "Well, it's time I learned about this." . . . I turned vegetarian and got involved in the [local] animal-rights coalition and have been involved ever since.

Not only does Wicklund continue to promote a vegetarian lifestyle by leafleting outside concerts, on college campuses, and at other youth-oriented venues, he has also faced some thirteen arrests for such actions as chaining himself to the entrance of a fur shop and protesting factory farming.

Sometimes it is difficult to differentiate personal suffering from political injustice. For "Veronica," sheer coincidence of events blended the personal with the political, as she explained to me:

> In March 1979, I went to [my] work at a restaurant where I was training women to be cooks and chefs . . . and I was beaten up by my boss. I was kind of in shock. I went home [and read] that Three Mile Island blew up. I was reading information about the nuclear power plant, and one of the headlines was about how the American government had lied to the American people. But my thing was really, "What is the [connection between] violence against women—in particular—and the violence that our government perpetrates toward our environment?" I immediately drew a connection. And that really changed my life, because after that I made certain vows that I wouldn't—I just changed my life.

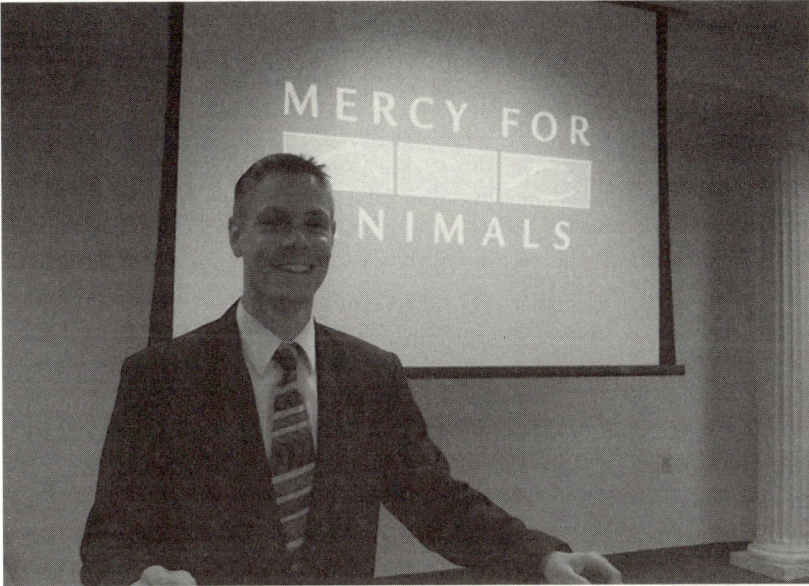

Freeman Wicklund of Mercy for Animals. (www.mercyforanimals.org; www.freemanwicklund.org)

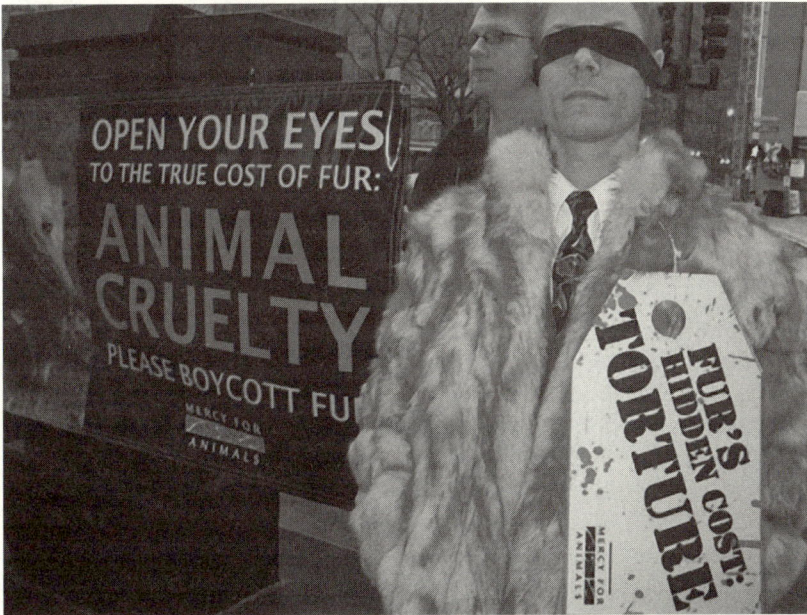

Freeman Wicklund protesting the sale of fur. (www.mercyforanimals.org; www.freemanwicklund.org)

This life-changing event caused Veronica to seek out Philip Berrigan, a Jesuit priest famous for his antiwar and antinuclear activism. In 1967, Berrigan joined three other activists in a protest in which they poured blood on Selective Service files in Baltimore. Eight months later, Philip and his brother Daniel made national headlines when they joined seven other Catholics in the burning of draft files in Catonsville, Maryland, using homemade napalm. Having quickly become leaders of sorts in the antiwar/antinuclear movement, in 1981 Veronica decided to join the Berrigans in a die-in at the Pentagon to protest nuclear weapons—an event that marked her first political demonstration. She has since been arrested over twenty times for various acts of dissent.

If individuals are willing to risk arrest while protesting the suffering of others (including animals), then it stands to reason that the contemporary activist is probably not a nihilist who rejects all proclamations of morality but instead is someone committed to a strong belief in universal values. It is one of trappings of modern social movements that they too often appear as campaigns that attempt to negate or nullify an existing policy or practice. A closer examination reveals that every act of rebellion is simultaneously an affirmation of some competing ideal or countervailing value. Those activists who say no to abortions argue that they are really saying yes to the Gospel. Similarly, those who say no to war assert that they are simultaneously saying yes to peace. It is this assertion of values that fuels enthusiasm for the future, as evidenced in the comments of one abortion protester I met who told me that "it's only a matter of time" before abortions become illegal. Quoting scripture, she told me that "the gates of Hell cannot prevail against the body of Christ." She concluded, "And that's what sustains me."

For Camus, then, if individuals rebel, it is only because they believe that civilization has something worth saving. This perspective is similar to that of Eric Hoffer, who has argued that "discontent by itself" cannot spark a mass movement. Instead, individuals must have "faith in the future."[46] That is, they must be guided by some belief system worth putting into social practice. Here, the role of ideology becomes important, for one of the appeals of participation in mass movements is the promise of having one's ideological framework realized through political action. For purposes of simplification, ideology may be understood here to mean any shared set of values, morals, norms, or beliefs that mobilizes an activist community to action. These values may be religiously inspired or based on a secular political philosophy. They may be well articulated and understood by the political actors, or they may constitute loosely shared assumptions among the various protest participants. It is also quite possible that the ideologies adopted by various mass movements lack what outsiders would consider to be internal consistency. Thus, as Hans Toch wrote in *The Social Psychology of Social Movements*, "A social movement can defend the underdog while being blatantly anti-Semitic."[47]

Jeff Dietrich is a community member of the Los Angeles Catholic Worker—a radical, anarchistic, and pacifistic religious community that not only provides homes for the downtrodden and soup kitchens for the hungry but that also participates in protests for peace and nonviolence. He explained to me the ideological appeal of his involvement in a mass movement:

> I had been raised Catholic, but you go to college and take a few philosophy courses and you go through your period of existential angst. So I was at a point [in my life] of intellectual reflection [that] when combined with the war in Vietnam, I had a sense that the Church and Christians—I didn't really expect them to stand up for anything. It just confirmed my sense that Christianity didn't have anything to say.

By the time Dietrich discovered the Catholic Worker, he was in need of a religiously inspired political vision, or a politically inspired religious vision.

> So here was this group, the Catholic Worker, and not only did they share my political perspectives about the war and social justice, but they also shared this kind of history and tradition of Christianity that I'd been steeped in but thought was pretty irrelevant. And here were people practicing it in a very relevant way and inviting me—actually *desperately* inviting me—to join them.

One thing that becomes readily apparent when talking to activists across the political spectrum is their commitment to ideology and their willingness to struggle for its realization despite personal risk and seemingly overwhelming obstacles. This commitment is most obvious when speaking to activists such as Dietrich whose ideology is religiously inspired. Two of the abortion protesters I interviewed justified their dissent solely in religious terms, as evidenced by the following statement: "We do not expect [government] to end abortion. That is the job of the

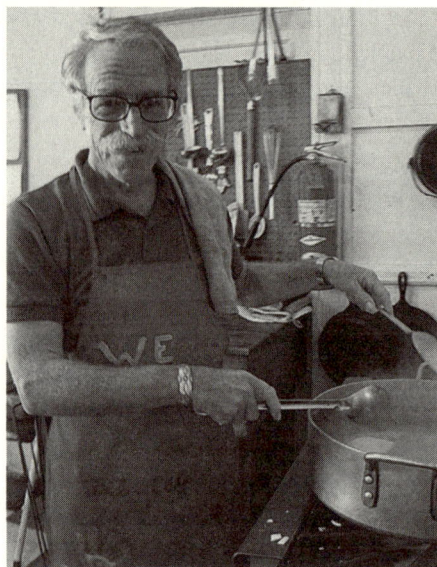

Jeff Dietrich of the Los Angeles Catholic
Worker. (Photo by Mike Wisniewski)

Church. . . . So here we are, engaged in this battle." Sharon Delgado similarly couched the reasons for her activism against corporate globalization and the WTO in religion: "I guess when I got started in activism and all through these years, my focus has been a faith perspective. . . . I want to be faithful. The idea of faithfulness rather than effectiveness is what is most important to me." Sanderson Beck is an antiwar/antinuclear activist who had a somewhat different experience. For him, it was his opposition to the Vietnam War that led him to religion, rather than the other way around.

> When I read the *Dao De Jing* by Laozi, it really blew my mind. So I was trying to define "being." I ended up saying I believe in Dao [Tao]. I had never met a Daoist or been to a Daoist church or service, but the philosophy felt right to me. So Vietnam led me to Daoism rather than Daoism leading me to oppose Vietnam. My unwillingness to go into the military and kill people led me to the study of religions—to all of the religions. And now I'm a very spiritual person, but it's all tied in with war and peace because my spirituality came out of Vietnam.

Although religion plays a prominent role in the lives of some activists, the values for which they strive need not be based in religious teachings. Participation in activism largely stems from recruitment through social networks, religious and secular. These social networks provide individuals with "systems of meaning" and help to create the opportunities to convert predispositions into action.[48] This process is not unlike the findings from criminological research that show strong linkages between friendship groups and crime such that the rationalizations, techniques, and opportunities for participation in criminal activity are acquired through social interaction. For example, James Tracy was working as a truck driver for a San Francisco thrift store during the aftermath of the dot-com bubble when he first began to think seriously about politics and become exposed to political doctrine. "We didn't do deliveries. . . . more often than not, we were asked by landlords to come and pick things up from people who were just evicted." It was through a co-worker that Tracy began to gain a sense of collective action and political resistance. "I had found out a lot about the unemployed workers' movements of the 1930s because my co-worker was a Trotskyite who was always trying to recruit me into his sect." Although Tracy may not have shared his co-worker's exact brand

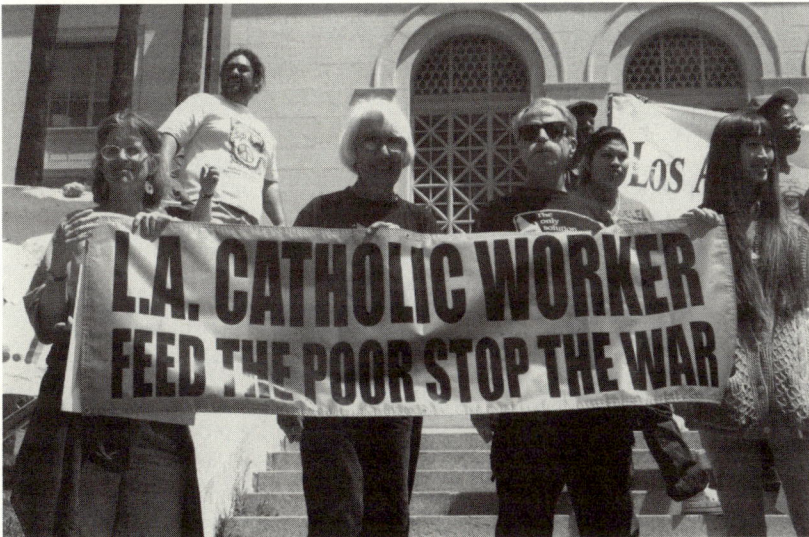

Martha Lewis, Catherine Morris, and Jeff Dietrich of the Los Angeles Catholic Worker. (Photo by Mike Wisniewski)

of politics, his co-worker did prove effective in exposing him to the potential success of direct action, as Tracy explained: "It was a large social movement during the Depression era that basically militantly un-evicted people, fought the police, did sit-ins and sit-downs in courthouses. [They] kind of raided the relief offices when folks got kicked off of aid during the Depression, and it was really inspiring." It was shortly after learning about direct action that Tracy organized with some of his friends to create an eviction defense network that relied on social networks for information about upcoming evictions.

> [A]ll we did was direct actions where our specialty was, if someone was getting evicted and their landlord happened to own a business or realty, wherever the public face of the landlord was, we'd just get a bunch of people and occupy the building. . . . it was actually quite successful. . . . We didn't really have a strategy except [to] get all of your people together and go get this fool. . . . We would get pipeline referrals from tenant lawyers and existing housing counseling groups, and they'd say, "Hey, we're working with these people. You should go talk to them because they are being evicted and we think we're going to lose in court."

It is a firm commitment to the tenets of anarchist thought that keeps war tax resister Ed Hedemann active in the antiwar movement, but the seeds of his dissent were planted by his peers while attending the University of California at Berkeley.

> I was apolitical, but my family was Republican, conservative. But as an undergraduate . . . I was motivated to oppose the war in Vietnam. Initially I was in support of it, but it wasn't an active support because I was busy with my studies, which weren't political. I got involved in opposition because of a lot of friends, because of what was going on, what was happening on the university campus. . . . All of that had a major impact on me.

Hedemann admits, though, that it was not until he received an induction notice in January 1969 that he became an activist. At the time, he was forced to make a decision: report for service, flee the country, or try to apply for conscientious-objector status. He opted for the latter but was denied. So he refused induction and was told that he would hear from the government in three months. Fortunately for him, he never did. As he surmises, "I was lucky to have been raised in the Bay Area. There were more induction refusals there than anywhere in the country," rendering enforcement somewhat problematic.

Years later, Hedemann considers draft resistance his first act of civil disobedience and his first taste of political activism. Moreover, despite having been raised in a politically conservative household, he now considers himself to be a philosophical anarchist. As such, his activism is always nonelectoral.

> I don't vote. I'm an anarchist. As an anarchist—a philosophical and political anarchist—I think we're only going to get a world without wars and stop this country from war by not endorsing the basic system. . . . To me, the problem is the system itself. I remember once there was an ad on TV that was trying to encourage young people to register to vote. It said, "It doesn't matter who you vote for, just vote!" And I thought, "That's exactly right! It doesn't matter. The system is sustained by voting!" So that's why I don't participate in electoral politics. [It's] not apathy. . . . It's more of a philosophical stand that I don't believe in the system itself, and I want the system to come down nonviolently.

Finally, it is worth noting that for some people dissent is itself patriotic and is in keeping with the very ideology of "We the People" on which the United States was founded. Recall that Bob is a tax resister who refuses to pay for war and abortion. For him, his tax resistance is completely in keeping with the tenets of American democracy: "[I]t is an obligation to exercise your rights as an American citizen. You need to vote, you need to be politically active, whether it's running for office or doing what I do. It is our obligation, our duty to do that. If we're not doing that, we're derelict." When I met with Bob, he was quick to tell me that he supports the American legal system, its law enforcement, and its electoral system. "But," he added, sometimes "they need to be massaged back into the condition [in which] they're supposed to be." Moreover, we all have to do this. "We have to keep exercising our rights. It's just like a muscle. If we don't keep exercising it, it atrophies." Other activists I met take umbrage at the characterization of civil disobedience and direct action as nontraditional forms of political expression, especially when this characterization is spoken in the context of American democracy. They are quick to point out that the tradition of dissent is written into the very language of the Declaration of Independence, which asserts the right of the people, after having first petitioned government for redress of grievances, to "alter or to abolish" the very government that becomes destructive to the ends of life, liberty, and happiness. Since then, major social and political change, everything from women's suffrage to the Civil Rights Act of 1964, has been gained using the very traditional strategies of civil disobedience and other means of illegal dissent, even if conventional textbooks try to downplay these strategies.

It should now be apparent that the contemporary activist is not someone driven by sheer selfishness or by a desire to be contrarian for the sake of the contrary. The protester is not the individual without a cause or a purpose, nor is he or she someone whose praxis is unguided by principle. The protester does not seek to destroy civilization so much as to revolutionize it. Finally, the protester acts not purely from a sense frustration but also because he or she is a visionary who sees the promise of a better tomorrow. Yet given this understanding of the activist, we are still left with generalities. "Why is it that some people refuse to go along and others do despite their discomfort at obeying the government and the law?" Hedemann asked rhetorically. That question is explored in more detail throughout the final chapter of this book. For now, the next chapter examines the strategies used by the people who simply refuse to go along with the government and law.

3

Dissent as "Pure" Crime

Glorify the crime as virtue.

—Sophocles, *Antigone*

In socially diverse and highly industrialized settings where a political consensus is difficult to achieve, individuals unrepresented by a political majority must choose between compromise and conformity on the one hand and resistance and rebellion on the other. *Crimes of dissent* embody strategies through which political resistance can be manifested. Collectively, the crimes serve as open challenges to the laws and practices of the prevailing political climate. To that end, the acts are often staged to trigger a response from the justice system so that the people dissenting have access to a public forum where they can challenge the legitimacy of a law or social custom. And because the challenges are launched as a means of exposing existing injustices, those who engage in these behaviors defend their actions as "crime as virtue."[1] Theirs is the staging of what can only be deemed pure crime.

Political dissent as pure crime: it is a curious characterization, to be sure, especially since criminal behavior is rarely described as a form of political expression, let alone one that is wholesome. At the same time, some of the most celebrated fictional, political, and religious figures in Western civilization are those whose disobedience was deemed to be criminal by the reigning authorities. Consider Antigone, the eponymous heroine in Sophocles's much-studied Greek tragedy. In the play, the connection between crime and dissent is evident. The story is rather simple. After having been accused of being a traitor, Antigone's brother is denied a proper burial upon his death, in violation of the law of the gods. Instead, the king orders that "he must be left to lie unwept, unburied, for hungry birds of prey to swoop and feast on his poor body." Antigone must choose between obedience to the king and obedience to her conscience. Ultimately, she opts for the latter course and provides her brother with a proper burial. All the while she makes no attempt to hide her action from the king. On the contrary, she sees the staging of her dissent as an opportunity to expose to the citizens of Thebes the injustice of the king while highlighting the virtue of her decision. Thus, when Antigone has firmly chosen her course of action, she proclaims her disobedience "pure" crime since her intent is to expose the exploitation of political power, especially when it clashes with the laws of the gods. "I shall bury him. And if I have to die for this pure crime, I am content. . . . But you, if so you choose, may dishonour the sacred laws that heaven holds in honour."[2] Meanwhile, for the audience, there is no misunderstanding that Antigone's action is to be celebrated—not despite its inherent criminality but, rather, because of it.

The Greek philosopher Socrates is also a celebrated figure who in 399 B.C. was convicted of what can be considered a pure crime, namely, for expressing beliefs not recognized by the State. During his trial, which is recounted by Plato in *The Apology*, Socrates defends his disobedience by arguing that God ordered him to fulfill the philosopher's mission of seeking truth, even when truth conflicts with the teachings of the State. For his unwavering principles he is sentenced to death, a fate that he readily accepts even when presented with an opportunity for escape. As Socrates reasons, "A man who is good for anything ought not to calculate the chance of living or dying." Instead, he ought only to consider "whether in doing anything he is doing right or wrong."[3]

Contrary to the title of Plato's retelling, Socrates never does apologize for his actions, a point that is central to an understanding of dissent as pure crime. An apology would constitute abandonment of virtue and would undermine the wholesomeness of the act. Nor does Socrates attempt to avoid punishment once it is meted out. Avoidance is something more befitting the street criminal than the pure criminal. Instead, Socrates accepts punishment as a necessary action that will expose the violence that is inherent in the State. Thus, as he prepares to die, Socrates speaks of himself: "Now you depart in innocence, a sufferer and not a doer of evil; a victim."[4] Millennia later, the subversive rhetorical device that branded Socrates a criminal has—ironically—become a celebrated and favored pedagogical device within schools of law, and it has become the dominant means by which nations practice jurisprudence.

Even Jesus of Nazareth was guilty of pure crime. The Gospel According to Mark tells us that Jesus was punished as a common criminal. He was crucified along with "two robbers, one on his right and one on his left." Yet his actions were hardly that of an ordinary pickpocket or beggar. Rather, his crime was blasphemy, which under Jewish law was punishable by death. Yet the Roman governor Pilate did not immediately rush to this outcome. Instead, he questioned Jesus, asking if he still claimed to be the king of Jews, thereby providing him with perhaps one last opportunity for renunciation. "And Pilate asked him, 'Are you the King of Jews?' And he answered him, 'You have said so.' . . . And Pilate again asked him, 'Have you no answer to make?' . . . But Jesus made no further answer."[5] Like Socrates, Jesus refused to apologize and saw arrest and punishment as necessary to raise the consciousness of the masses. It was then, and only after Jesus's recalcitrance, that Pilate ordered the crucifixion, therein exposing the violence of the State while rendering Jesus among the most celebrated of pure criminals in the annals of tragic figures.

Pure Crime, or Crime as Virtue

When we think about crime, it is reasonable to assume that the accused will prefer anonymity to publicity and acquittal to conviction.[6] But that is not so for people guilty of pure crime. Unlike street offenders, who might go to great lengths to conceal their culpability, people guilty of what Antigone called pure crime always perform their actions openly. They even stage them so that through the visibility of their actions they might call into question the behaviors of the State. In many cases, they may even seek arrest because the subsequent trial—should there be a trial—will provide them a forum to challenge power in front of a jury. Finally, people found guilty of pure crime often accept any punishment that might ensue, because it is largely through punishment that the violence inherent in the law becomes patent. Criminals guilty of pure crime may therefore welcome arrest and punishment as necessary steps not only to display to the masses the violence of the State but also as a means toward the undoing of political power.

Pure crimes by their very nature are largely nonviolent actions,[7] because it is through a commitment to nonviolence that that those who commit pure crimes can more persuasively communicate the virtue of their actions. Moreover, if we accept the anarchist diagnosis of the State, then we recognize that political power is always backed by the threat or use of violence. Therefore, the State only knows how to respond to dissent with force. Yet violence inflicted on people who clearly pose no violent threat in return only proves to weaken the respectability of those who govern while raising the virtue of those who resist. At the same time, the strict adherence to nonviolence that is central to pure crimes falls completely outside the expectations of the people who govern, who anticipate their enforcement of law to be met by violent resistance. In the book *The Power of Nonviolence,* which introduced the Gandhian principles to a Western audience and established the rules for the civil rights movement, author Richard Gregg referred to the strategic use of nonviolence as an exercise in "moral jiu-jitsu." As he explained, when engaged in a physical battle such as a jiu-jitsu match, most fighters expect their acts of violence to be met with physical resistance. What if, however, the opposing fighter simply steps back—thereby not allowing the thrown punches to connect with any act of resistance? This tactic will merely cause the aggressor to stumble and lose his balance and, in turn, lose the match.[8]

Antigone's willingness to accept the violence of the State without returning violence serves as an example of moral jiu-jitsu, and it catches the king completely by surprise. In fact, unable to comprehend her lack of physical resistance, the king perceives Antigone to be mocking the power and authority of the Crown. "[S]he transgressed the laws that I established; And now she adds a second outrage—to boast of what she did, and laugh at us."[9] The king's assessment is not far off the mark, as it is the goal of dissent to usurp the authority of those who govern, and like nonviolence this goal can also be accomplished through the use of humor, mockery, and satirical excesses. Mikhail Bakhtin's description of the carnival of the Middle Ages, replete with the crowning of a fool as king, reminds us about the power of these devices. Today, humor, mockery, and satire have become essential components of crimes of dissent. In *Rules for Radicals,* Saul Alinsky writes that "*Ridicule is man's most potent weapon. It is almost impossible to counter-attack ridicule. Also, it infuriates the opposition, who then react to your advantage.*"[10] The king, not knowing how to keep his reaction in check, overreaches his power and sentences Antigone to death, an action that ultimately leads to his own political and personal downfall.

Although it remains unclear in the text of the play whether Antigone had predicted the king's downfall, Socrates clearly understood that his own punishment would "increase the impact of his character and principles far more than anything he could accomplish in the remaining years of his life."[11] Like Antigone, he too confesses his crime, offering no more resistance than that which comes in the form of a rhetorical defense. All the while, he badgers and antagonizes the judges before him, thus giving him a final opportunity to ridicule the men of Athens for failing to embrace the virtue of truth. Even when faced with an opportunity for escape, he chooses punishment. Escape would have undermined the virtue of his crime, whereas martyrdom through the violence of punishment only served to strengthen it.

Finally, in the Gospel According to Mark we learn that Jesus had no choice but to perform a pure crime. Rather than display resistance, he had to admit guilt and suffer for his act, otherwise he would not have been able to attain the status that he did. That is, had he not been rendered a martyr, he would not have been able to exit the earth as the suffering servant, as the divinely innocent, and as the savior for all humanity. In Jesus's view, then, resistance as a means of acquittal would have been disastrous for mankind. Therefore, like the aforementioned pure criminals, Jesus disobeyed the State nonviolently in favor of obedience to God. And like Antigone and Socrates, he accepted his punishment. As such, his act of dissent triggered "a radical social transformation," one that exposed the limits of State authority and the follies of political power.[12] And this result was no accident, for as the next section illustrates, crimes of dissent—that is, pure crimes—are designed to accomplish exactly that.

Power to the People

Whether today's activist is studying the fictional account of an unruly woman in a Greek tragedy or assessing the actions of a philosopher-poet who denounced the unexamined life, nothing is more important for the activist than an understanding that the foundation of all political power rests on the obedience of the masses. *Power* in this discussion refers to "the capacity to control the behavior of others," and one of the great fallacies of our time is the assumption that political power exists solely within an individual.[13] Thus, the typical textbook or movie-house biopic erroneously portrays history as the product of unique and powerful figures who single-handedly lead the masses to victory, salvation, even ruin. But if this portrayal is accurate, then the only way people can overcome a brutal or corrupt political figure is to confront him (it is typically a "him") with a countervailing personality of greater character or charisma. With power characterized this way, the masses are presented as largely ineffectual at exacting social change and are simply relegated to the margins of history.

Unfortunately, many constituencies around the world endure countless political, social, or economic injustices in part because of this false assumption that power rests within a singular entity. Although many political leaders are indeed imbued with exceptional personality, intellect, and talent, the fact remains that those who govern are no different from the governed; they have their strengths and shortcomings like everyone else. What makes political leaders unique is that they also possess the consent of the governed. Musing on the nature of political power, the sixteenth-century French writer Étienne de La Boétie noted that even the most powerful political figure "has only two eyes, has but two hands, one body, and has naught but what the least man of the great and infinite number of your cities, except for the advantage you give him to destroy you."[14] Politically speaking, then, the primary quality that people in power have that no one else can claim is nothing more than the will of the people. Even the resources that are made available to a political figure are dependent on the obedience of his constituency, who amass them and who agree to use them to carry out the directives of the powerful. From this discussion, it should be understood that political power is actually a relationship between the government and the governed. It is a bond between persons in which one agrees to be in control while the other agrees to be controlled, albeit with restrictions and protections in place. Power, therefore, is a variable, and it is one that is less adversarial than consensual. From a criminal justice perspective, then, what we understand as order or "policing" is little more than a willingness of the masses to have their behaviors "policed."[15] And as can be seen through the history of corrections, even prisoners maintain a level of political power, as they can withdraw their consent to be disciplined, causing much disruption to the governance of prisons, as evident in the various riots that plagued state facilities throughout the twentieth century.

Once we view power as a relationship, we begin to recognize an ironic though essential concomitant characteristic of political power: freedom. Michel Foucault argued in his many lectures and essays that "power is exercised only over free subjects." In other words, it is always exerted over individuals who have a field of possible actions from which to choose but who choose to abide by the authority of another person. Thus, as Foucault notes, slavery is not a power relationship when a man is in chains but only when he has the possibility of autonomy. "A man who is chained up and beaten is subject to force being exerted over him, not power." This point is essential. For Foucault, "There is no power without potential refusal or revolt." Understood this way, we can see that the masses play an equal role in the maintenance of political power, and it is through "refusal and revolt" such as that displayed by Antigone, by Socrates, and by Jesus that they exercise their freedom and withdraw their consent and that they remove power from the political leadership.[16]

But if power is equally shared by people who at their core are really free, why do more people not exercise their power and dissent when presented with an injustice? What is the explanation for so much obedience even when obeying appears to be against our better judgment? One critique of the characterization of power as a relationship is that it is overly simplistic in that it neglects the central role of fear in fostering compliance. On one level, it is the fear of not fitting in and being viewed as different that fosters conformity. Stanley Milgram argued in his study on obedience that obedience is a "prerequisite of . . . social organization" since contemporary social life requires respect for authority. This socially ingrained respect for authority over the course of a lifetime explains why even in the most extreme of circumstances, the very contemplation of minor (or even civil) disobedience can provoke extreme anxiety, psychological discomfort, and fear.[17]

Similarly, Erich Fromm viewed obedience (or conformity, as he described it) as a means of escape from the pressures wrought by free will and personal choice. To be free is to be independent, yet to feel independent is to experience one's "insignificance and smallness" in comparison to the mass. For Fromm, there exists in all people an impulse to avoid individuality and to submit completely to an authority. Doing so relieves the burden that comes with freedom and independent thought and action. For many people, Fromm argued, the State takes on the role of a surrogate parent or family member (e.g., Uncle Sam, the Founding Fathers, and the Queen Mum) to whom they can turn for protection, all the while understanding that with a strong State, there is no need for much independent political thought or action.[18]

On another level, obedience can be explained by the fear of violence and coercive sanctions that can result from a failure to obey authority. Even when compliance to the State and to the rule of law is based on willful consent, there always remains the threat of punishment should one ever cease to conform. Whether democratic or despotic, the State is always backed by some degree of coercion, which explains why Gandhi argued that the State "cannot be weaned from the violence to which it owes its very existence."[19] Simply put, fear of sanctions always buttresses legal compliance, which is evident by the sheer expansion of government expenditures for law enforcement and for prisons within the most democratic and "free" of societies.[20] Fear must therefore be acknowledged as a significant cause of obedience that is central to the power relationship, understanding that as leadership diminishes in legitimacy, fear takes on an increasing role in the maintenance of obedience.

Still, political power can never rest on fear alone, for fear of punishment has never been sufficient to induce compliance to the law. Indeed, the mere fact that the United States has a prison population of more than two million people is evidence that fear of sanctions alone is an insufficient means of securing compliance to the law. Moreover, although disobedience and dissent in an age of conformity can be incredibly fear-inducing, fear is often a source of power or energy, and the energy it induces can often prove revolutionary. Disobedience therefore becomes a possibility once citizens of a State position themselves to confront their fears and "plunge headlong into an undertaking" of both personal and political consequence.[21] It is only when we emancipate ourselves from fear that the crime of dissent becomes possible. When fear is indeed overcome, the people can begin to devise strategies of resistance that remind the political leadership of the mutuality of political power. When carried to fruition, the crimes of dissent that result from these strategies restore the balance of power to where it belongs: with the people.

Civil Disobedience: A Starting Point

When we think about the various strategies that activists use to restore the balance of political power, conventional wisdom suggests that we begin by turning our attention to the practice of civil disobedience, perhaps the most well-known form of political dissent. At the same time, there remains no shortage of confusion over the definition and scope of civil disobedience in contemporary society. As one activist told me, "I use [the term] *civil disobedience* with the caveat of 'let me explain what I mean by that.'" The preceding discussion notwithstanding, there is even some confusion as to whether the actions of Antigone, Socrates, and Jesus qualify as civil disobedience, at least as defined in the conventional sense. For one, Antigone does not deliberately publicize her disobedience; she simply makes no attempt to conceal it. Meanwhile, in the *Apology*, Socrates justifies disobedience as a means of achieving justice (i.e., the truth), but in the *Crito*, he argues against it. For Jesus, his disobedience was never designed to reform the laws of State. Rather, his transgression served the purpose of affirming his role as the messiah. Some scholars therefore argue that because of his "special status as the Christ, his actions cannot always serve as models for human conduct."[22]

Much of the confusion over civil disobedience stems in part from the fact that people often apply the label indiscriminately. They fail to distinguish between acts in which laws are deliberately but civilly violated from acts involving violence and an unwillingness to submit to arrest.[23] Such misapplication of the label is not new. The Boston Tea Party is often celebrated in American history as an early example of civil disobedience. Yet like the actions of Socrates and Jesus, it hardly represents a definitional fit. Not only did the fifty men who boarded the East India vessels conceal their identities by masquerading as Mohawk Indians, but they also evaded arrest and punishment upon completion of the task, rendering their actions impure and virtually indistinguishable from everyday crime. Some scholars and activists also take issue with the property destruction inherent in the Tea Party as constituting a "civil" act. In fact, at least one debated meaning of the term *civil* with reference to disobedience implies purely peaceful and nonviolent behavior and a rejection of uncivilized or destructive behavior.[24]

Whether or not the actions of Antigone, Socrates, Jesus, or those responsible for the Boston Tea Party qualify as case studies in civil disobedience, they nevertheless all qualify as acts of dissent staged against the State. Most of the strategies of resistance detailed in this book can loosely be categorized as forms of civil disobedience. It is important, then, to begin to clarify the meaning and scope of civil disobedience so that we can avoid conceptual misapplications while distinguishing it from more specific strategies of resistance.

Broadly speaking, civil disobedience is the deliberate violation of a law carried out as a form of protest. Moreover, its practice is nonviolent and is performed with the intent to educate or persuade a political majority of a perceived injustice.[25] Its staging can reveal itself in any number of ways, and it is this diversity in strategies that is a likely cause for the lack of conceptual specificity and misuses of the label. To begin, civil disobedience can constitute either *active* dissent marked by a strategy of political intervention, or it can constitute *passive* dissent through a strategy of noncooperation with a policy. Thus, individuals may choose to engage actively in legally prohibited behavior (active dissent), or they can fail to perform that which is legally required through an act of noncooperation (passive dissent).[26] The decision of southern civil rights leaders deliberately to sit at segregated lunch counters in violation of Jim Crow laws is an example of active disobedience, and Henry David Thoreau's decision not to cooperate with the government and to withhold his federally mandated poll tax is an example of passive disobedience. More contemporarily, people who trespass onto a military base or nuclear testing site are engaging in active resistance, and reporters who refuse to reveal the identity of their confidential sources are engaging in passive resistance.

Strategies of civil disobedience also range from the purely *symbolic* protest to those that constitute forms of *direct action*. Symbolic actions express a level of political or social discontent without significantly disrupting the real carrying out of the protested policy or practice. Conversely, direct action represents a strategy designed to target the carrying out of a disputed policy. Thus, marching without a permit in protest of an ongoing war may interfere with the regular flow of street traffic and create other forms of disruption to local municipalities, but such expression of dissent does not directly affect the continued carrying out of international policy. In contrast, blocking access to a family-planning clinic prevents the carrying out of abortions, if only temporarily and on a small scale. All these distinctions are somewhat fluid, as marching without a permit may begin as active dissent, but failing to disperse when ordered converts one's actions into noncooperation. Likewise, a sit-in in an academic administration building may have been staged solely to display symbolically a level of student commitment to a cause; but should the administration respond by canceling classes for the day, one could argue that the symbolic action has begun to cross the threshold to direct action.

Whether we call the dissent active or passive, symbolic or direct, what unites all these examples is that in each instance, a person or persons willingly and deliberately violates a known law as an act of political dissent in order to direct public attention to a perceived injustice. But noncompliance to the law is not enough to render dissent civil disobedience. The activity must also be made public to distinguish the protester from the common criminal as well as to bolster the virtue or purity of the participant's behavior. Thus, as one activist explained to me, "We are a public proclamation, not some clandestine operation." One of the more expedient ways of achieving this level of virtue is to use the imprisonment of the body as a means of bearing witness to an existing injustice. To that end, people who engage in civil disobedience typically seek out an arrest (though some strategies such as tax resistance represent important exceptions that are discussed under a separate heading). In fact, it is not uncommon for the civilly disobedient to negotiate with law enforcement regarding the time and manner of the arrest prior to the staging of an action. Postarrest, the civilly disobedient may continue to bear witness through a refusal to post bail, to accept plea bargains, or to shirk culpability for their actions.

This practice of bearing witness—that is, the practice of becoming a martyr—plays a crucial role in the staging of civil disobedience, for one of the objectives of the political dissenter is to ensure that the injustices of the body politic symbolically leave their mark on the body of the detained. To understand this objective, consider the words of an activist I met named Steve Clemens, who served three months in federal prison for trespassing onto the grounds of the notorious School of the Americas (SOA) training camp in Fort Benning, Georgia. Clemens described the image of activists bearing witness at the SOA as "the power of voluntary suffering":

> [S]omehow being willing to suffer on behalf of one's convictions or particularly suffering on behalf of others speaks to the hearts of people; it doesn't just speak to the mind. Sometimes our dialogue in politics leaves the conversation only on the intellectual level, and we need to also address the heart, particularly the heart of those who are doing the oppressing. And somehow the willingness to go to jail for one's beliefs has a way of deepening the conversation or changing the conversation at a deeper level. It also . . . tends to reveal the violence that's already in the system. . . . Sometimes when the police are beating you or the dogs are attacking you—these are extreme cases—sometimes the humanity of the police officer does come to the surface, and they have to stop and rethink "who am I protecting and why am I protecting it?"

In this regard, the tactics of the civilly disobedient can indeed be traced back to those described in Sophocles's *Antigone*, in Plato's *Apology*, and in the Gospel, in which an individual must suffer to ensure the prosperity of future generations. It is hoped that through martyrdom, the proclaimed injustice inherent in a given interpretation or application of law will reveal itself to the masses, resulting in a reconsideration of legal practice.

It is also the case that as traditionally conceptualized, people who engage in civil disobedience are certain to restrict their behavior to "carefully chosen and limited means" of action.[27] Tactics can range from staging sit-ins to creating physical blockades, but as discussed previously, the civil disobedient is committed to the principle of nonviolence. Yet the line of demarcation between violence and nonviolence as it pertains to property destruction represents an additional source of definitional confusion even among people involved in the staging and carrying out of civil disobedience. Howard Zinn has advocated for a clear distinction between violence to people and violence to things, suggesting that violence only be thought of as applying to people. He cautions that the treatment of property as equal to people, "when carried to its extreme, leads policemen to shoot to death black people who are taking things from stores."[28] Similarly, activists within the Ploughshare's Movement, who heed the prophet Isaiah's call to beat swords into plowshares, argue that when they illegally sneak onto military bases and hammer on warheads, their actions serve to prevent future acts of violence. This argument is similar to the rationale proffered by David O'Brien, who was convicted in 1966 for burning his draft card in protest of the Vietnam War. Others, such as Medea Benjamin, who is a longtime activist and founder of the antiwar/feminist group Code Pink, contend that although the destruction of property may sometimes be symbolically or practically warranted, these actions nevertheless create the impression among police that violence is afoot.[29] Although many of the activists I interviewed confessed admiration for the property destruction wrought in Seattle by the Black Bloc, they acknowledged that a strategy of property destruction can often prove naive because it can trigger in law enforcement a response far greater than that which is typically warranted.

To summarize, civil disobedience involves the deliberate violation of law committed in public as a form of political or social protest. Its practice is nonviolent but may or may not involve property destruction. Further, the act of disobedience may be either active (i.e., intervention) or passive (i.e., noncooperation) and may be merely symbolically disruptive or constitute direct action against a government practice. Finally, acts of civil disobedience are designed and carried out to educate or persuade a political majority of a perceived injustice.

With the parameters of civil disobedience delineated, it is worth mentioning that not everyone interviewed for this book accepted the label of civil disobedience as a descriptor of their actions. Their reasons were varied. Some activists rejected the notion that they ever act in an uncivil or disobedient fashion, a position that I encountered early in my research when Sanderson Beck, a career activist, an author, and one of my initial contacts for this study, warned me against continued use of the label *civil disobedience*: "There are a lot of people who object to the term *civil disobedience*. This is really civil *obedience* in many cases. It is obeying either a higher law, or it is the government that is in fact breaking the law." Although Sanderson had been arrested some sixty times for various antiwar/antinuclear protests, he told me that as far as he is concerned, he has never performed an illegal action when juxtaposed with the actions of his government. As he explained, when the State is in violation of its own laws, it is the duty of the citizen to take steps to prevent illegalities committed in the name of the people. This position is commonly referred to as the "necessity defense." This defense raises an important definitional clarification since it signifies the objections that many protesters have to the term *civil disobedience*. Thus, Sanderson continued, "When I was protesting the Iraq War, I don't think I've broken any law. And I don't think I was guilty, and I usually go to trial and talk about all of that."

Other activists I interviewed tended to agree with Sanderson's perspective and reject the characterization of disobedience—let alone the term *civil*. Abortion protester Flip Benham of Operation Save America made an important distinction between civil disobedience and biblical obedience and between acting out of commitment to Church and acting out of commitment to State. "We don't refer to it as civil *dis*obedience. We refer to it as *biblical obedience*. We make that distinction on purpose. We are not 'civilly' disobedient." Instead, he sees his actions as being true to his faith, whereas for him, people who seek an abortion are the ones truly guilty of disobedience—that is, disobedience to God's law.

One final objection to the term *civil disobedience* among the many activists I interviewed has to do with its association with politics. People who engage in civil disobedience are typically thought to be political activists. Yet some people within various religious communities reject the notion that they are engaging in a political activity when they engage in public dissent. Benham began his interview with the following categorical statement: "We do not practice political activism. We simply call it theology." He explained that "politics is . . . the art of compromise—compromising principle in order to come to some solution where both sides can agree." Yet for him, abortion cannot be considered a political issue; if it were, it would require compromise, and any compromise on human life is an exercise in immorality. Certainly, he acknowledges that there have emerged many different political manifestations of the abortion issue, but he believes the question of abortion "cannot be won politically": "that's why you won't see us as political activists."

Others within the religious community shared this disdain for politics, likewise viewing the political arena as an area where principles are forsaken for the sake of governance. Steve Clemens, the SOA protester mentioned earlier, is also a Mennonite whose commitment to morality makes him unwilling to bend on key issues of faith. As he explained, "For me, politics is very important, but I don't see myself in the role of seeking out comprises." He continued, "I do think in the political system we need to hear a prophetic or challenging voice in order to frame the debate so that politicians who do end up with compromises hear another side and hear a voice on behalf of the marginalized, on behalf of those who often don't have a voice in our society." Nevertheless, both Benham and Clemens engage in the political process through the ballot box simply because issues of abortion and militarism are often manifested in the voting booth. "Understand, we're going to vote because we must vote; we have to. We are part of the system. We don't pull out. We must be very involved in every facet."

Instead of using the term *civil disobedience,* people who are working for change through religious communities on the right of the political spectrum refer to their actions as part of an evangelical revival—the practice of biblical obedience—and those on the left refer to their activism as falling within the tenets of liberation theology. Before examining more closely the various manifestations of resistance, let me give voice to the people who are firmly rooted in the belief that their actions fall on the side of biblical law rather than in the realm of civil disobedience. I begin with an examination of what has loosely been termed the *religious Right* and follow that with a discussion of the actions of the *political Left,* though it is important to keep in mind that the people working within these communities are often uncomfortable with these political associations and instead view their (dis)obedience merely as acts of faith.

Biblical Obedience and Liberation Theology

In 1981, the evangelical writer Francis Schaeffer published the highly influential book *A Christian Manifesto.* Referring to the conservative swing taken in the United States with the election of Ronald Reagan as president, Schaeffer wrote, "Now the window is open and we must take advantage of it in every way we can as citizens, as Christian citizens." For Schaeffer, modern society has devolved into a contest between two worldviews: the

Christian worldview, which is rooted in morality and truth, and a materialist or humanist worldview rooted in the "impersonal." Because the latter worldview has been successful in the "takeover of government and law," it is the responsibility of Christians to return to their evangelical heritage and work feverishly to protect their own projects. "This brings us," wrote Schaeffer, "to a current issue that is crucial for the future of the church in the United States—the issue of abortion. What is involved is the whole issue of the value of human life." When the policies of government that protect the right to abortion conflict with the teachings of the Church, "there is not only the right, but the duty, to disobey the state."[30]

Certainly, Schaeffer was not the only Christian intellectual at the time to call for a renewed campaign to convert faith into government practice, nor was abortion the sole issue of Christian concern. In 1984, a student of Schaeffer's formed the Coalition on Revival. During the mid-1980s, the Coalition on Revival drafted position papers that outlined a political program based on "biblically correct" stances on issues as varied as taxes, public schools, and the arts.[31] Meanwhile, during the late 1980s, Operation Rescue and other "pro-life" activist groups began to bring their theology to the streets through strategies of resistance, once they realized that Vice President George Bush was rather quiet for their tastes on the issue of abortion during his 1988 presidential campaign.[32] All these groups combined to create a new level of activism through which Christians falling to the right of the ideological spectrum began to work outside conventional channels to bring their interpretation of the Bible into the halls of governance.

The point here is rather simple: for people whose activism is religiously inspired, there is little concern over "civil" disobedience when spreading the Gospel. For them, God's punishment is far greater than anything the justice system could mete out. There is also a belief that true Christians are compelled to disobey man's law when politics conflicts with religion, as Flip Benham explained to me:

> We've forgotten that we're *supposed* to do it. We hide in our caves that are our churches, and we don't dare peep our head out there too far. And boy if we get [too] close to the abortion mill, we know that we're going to get spanked [by the government]. And so we stay and have church—excuse me, *play* church—inside our little caves while a giant out there is saying "Abortion is a good thing."

What Benham believes he is doing, then, is far from disobedience. Instead, he is simply "bringing the Gospel of Christ to play in all spheres, be it economic or be it social." Another abortion protester, a woman in her late fifties who worked for a pro-life organization, expressed similar frustration with the dogged adherence to man-made law over God's law displayed in some Christian congregations.

> Believe it or not, there's a lot of Christians that don't understand at all why we do what we do with civil disobedience. But I say to those Christians, "When you applaud the fact that you are able to smuggle Bibles into China and you know it's against *their* law, what's the difference? . . . So it's a matter of perspective and allowing latitude here for the higher law. There is a higher law. I believe that God's law is much higher than man-made law.

To the left of the religious spectrum, people who engage in acts of dissent often refer to their behavior as the practice of *liberation theology*. Above all, liberation theology is predicated on the belief that "love is praxis, not theory."[33] If that sounds somewhat Marxist in origin, it is because liberation theology shares many of the assumptions of Marxist doctrine, though it would certainly be a mistake to confuse the two ideologies. Leonardo and Clodovis Boff, two leading scholars of liberation theology, have written that it "freely borrows from Marxism" but recognizes that Marx "can never be *the* guide" but instead "can be a companion" on the way to Christ.[34] Still, as they explain, liberation theology begins as a protest against misery and—in particular—as a protest against the conditions of poverty wrought by humanity's dogged commitment to capitalism. It is a belief that the gap between the rich and poor throughout the world is a contradiction to Christian existence. Therefore, according to liberation theology, it is the duty of all Christians to work toward undoing the harms of poverty.

Theology is typically thought to be the study of ecclesiastical and intangible concepts. Yet liberation theology has as its concern the "premature and unjust death of many people" in the present and in this lifetime.[35] It rejects the notion of a scripted providence and instead asserts the centrality of humans in the development and unfolding of history and its earthly conditions. In other words, there is an existential quality to liberation theology, which has as its concern "actual concrete human existence" and which insists that theological understandings "have bearing on, carry meaning for, and make sense to actual human existence."[36] Thus, neither the Church as an institution nor the individuals who compose the flock can deny their Christian obligation to serve God through the eradication of the many injustices that plague those created in God's image. For the adherent of liberation theology, then, the Christian cannot limit faith to prayer but must act.

The point of departure between traditional civil disobedience and liberation theology should now be clearer. Activists who deny their involvement in civil disobedience do so because of an insistence that their actions are not designed to break civil law so much as they are staged as a commitment to a divine or higher law. Nor are their actions designed to improve the machinations of government. Like anarchism, liberation theology seeks to reverse the harms wrought by the State by stepping away from politics and government. To that end, perhaps no other religious community has removed itself from the dependence of the State (while simultaneously working to reverse its harms through the praxis of faith) more than the Catholic Worker Movement.

The Catholic Worker Movement was founded in 1933 by Dorothy Day and Peter Maurin to alleviate the harms of the Great Depression and to provide support for labor unions, the working poor, and others needing assistance. Today, the Catholic Worker is perhaps best known for its Houses of Hospitality, which provide food, clothing, and shelter to the needy. These houses are completely volunteer staffed and operated and have come to constitute religious communes. The people who live and work within the Catholic Worker communities do not take salaries and do not have a health plan by design, for liberation theology has as one of its tenets that it is not enough to sympathize with the poor and disenfranchised. One must instead empathize, which can only be accomplished by being at one with the people society has left behind.

One of the defining features of the Catholic Worker is its attempt to separate itself completely from the government, that government's economy, and most important for present purposes, its laws, since it is the organization's belief that these are largely the causes of society's ills. In this regard, people active with the Catholic Worker Movement sometimes describe their ideology as that of "biblical anarchism." An article in the Los Angeles *Catholic Agitator* described biblical anarchism as a brand of theology that is "direct, non-bureaucratic, anti-state, hands-on compassion." Biblical anarchism sees political power and organizations as "necessities," but they are necessities that nevertheless attempt to usurp the power of God. When that happens, "we must challenge, deny and object" to it.[37] Thus, acts of dissent carried out by the Catholic Worker are not really seen as acts of political or civil disobedience. Instead, they are acts of faith designed to liberate humanity from poverty and oppression. Martha Lewis of the Los Angeles Catholic Worker explained her activism and her lifestyle to me this way:

> Civil disobedience is breaking the law. [But] you know it's weird. This will sound kind of nutty, but I always think that when I joined the Catholic Worker, I tried to step outside of the law just by doing that. I tried to step out of the government, stop paying taxes, and live under a different law: God's law.

Jeff Dietrich, also of the Los Angeles Catholic Worker, was a Vietnam-era draft resister who when visiting a friend discovered the group giving out coffee and donuts to people getting out of jail. He explained his community's activism this way: "We live in a community and largely devote our time and effort to operating our free soup kitchen and opening our house here to hospitality for the homeless. But a significant portion of our time is devoted to nonviolent campaigns and issues of peace and social justice."

Many times these nonviolent campaigns clash with the policies or practices of city, state, or even federal officials. That proved to be the case when in 2006 Los Angeles mayor Antonio Villaraigosa scheduled a press conference just outside the Catholic Worker's Skid Row soup kitchen to provide reporters with a first look at the city's new street sweepers in action. The media event was held mere weeks before the launch of the mayor's "Safer Cities Initiative." Borrowing a page from the "broken windows" model of policing, which argues that abandoned buildings, unkempt lots, and even homelessness are attractors of crime, the initiative sought to rid the downtown area of its burgeoning homeless population by linking sleeping on sidewalks with violent crime. To that end, the Los Angeles Police Department (LAPD) allocated an unprecedented fifty police officers to the 0.85 square miles of Skid Row. According to a study produced by the UCLA School of Law Fact Investigation Clinic, in just the first year of the initiative the police issued some twelve thousand citations, 85 percent of which were for jaywalking, a figure that is between forty-eight and sixty-nine times the rate at which citations were issued citywide. Most of the persons receiving the citations could not afford to pay the fine and thus faced arrest and jail time. During this same period, police made some nine thousand arrests, though less than 2 percent of them were for violent offenses. The majority of them, of course, were drug arrests, with a high percentage stemming from sting operations. And while the city spent some one hundred thousand dollars on housing for L.A.'s Skid Row population, the cost of the fifty extra police officers ordered to patrol Skid Row hovered at $10 million.[38]

To the staff at the Catholic Worker soup kitchen, the Safer Cities Initiative appeared designed to do nothing less than police homelessness away. For months, law enforcement had reportedly been confiscating the property of the area's homeless upon arrest. Then, three months before the press conference, the U.S. Ninth Circuit Court of Appeals ruled that unless adequate shelter was made available for area homeless people, the police could not arrest them for sleeping on city sidewalks because such arrests amounted to cruel and unusual punishment. Thus, the rollout of street sweepers and high-pressure water hoses appeared to be a back-handed attempt to rid the neighborhood of the downtrodden without having to provide the court-ordered shelters. So the Catholic Workers (and other homeless advocates) decided to make sure that the sweepers never moved an inch.

Before the Department of Sanitation even had a chance to rev up the engines of the street sweepers, several activists had lain down in front and behind all the tires of these multi-ton trucks, rendering it impossible to move the vehicles without crushing the activists. All the while, news cameras rolled. The story in the paper the following day highlighted the protesters' opposition to the city initiative and featured a color photograph of a Catholic Worker being carried away by police for the crime of supporting the city's disadvantaged. Thus, understanding that liberation theology teaches that "the living God sides with the oppressed" and that "true faith includes the practice of liberation," the Catholic Workers are not merely expressing frustration with the policies of government;[39] they are engaging in an expression of their faith, while offering themselves as martyrs in their quest for justice.

Strategies of Resistance

The term *civil disobedience* can be used to unite loosely the forms of illegal protest staged by the contemporary activist. At the same time and as has been discussed, people who regularly protest government policy similarly

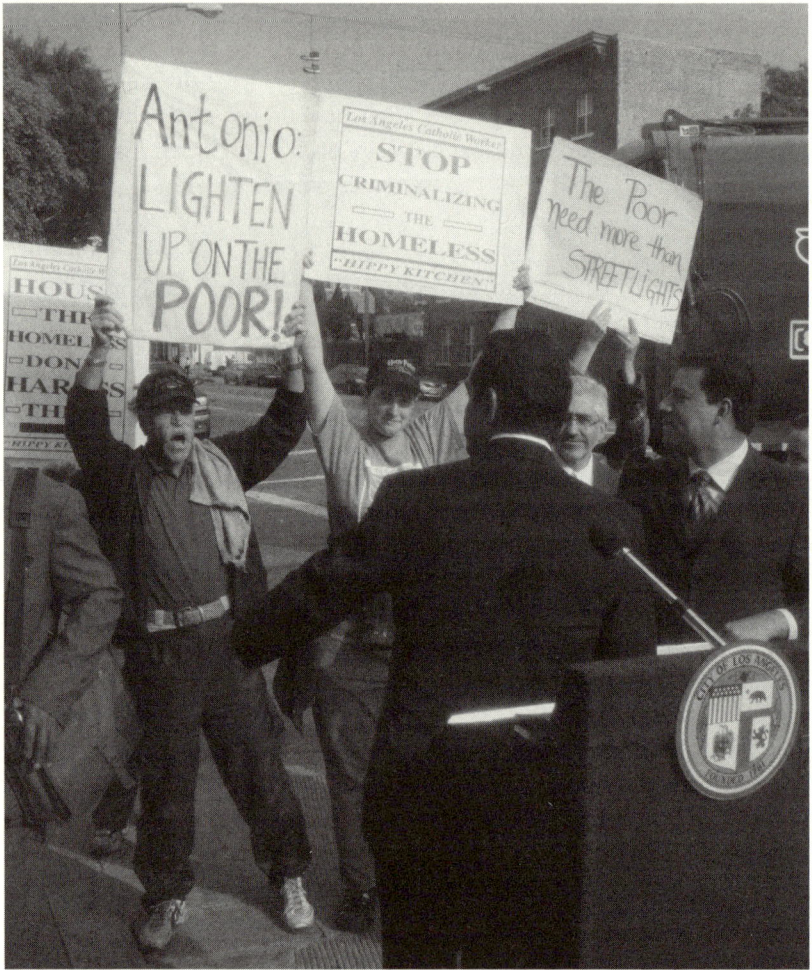

Jeff Dietrich (left) and the Los Angeles Catholic Worker interrupt one of several press conferences held on Skid Row by Los Angeles mayor Antonio Villariagosa. (Photo by Mike Wisniewski)

protest the very labels used to characterize their strategies. In fact, it is difficult to find a contemporary activist handbook that clings closely to the definitional constraints of civil disobedience. Ultimately, though, what is of utmost concern to the seasoned protester is the nature of the action itself and whether it communicates the intended message, whether it draws an awareness to an existing injustice, and whether it begins the process of effecting social change. It is these concerns, along with those of public perception, that largely determine the nature and scope of the strategy adopted, and it is these concerns, along with ideology, that largely determine the form in which dissent takes shape. The following sections examine these forms of dissent closely, beginning with those that are merely symbolic displays of dissent and concluding with those that are directly disruptive to the carrying out of government policy or practice.

Symbolic Actions

In the book *The Symbolic Uses of Politics*, political science professor Murray Edelman argued that the bulk of government activity is predominantly symbolic in nature. When examined closely, politics is more often about persuasion through emotional manipulation than through an appeal to reason and circumstance. This characteristic is particularly relevant in an age of mass media, when gestures and iconography are more befitting of the eight-second sound bite than is a full rhetorical explanation of policy and legislation. In the modern political arena, such disparate activities as flag waving, lapel-pin wearing, and even the staged landing of a fighter jet on an aircraft carrier are powerful visuals that tug at the emotions and are designed to influence policy debate. Politics, then, can be seen as "a passing parade of abstract symbols" planted in the political spotlight by various groups or figures wishing to convey a particular ideology or message.[40]

When it comes to activism, symbolic dissent is any illegal action staged to convey a commitment to political resistance, yet its staging does not significantly prevent the carrying out of the offending policy or practice. In fact, many times, symbolic actions do not directly target the offending law, policy, or practice. Instead, they may be carried out at some highly meaningful setting that nonetheless provides an opportunity to convey a message of disobedience or dissent. One activist I interviewed therefore made a distinction between protests, which directly target a law or policy, and symbolic (albeit illegal) actions that merely communicate dissent.

I've been arrested a couple dozen times, maybe twenty or twenty-five. . . . but many of the times it was not specifically civil disobedience in the sense that I deliberately broke a law in order to challenge that law. A lot of times I risked arrest to do a witness for my own faith and political convictions, where I knew the possibility was that I'd be arrested. Sometimes it was classic civil disobedience; sometimes it was more going and knowing that likely I'd be arrested. But my purpose in going was not to be arrested [while] challenging [that particular] law but more to go irrespective of the law because I felt my convictions demanded it.

This distinction is an important one. Whereas direct actions almost invariably target the offending laws or practices directly, symbolic actions seldom challenge the offending law head-on. It is this *indirect* challenge to the legal norm that renders the action symbolic. These symbolic displays of resistance may violate a separate policy or neutral law, but they nevertheless convey an unmistakable message of resistance to the offending legislation or custom.

TRESPASSING

The act of trespassing is a commonly staged symbolic (and active/interventionist) action that violates a neutral law in order to highlight a related legal injustice. This act of nonviolent intervention calls on demonstrators to enter and/or refuse to leave some place where they are not wanted or not permitted. Although the very physical nature of the intervention may cause some observers to consider trespass a form of direct action, typically the act of political trespass alone is insufficient to inhibit the carrying out of a policy or practice. Moreover, people engaging in these actions are challenging not laws prohibiting trespass but some related injustice. As an example, each year hundreds of antinuclear activists converge at the Nevada Nuclear Test Site and trespass onto the site by crossing a line literally drawn on the pavement. Here, the action is purely symbolic, as police are notified of the event ahead of time and await the protesters on the other side of the line. Of course, the purpose of the action is not to challenge laws against trespassing. But through the act of criminal trespass, the activists are able to convey symbolically a broader dissatisfaction with continued nuclear weaponry development and testing. Similar forms of symbolic action take place at military bases and test sites across the country and around the world.

Although the First Amendment to the U.S. Constitution guarantees the freedom of speech and of assembly, the Supreme Court has allowed policymakers to regulate the time, place, and manner of all speech—including political speech. As is discussed in chapter 4, on policing protest, many local municipalities require individuals and organizations to obtain a city permit to stage a march or rally when the turnout to the event promises

Activists converge at the entrance of the Nevada Nuclear Test Site—"the most bombed place on earth"—moments before a trespass. (Nevada Desert Experience)

to be sizeable or to disrupt area traffic. Yet many political events unfold more quickly than the slow wheels of the government agency issuing permits, and many groups protesting government policies see the process of obtaining a permit as akin to asking permission to voice one's complaint. Nonpermitted marches and rallies therefore constitute an active or interventionist protest (i.e., actively engaging in a prohibited activity). The protest is symbolic in that even when the attendance of the event is sizeable, its staging will not bring the offending policy or practice to a standstill. Instead, the event is designed to allow a constituency to voice its opposition and to do so in an illegal fashion if deemed necessary.

In the wake of media publicity surrounding the murder of Matthew Shepard, who in 1998 was beaten, tied to a fence, and left to die in the Wyoming night by locals upon the discovery that he was gay, activists in New York City staged an impromptu funeral for Shepard at Manhattan's city hall. Ben Shepard (no relation) was one of the attendees. He told me that the mock funeral was one of the first area rallies to be promoted almost entirely by way of the Internet, and he described the event this way:

We thought hundreds of people would show up. Instead five to ten thousand people showed up, and there wasn't room for everyone. The police arrested all of the organizers. I saw a lot of people that I liked being pulled off [of the streets] into the [police] wagon, so I hit the streets, too. I was pissed off at the cops for, I mean, the symbolism of stopping a funeral march is kind of tacky. . . . It shouldn't be illegal to have a funeral march.

In this case, the nonpermitted march/rally was sizeable enough that law enforcement felt it warranted a response, though instead of directing traffic around the event so that impromptu free speech could occur, they opted instead for mass arrests. Yet as dramatic a protest as it was, it was nevertheless merely symbolic in that its staging was not designed to prevent the carrying out of a particular legislative item. Instead, its goal was to highlight the reality that homophobia and hate are still threats in our open and free democracy.

SIT-INS

Unlike many forms of trespass-as-protest, about which police may be notified ahead of time and for which arrest is immediate, sit-ins constitute a more disruptive form of interventionist action. Depending on the setting, sit-ins may also constitute a form of direct action. One of the more common settings of a sit-in is in an administrative or congressional office. Students may stage a sit-in in the office of a university president in protest of higher tuition, or constituents may stage a sit-in in the office of their representative in protest of his or her voting record. For these actions, the protest is purely symbolic. Although occupying an office is certainly disruptive, it does little to disrupt the governance of a university or of the nation.

During the late 1990s, when New York City mayor Rudolph Giuliani began dramatically altering the character of the city's famed Times Square, many city residents were thrilled to have the area cleansed of crime and the many sex shops that peppered the landscape, but others felt that the mayor's attempt to make the area family friendly went too far. So when the adult theaters gave way to such retail giants as The Gap and Toys "R" Us, quite a few New Yorkers took a symbolic stand by staging a sit-in inside the 42nd Street Disney Store. Ben Shepard was among them.

I am really scared of the idea of living in a strip-mall country. . . . I really think [our culture] doesn't have to be a monoculture. It scares me. I don't want to be in a shopping mall. I don't know that we stopped the Disney

Martha Lewis of the Los Angeles Catholic Worker at
a sit-in for area homeless at city hall. (Photo by Mike
Wisniewski)

Store. Who knows? But I think sometimes [you protest] because you have
to, because a feeling in your heart tells you that you have to. You follow
that gut, and I think that's very valid.

During the Iraq War, one of the more popular manifestations of the sit-
in has been that staged by the Raging Grannies, a social group that uses
street theater to garner media attention to raise awareness of issues relating to peace, the environment, and social justice. "Of course, you don't
have to be a grandmother to join," one Grannie told me. All that is needed
is a great costume: funny hats, gray wigs, and stereotypical grannie outfits.
In full attire, these spirited activists head out to various military recruiting
centers and attempt to enlist for service. Their goal: by taking the place
of the young, they hope to save future generations from war. When the
Grannies are refused induction, they hold sit-ins at the recruiting centers
and refuse to leave until carried away by police. "The New York Grannies

A Calgary chapter of the Raging Grannies protests the Iraq War outside the U.S. consulate. (Photo by Robert Thivierge)

actually set out to get arrested because arrests make news. It's [all] about media. The irony of arresting Grannies is really funny when they're trying to say 'stop recruiting our young people.'"

In the summer of 1957, a group of avant-garde artists from across Europe formed the Situationist International for the purpose of sparking a cultural revolution. Tired of passively accepting what society had to offer, these students of Dadaism and Surrealism were determined to create new cultural messages—ones more to their liking. To that end, they advocated the use of art, cinema, graffiti, and street theater to redefine reality. One of the leading Situationist intellectuals, Raoul Vaneigem, described this strategy as a means of bringing about a widespread reversal of perspective. To reverse perspective is to stop seeing things through the eyes of the powerful; it is to create a new vision of possibilities.

To be sure, the Situationists were highly critical of a society in which mediated experience ("the spectacle") replaced lived experience, and they viewed spectacle as a means of propaganda to manufacture consent. At the same time, they felt an obligation to replace the capitalist/corporate spectacle with something new. And as artists, they were not averse to using media against it, a practice they referred to as *detournement*.[41]

Following in the Situationist tradition, many contemporary acts of resistance are designed simply to create a visual of rebellion that can be replayed in an endless loop and spread like a virus in today's highly mediated culture. Consider the following: the San Francisco group The Billboard Liberation Front scales highway advertisements and alters their messages to ensure that capitalist propaganda tells the truth. Thus, after it was revealed in 2006 that telecommunications giant AT&T was secretly cooperating with the National Security Administration's (NSA) domestic spying program, one of its billboards that had said the corporation was hard at work in your hometown was changed to say that it was hard at work in "NSA Headquarters," a perfect *detournement*.[42] Or consider the staging of "Jesus Loves Children Day" by a group of abortion opponents as an attempt to create "a living billboard" of their own. With a loud-speaker, music, dozens of children, and even helium balloons, they set up a show outside a clinic and sang songs of childhood—"Jesus Loves Little Children," "This Little Light of Mine"—all designed to "prick the heart of the people going in." There are also the antiwar activists who, in the midst of the invasion of Iraq, performed an "exorcism" in front of a downtown federal building in a strategy reminiscent of the Yippies. When they entered the building to "finish up the job in case we missed any evil spirits," they were threatened with arrest. Insisting that they "have work to do," they were carried off to jail in handcuffs.

One of the more popular ways of creating a visual of rebellion is through a banner drop in a highly populated setting. With the virtual exclusion of antiwar voices from news media in the lead-up to the war in Iraq, the banner drop became a signature action of the organization Code

It may be hard to tell, but this advertisement has been altered by the Billboard Liberation Front to highlight AT&T's complicity in the National Security Administration's domestic spying program. (www.billboardliberation.com)

Pink for Peace, as was the case in June 2003 when Code Pink dropped a forty-five-foot "pink slip" down the front of the Century Plaza Hotel in Los Angeles, where President George W. Bush was holding a fund-raiser. When initiating a banner drop, activists typically affix a weight, water balloon, or water bottle to the bottom edges of a large cloth banner containing a political message and unfurl it from the side of a large building or high-rise, creating a do-it-yourself billboard guaranteed to garner public exposure if not media exposure.

Additional ways to create spectacle include the staging of a critical-mass bicycle ride, a bicycle (or rollerblade) parade in which the objective is to reestablish a presence of alternative modes of transportation that decrease our dependency on foreign oil and reduce greenhouse emissions. Typically, the parade is staged without the knowledge of law enforcement, placing riders at risk of arrest for—of all things—blocking traffic (though some cities have made accommodations for scheduled rides). When the parade does indeed reach a critical mass, it has the effect of bringing automobile traffic to a halt, converting the streets into one big bicycle party. It also serves as a source of tremendous pleasure for those involved since it signifies a complete subversion of the rigid patterns of everyday street life. Similarly, a Reclaim the Streets action "hijacks public space" without warning and therefore works much in the way that a critical mass does. As a "radical, do-it-yourself street carnival" equipped with music, food, props, and games, Reclaim the Streets shows some of the ways public space can be used for creative, rather than for commercial, purposes.[43] Because many attendees of these events do not seek out arrest (nor do those who perform billboard liberations, which typically take place incognito and under the secrecy of night), these activities fall outside the scope of traditional civil disobedience. Nevertheless, these crimes of dissent highlight the injustices of everyday life and do so in a manner that uses the system against itself.

CONTEMPT OF COURT

Whereas many of the preceding strategies of symbolic dissent may be characterized as the performance of prohibited behaviors, some forms of symbolic dissent call for the *failure* to perform legally required actions and are therefore labeled as strategies of passive noncooperation. These strategies are passive because they do not require the staging of dissent, and they are noncooperative because they usurp State power through noncompliance to an official order. These types of symbolic actions can include such forms of noncooperation as contempt of court or failure to disperse. In 2007, independent journalist Josh Wolf spent 225 days behind bars for failing to reveal his sources to federal law-enforcement officials investigating a case, and *New York Times* reporter Judith Miller spent twelve weeks in jail for refusing to reveal her source regarding the leak of the name of CIA operative Valerie Plame. In many instances, contempt-of-court gestures are merely symbolic in that they do not infringe on court proceedings or government investigations, though they come at a heavy cost to the resister. Some observers, though, may consider contempt of court to have a more direct level of impact since the target of resistance is the offending policy or court order itself.

Direct Actions

If symbolic actions are primarily staged to communicate the volatility of political power, then direct actions raise the stakes of dissent by directly targeting the offending policy, practice, or social trend. As discussed in the preceding chapters, direct action entails acting for oneself to fix a problem, whether that entails tackling hunger directly by setting up a local Food Not Bombs collective, or distributing leaflets that promote alternatives to military enlistment in front of a military recruitment center. Strictly speaking, then, direct actions need not be illegal, though when people act for themselves, it tends to raise the ire of those who benefit from our dependency on them.

Regardless of legal status, strategies of direct actions are invariably politically disruptive, because they are explicitly designed to prevent the carrying out of governance and to bring about a change in the status quo, at least in the immediate term. With direct action, the operative word is *disruption,* as one activist explained:

> I would say direct action is any time that you step outside of the formal legislative and electoral process in usually a disruptive way as a political tactic. . . . although direct action can be nondisruptive, as simple as, you know, Food Not Bombs that builds up self-reliance outside of the State— but most of the time direct action is when you actually stop the functioning of oppression.

Because direct actions target the offending practices specifically, rather than symbolically or metaphorically, many activists favor them over symbolic gestures, as Ed Hedemann—the war tax resister—explained to me: "I'm not much into the bearing witness kind. That doesn't interest me much. But I have done that, and I'm willing to do that in certain circumstances. I'm more interested in doing the actual blocking—to use that term in a loose fashion." Sharon Delgado, the anti-corporate-globalization activist introduced in the previous chapter, shared this bias in favor of direct action, though she acknowledged the importance of symbolic actions, especially for newcomers:

> The purely symbolic actions are less exciting to me. I do engage in symbolic actions when someone else organizes it. The least I can do is participate. It's one step beyond a protest march. And for people who have not participated in nonviolent resistance and it's their first time, I think symbolic actions can give them the experience of crossing the line without a high level of risk.

Like symbolic strategies, direct actions are of two kinds. They can be manifested as *interventions* (i.e., performing some behavior that is legally prohibited) such as using one's body to block a military recruitment center or abortion clinic or chaining oneself to a demolition tractor, or they can be manifested as strategies of noncooperation (i.e., not performing a behavior that is legally required) such as failing to pay one's taxes or failing to report for military service. When performed singularly, these direct actions may not appear significantly to thwart the carrying out of business as usual, but that attribute is not unique to dissent. One employee's failure to show up for work typically does not cause the collapse of an enterprise, but if employees do not show up en masse, business cannot continue as planned. This same principle applies to direct action, which works best when its staging reaches some critical mass. At the same time, the beauty of direct action is its ability not merely to communicate but to demonstrate the impact that a handful of individuals can have in monkey wrenching the system.

TAX RESISTANCE

As a means of direct action, tax resistance is one of the oldest "American" strategies of noncooperation, with objections to war serving as the primary motivation for resistance. In 1637, the Algonquin Indians refused to pay taxes to the Dutch to support their colonial efforts. During the

American Revolution, there was widespread resistance to the Stamp Act, which was to serve as a source of revenue for the British Army, thus perpetuating British rule. The Quakers and later Henry David Thoreau refused to pay a poll tax designed to help finance the Mexican War, which was an imperialist conquest that expanded slavery into the West. With the emergence of a federal income tax, modern war tax resistance entails the public refusal to pay some or all of those federal taxes that contribute to an offending policy or social practice.

In lieu of payment, tax resistance can be manifested in any number of ways. The most popular form of tax resistance is to withhold payment of the federal telephone tax. To refuse this federal excise tax, resisters simply subtract that amount of the tax from their monthly telephone bill and include a note of explanation to the phone company each time they pay the bill. According to the War Resisters League, "the phone company is required (by FCC regulations) [to] credit your bill and report this amount to the IRS, but not cut off your telephone service."[44] Filers may choose to withhold merely a portion of federal taxes from their annual returns. Since current military spending constitutes roughly 30 percent of federal spending, many tax resisters choose to submit only 70 percent of their owed taxes along with a letter of dissent, thus withholding that percentage that would otherwise finance war. Other resisters choose to file a blank income-tax return along with a note of explanation as to the nature of the tax resistance, and still others divert the amount owed to charities and submit documentation of these contributions as a substitute for payment. Moreover, with a permanent military budget, war tax resistance need not occur solely during times of open or "hot" warfare. On the contrary, it can take place annually through small but nonetheless direct measures that impede the collection of revenue, as Ed Hedemann explained:

> Being a war tax resister—despite the myths about this—does not require a change in one's life. You could refuse to pay a dollar of your income tax, and there's no sacrifice in that, although it's a dollar or ten dollars that the government is not going to ignore. You send a letter along with it. It doesn't require anything excessive on your part or a change in lifestyle. So what if they seize a dollar plus interest in penalties?

At the same time, when carried out to the fullest, tax resistance can require major sacrifices in one's life, as Hedemann explained:

I refuse to pay any of my federal income tax because I just don't want to have any part of [my income] willingly going over to the government. Now, this does require some sacrifice. For example, if I take a salary job, the chances are that the IRS will eventually find out who I work for and seize the money from my paycheck. So I've been avoiding salary jobs. I work as an independent contractor for a variety of nonprofit groups. . . . I can't have a bank account with a Social Security number on it. . . . So I have my money in somebody else's Social Security number in an account in another state. I also can't own a house or a car because I don't want that seized. So I've rearranged my life to some degree because I'm so determined to go the extra mile and not allow the government to [pay for war].

War, however, is not the only motivation for tax resistance. Recall that in the previous chapter we met "Bob," whose tax resistance centered in part on the issue of abortion. When he returned from his tour in Vietnam, he made a decision never to lend his support to a policy that allows for killing, which for him simply meant war. "I wrote letters to the secretary of the Treasury, the IRS, the Department of Defense outlining my opposition, telling them that I'm not part of the game anymore." It was around that time that Bob found out that his pregnant girlfriend was seeking an abortion and that the U.S. Supreme Court was reviewing *Harris v. McRae*, a case that questioned the constitutionality of the Hyde Amendment, which placed restrictions on the federal funding of abortions through Medicaid.

For a time, Bob worked with Operation Rescue obstructing access to abortion clinics, but he quickly felt that the organization attracted elements that betrayed his stance on nonviolence. Eventually, the confluence of his experience in Vietnam, the national debate over the funding of abortion, and the discovery of his girlfriend's pregnancy all led to his move toward tax resistance, which for him was the most direct and nonviolent means of intervening in the carrying out of policy. So he began making life arrangements that allowed him to earn less than the taxable income while being able to continue speaking out about the "voluntary nature of taxes." As Bob sees it, it matters not whether the issue is war, abortion, or any other government program:

If people continue to fund the monster, the monster is going to continue to grow and do its evil deeds. It's gotten to the point where the number, depth, and quality of the evil deeds have gotten so huge that we need to defund it. That's how we can really make this thing turn around: defund it.

DRAFT RESISTANCE

"In the beginning all wars are popular." Thus begins Willard Gaylin's study of draft resistance, the refusal to perform government-mandated military service during times of war.[45] Although many people who enlist in the armed forces do so out of financial necessity, the United States can nevertheless boast about having an all-volunteer military. Yet at crucial times during the country's history, when the reality of war sets in, the U.S. government has been forced to institute compulsory military service through the use of a draft, through which all able-bodied men falling within a specified age demographic can be selected by lottery to perform military duty. Unless a person has established a lifelong record of religious or conscientious objection, the only option out of service is through illegal means. In this regard, many people who became antiwar activists were literally "conscripted into resistance," as Jeff Dietrich described his initial encounter with activism:

> During the Vietnam War, I don't think I was particularly politically active. I wasn't involved in any of the political activities at the time. The main thing was the draft, and I got inducted, and you know, I tried to get a conscientious objector status. I [even] went to a conscientious objector lawyer. [When this strategy failed,] I ultimately refused induction into the military. I thought I would be going to jail. . . . The FBI said they'd be seeing me.

After leaving the country for about six months, Dietrich returned and became active in various peace movements, until he ultimately discovered the Catholic Worker Movement.

Like Dietrich, several of the activists I interviewed were politically disinterested prior to the Vietnam draft. Yet the prospect of mandatory military service caused draft-age men immediately to break the law by burning draft cards, fleeing the country, or going underground, all forms of direct action through noncooperation with a government policy. Ironically, those previously disinterested college students who illegally avoided military service suddenly found themselves participating in many of the marches, rallies, and other forms of dissent building across the United States. In sum, not only is draft resistance in itself a means of direct action, but the act of getting called for compulsory military service also proves to be a catalyst for the creation of future activists. This observation clearly has not been lost on subsequent war presidents, who have avoided reinstating a draft for fear of Vietnam-era political backlash.

BLOCKADES

Clearly, the most recognizable form of direct action is the blockade, in which activists physically intervene in the carrying out of a policy, often by using their bodies as barriers to deny individuals access to the source of the offending practice. Earlier in the chapter, we learned about members of the Los Angeles Catholic Worker using their bodies as barriers to prevent a street sweeper from removing the possessions of the homeless from Skid Row. Elsewhere in the text, Flip Benham of Operation Save America and Ellen Barfield of the War Resisters League have spoken of using their bodies as human chains to block access to abortions and military recruitment centers, respectively. All these actions are examples of blockades, as are the actions of the WTO protesters who blocked delegate access to the trade negotiations in Seattle.

Unlike other forms of dissent, the blockade places the activist at greater risk of physical harm, since the activist literally places his or her body on the line, as Sanderson Beck did when he placed his body on railroad tracks to prevent a train from delivering weapons to Central America. People who form blockades sometimes lock arms with fellow activists or use accoutrements such as chains or PVC piping to create "lockbox" devices: two protesters typically place their arms inside opposite ends of PVC pipes, and both hands may be attached to a mechanism inside the box. Not only do the lockboxes expand the width of a human chain, but they also make it extremely difficult for law enforcement to remove protesters, who are literally locked together and perhaps also locked to the scene.[46] Often, police must cut the PVC pipe and remove protesters, but doing so places both police and protesters at high risk. As for blockades in general, it is imperative, therefore, that activists who utilize lockboxes be well trained in the principles of nonviolence, since the risks of provocation are always higher when bodies are on the line.

ECONOMIC NONCOOPERATION

A previous section of this chapter explained that political power is a relationship. In contemporary contexts, this relationship is almost invariably economic. It is based on the obedience of a constituency that provides the

Antiwar activists form a blockade in front of an Armed
Forces Career Center in Hollywood, California. (Photo
by Mike Wisniewski)

leadership with the monetary and material resources necessary to govern.
Economic noncooperation is therefore a strategy of withholding the resources in an effort to undermine political power. As a strategy of dissent,
it ranges from purely legal actions to those that are potentially illegal.

Boycotts represent a legal strategy of economic noncooperation. In
free-market economies, consumers are free to choose how to spend their
money. Consumer boycotts therefore entail a commitment among a constituency to avoid purchasing goods or services from offending businesses
or service providers in an effort to generate economic pressure for reform.
Between 1955 and 1957, black residents of Montgomery, Alabama, set up a
well-orchestrated carpool network and avoided the public buses to protest
the segregated transit system after Rosa Parks was arrested for refusing to
give her seat to a white passenger. The boycott cost the bus company thousands of dollars a day and created major financial losses to white-owned
businesses. This economic pressure was not enough to end segregation on

Sanderson Beck (right) in Concord, California, blocking access to a train transporting weapons to Central America in June 1988.

public transit outright; that came from a Supreme Court decision. But the Montgomery bus boycott did cause a number of southern cities to integrate their transit systems to avert consumer boycotts within their own jurisdictions, while the rest of the country waited for the legal machinations to work.[47] In South Africa, the Port Elizabeth Black Civic Organization spearheaded a powerful boycott of white businesses in protest of apartheid policies. White store owners lost roughly 30 percent of their business, yet there was little the police could do to stop the boycott, as the police intelligence chief then acknowledged: "If they don't want to buy, what sort of crime is it?"[48] The Port Elizabeth boycott proved an effective tool in winning the release of black leaders from police custody, and it forced South African businesses to acknowledge the influence they had in affecting the policies of government. It also led to a realization by the rest of the world that it too could use the economic boycott with much success to divest from corporations doing business in South Africa.

Consumer boycotts are legal, but other forms of economic noncooperation are less so, though there is little that can be done to force protesters' compliance with the law when illegal economic noncooperation is well orchestrated. Such was the case when thousands of families in apartment buildings across New York City participated in a withholding of rent to

protest the failure of landlords to address the disrepair of their living conditions. Recognizing that the arrest of families would not bring about a
favorable resolution for anyone, a judge ordered the tenants to pay rent to
the court, which would only release the money to the landlord upon proof
of repair. As one observer of the strike noted, the coordinated efforts of a
large number of tenants during the New York City rent-withholding in
essence made rent strikes "legal."[49]

In addition to the rent strike, there are other forms of economic strikes
that exist in a state of legal limbo. Employees in certain trades are legally
prohibited from engaging in labor strikes, though these prohibitions
are not easy to enforce when masked by slowdown strikes or sick-outs.
Whatever the strategy and legal ramifications, the goal is the same: to
undermine political power through the withholding of the resources that
sustain that power. In that regard, economic noncooperation is really no
different from tax resistance. It is a form of direct action that targets a
specific offending law or practice. Like all direct action, when carried out
successfully it raises the political stakes and makes it both risky and economically unwise to continue with governance as usual.

Postscript: Raising Social Cost

The strategies of resistance outlined in this chapter represent but a few
of the many ways dissent is communicated in the contemporary political
climate. They do not represent a comprehensive list of the myriad forms
of dissent available to protesters, in part because the strategies are ever
changing and are as limitless as the human imagination. As technology
continues to proliferate, activists in turn continue to find new ways to
communicate their messages of dissent in new and creative ways—some
illegal, some merely deceptive. Thus, the Yes Men (i.e., Mike Bonanno and
Andy Bichlbaum) pass themselves off as spokespersons for multinational
corporations and infiltrate stockholder meetings, globalization conferences, and even BBC news interviews. There, they make outlandish claims
about corporate power that are designed to spark public outrage and initiate policy debate. Meanwhile, the Reverend Billy and the Church of Stop
Shopping hold guerilla-theater prayer services in Starbucks and other
large retail chains, where they pray for the souls of corporate America.
And the Critical Art Ensemble uses multimedia to engage in what it calls
"electronic civil disobedience," which involves visual displays designed to
"explor[e] the intersections between art, technology, radical politics, and

critical theory."[50] As visual and communication media continue to evolve, so too will the strategies of dissent.

If there is one element that unites the myriad crimes of dissent discussed in this chapter, it is that each is designed and executed in a manner that seeks to "raise social costs."[51] But what exactly does that mean? The answer is rather simple: resistance must display to those in power the very real costs of continuing with politics as usual. These "costs" can most directly be measured in economic terms through decreased revenue from tax resistance, declining business sales from retail boycotts, and excessive overtime pay for law-enforcement officers who police mass protests. Social costs can also be measured through less readily calculable ways. For instance, what is the cost of bad public relations stemming from a campaign against a particular corporation? What is the cost of declining public opinion polls stemming from the seeming inability of public officials to keep order in the streets? Whatever the actual costs, the goal of dissent is and should be to raise the stakes for political officials who decide to continue with politics as usual.

This point is crucial, and it is one made by Michael Albert in his book *The Trajectory of Change*. For Albert, what provides dissent its effectiveness is not the level of its militancy; it is the threat to the targets of dissent that "such events forebode a threatening firestorm of still more activism." Activism therefore cannot "plateau."[52] It must constantly build in visibility and numbers and must be attractive to new recruits. The incorporation of humor and spectacle since the days of the Situationists and the Yippies is not only a response to a media-saturated climate. It is also recognition of the need to keep activism fun and fresh in order to stave off burnout. Thus, Albert concludes, "dissent that appears to reach a plateau . . . has no forward trajectory and is therefore manageable. Plateau-ed dissent is an annoyance that the state can control with clean-up crews or repression."[53] The next chapter takes up this subject of the control of dissent through policing and repression.

4

Policing Dissent

> Police . . . they're sort of becoming the Roman guards of the Empire right now. They're really all about protecting capital.
>
> —activist Benjamin Shepard

The location was Floyd Bennett Field, New York City's historic municipal airport, which first opened for business in 1931. Located at the southeastern end of Brooklyn, it is named for the aviator who flew Admiral Byrd across the North Pole in 1926. Because of its long runways and agreeable weather conditions, the airport quickly became popular among pilots who sought to establish speed and distance records. Although it never became a commercial success, in its prime the airfield ushered in the aviation era by hosting visits from such pilots as Howard Hughes and Amelia Earhart. Today, with over twenty-five species of bird calling it home, the field is preserved by the National Park Service, and it hosts a number of tours for members of the Audubon Society and other avid birdwatchers. It also happens to be a site used by the New York Police Department (NYPD) to rehearse protest-containment drills, crowd-control maneuvers, and an array of antiterrorist police tactics.

In the months before the Republican National Convention (RNC) was set to convene in New York City in August 2004, the NYPD launched a preconvention media campaign that exaggerated the likelihood of protest-related violence while illustrating its officers' preparedness for whatever calamity they may face. For months, reporters had been feeding off police-issued sound bites suggesting that the demonstrations scheduled to coincide with the political convention were certain to turn violent. One headline in the *New York Post* declared the Big Apple to be under a "RAD Alert" since radical groups were surely preparing to make mayhem and violence in the streets.[1] Citing undisclosed sources, the *New York Daily*

News reported knowledge of "fringe elements" planning "a series of 'sneaky tricks'" set to unfold during the RNC, such as a plot to fool bomb-sniffing dogs with ammonium-nitrate-laced tablets and a strategy of using sling-shots to pelt police horses.[2] Not coincidentally, many of the news accounts juxtaposed fears of an Al Qaeda–like attack with concerns that protesters would rain violence on the city. One newspaper article lamented that "in addition to guarding against the most vile, organized and destructive ter-rorists," police commissioner Raymond Kelly and company would have to combat "a shadowy, loose-knit band of traveling troublemakers."[3]

To offset fear of pending mayhem and to illustrate preparedness in the face of this certain menace, just days before Republican Party delegates were scheduled to arrive in the city, the NYPD invited the media to Floyd Bennett Field, where reporters were privy to a preview of the high-tech equipment, gadgetry, and crowd-control drills to be employed through-out the RNC. One drill featured a Ryder truck filled with explosives that was soon surrounded by law-enforcement agents with their weapons drawn. In another scenario, cops acting as protesters rushed a bus filled with convention delegates in an effort to prevent it from moving forward. Fortunately, the NYPD was able to move in and successfully arrest the protesters. Throughout, bomb-sniffing dogs, high-definition cameras that photograph the undercarriages of trucks, Italian-made helicopters with night sun floodlights, and other police accoutrements were on view in a massive display of choreographed police use of force.[4]

By the time convention delegates arrived, the conflation of terrorism with protest was complete, and the NYPD was ready for the protesters. Having predicted waves of violence and unruly behavior and with some ten thousand officers deployed during the convention, an unprecedented number of arrests was a forgone conclusion, as they were needed to jus-tify the unparalleled level of policing resources allocated for the political event. To that end, the NYPD did not disappoint.

Over an eight-day period, the NYPD made more than eighteen hun-dred arrests—the largest number of arrests at any political convention in U.S. history. Most arrests were for minor charges such as disorderly conduct—a catch-all for such violations as parading without a permit or picketing outside a designated "free speech" zone. The arrest of protest-ers for parading without a permit is ironic given that protest organizers were denied a permit to hold a large rally on the Great Lawn in Central Park—a cite that in previous years hosted such large-scale public events as a concert by Paul Simon and even a Mass conducted by Pope John

Police anticipate mass arrests as protesters arrive in New York City on the eve of the 2004 Republican National Convention. (AP Images)

Paul II. Instead, the city allocated space on the West Side Highway on the outskirts of the city and far removed from public (or media) view. Widely considered an unacceptable location for a permitted protest, event organizers decided to cancel plans for an antiwar rally, thus leaving protesters with no central point of assembly and subsequently more vulnerable to arrest.[5]

Of course, city-imposed limitations on the lawful right to assemble did not end with permit limitations. Even prior to the RNC, the NYPD had been enacting a policing strategy designed to limit the size of crowds assembling at protests by setting up lines of interlocking metal barricades (or protest "pens") that when used have the effect of dividing a crowd and segmenting marches into separate groups.[6] This strategy was employed during the RNC with dramatic results. In one incident, and reportedly without warning, the police rushed a line of metal barricades through a crowd in an effort to segment it and create several three-sided pens. But this police act of fencing in activists only caused confusion among protesters, who believed they were unlawfully being arrested, prompting riot police to use their batons against the crowd. Elsewhere, the use of metal barricades served to deny the public access to marches and rallies outright.[7] Meanwhile, individuals—including me—who were found to be demonstrating outside these makeshift protest pens were arrested en masse as police used orange netting to engulf and arrest people on the streets, resulting in a large number of wrongful arrests. In fact, over 90 percent of RNC arrests—including mine—resulted in dismissals or in acquittals at trial. Finally, in a throwback to the days of the FBI's repressive counterintelligence program known as COINTELPRO, throughout the week of protests, police officers engaged in acts of crowd infiltration and surveillance, using plainclothes officers, perhaps as provocateurs.[8]

During the RNC, then, the arrest tactics used by the NYPD were intrusive and preemptive, if not outright aggressive, even when crimes of dissent were not occurring. Of course, various activist groups *had* planned numerous acts of dissent during the weeklong convention, but many of these strategies were either well publicized or involved prior negotiation with police. Clearly, their staging was hardly a public threat. Still, protesters often found their attempts at free speech completely thwarted, which became most evident on August 31, when the War Resisters League (WRL) attempted to march from Ground Zero to Madison Square Garden, where some marchers were reportedly going to engage in civil disobedience by

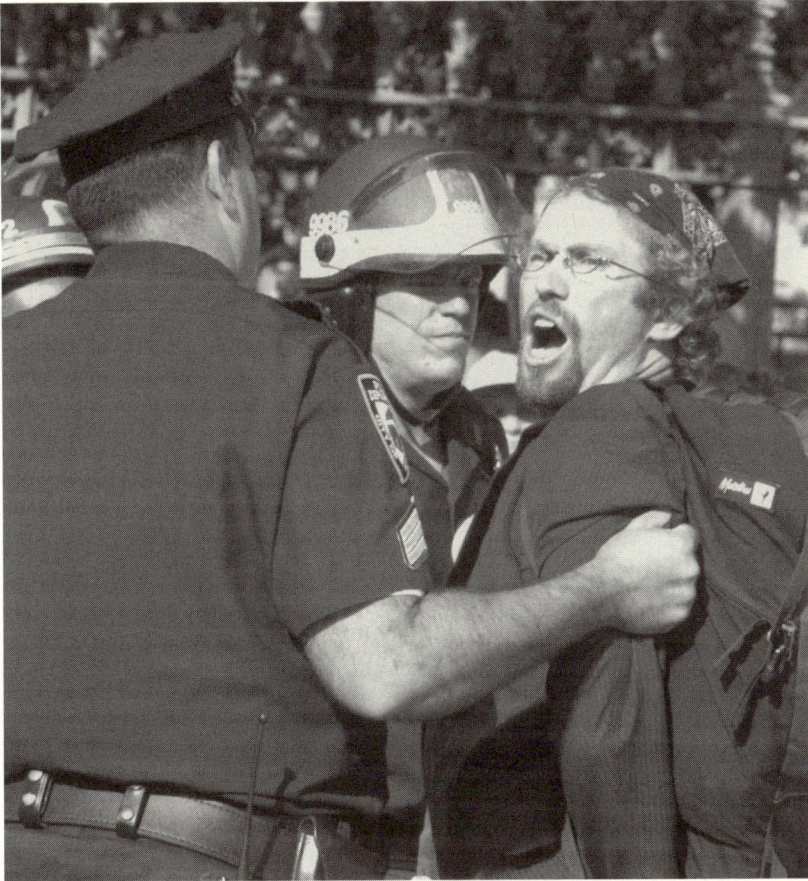

A handcuffed protester is pushed by the NYPD after being arrested at a demonstration during the 2004 Republican National Convention. (AP Images)

staging a symbolic "die-in." To be sure, the march itself was legal; in fact, protesters reached an agreement with the commanding officer on the scene whereby the group could march without a permit so long as it remained on the sidewalk with no more than two people abreast. According to an investigation launched by the New York Civil Liberties Union (NYCLU), the police even announced the rules of the agreement with a bullhorn. An officer concluded these announcements by telling the protesters, "Have a nice march." But once the first steps were taken, the police began making arrests.[9]

Ed Hedemann, the war tax resister featured earlier in this text, was among those arrested as part of the WRL contingency. Having been arrested some forty times for civil disobedience since the days of Vietnam, he was certainly familiar with crowd-control tactics and police-protester negotiations. Nevertheless, he was surprised to find his right to free speech completely thwarted. "We were arrested *before* we even committed civil disobedience! There was one high-ranking officer who lost his cool. He started screaming at people. And the police had blocked us from going anywhere. We were stopped; we hadn't done anything illegal, and he just completely lost it." Sharon Delgado, who was at the RNC protests and who had also been among those arrested at the WTO protests in Seattle, said that she witnessed people being encircled and arrested as soon as they started out on the WRL march. But she was hardly surprised by the intrusive nature of the police tactics, for she sees this as part of a larger, emerging trend in the manner in which law-enforcement agencies police dissent—a trend such that the use of protest pens, free-speech zones, surveillance, and preemptive arrests is making dissent (including civil disobedience, nonviolent resistance, and direct action) exceedingly difficult to express: "People used to be able to take to the streets, but no longer. Now, you can't get anywhere to protest. . . . The police are just trying to make it impossible. In New York at the RNC it was impossible. The streets were full of police. How could you protest?"

Police and Protests: Tension and Transition

Strategies of protest policing have undergone a number of qualitative changes since the establishment of the modern police department in the mid-1800s. These changes are best characterized as a transition—or, as was evident at the RNC, a tension really—between historically early strategies that called for the use of force against protesters in an effort to quell dissent and more recent strategies that call on police to negotiate with protesters regarding the time, place, and manner of marches, rallies, and even civil disobedience.[10] Today, protest policing appears to be a far more choreographed and technologically advanced application of the use of force, leading many observers to question whether law enforcement has abandoned negotiated management altogether in favor of a more militarized approach toward crowd control.

Because the pendulum representing the method by which police address large-scale protests once again appears to be swinging away from negotiated management and toward the use of force, it is perhaps appropriate to have a more comprehensive understanding of various strategies for policing protest. The following sections briefly review the history of policing protest in greater detail, beginning with the application of force as a means to address political domestic unrest. That discussion is followed by an examination of more contemporary police practices that use the negotiated management system, which is followed by an overview of recent trends in protest-policing practices, such as the use of military-style tactics. Finally, the chapter concludes with an examination of protester behavior in light of current policing practices.

The Use of Force: "A Drop at Every Whack!"

For much of the nineteenth and twentieth centuries, protest-policing strategies called for a large police presence to act quickly and with force to disperse gathering crowds. Most civil disturbances during that time were labor related and stemmed from the growth and expansion of the factory labor force during the nineteenth century. During the nineteenth century, the number of factory workers in the United States expanded from the thousands to the millions.[11] Conditions in these new factories were far from idyllic. Low wages, long hours, and unsafe working environments were commonplace, rendering domestic unrest inevitable. Workers who chose to picket or take to the streets were characterized by police as subversives. More accurately, they were simply members of an ever-expanding working class collectively responding to the harsh conditions of early industrial America. Either way, police viewed protesters as dangerous persons who must be dealt with by using certain force. As such, newspaper reports of indiscriminate police violence were typical. One newspaper feature reporting on the police response to an 1874 labor parade in New York City noted that "police clubs rose and fell" while women and children ran screaming from the parade. The article continued: "Bystanders were ridden down and mercilessly clubbed by mounted officers."[12] This incident was just one of many in cities across the United States that witnessed the police employing the use of force against striking workers during the early days of industrial capital.

Then in 1877, a monumental series of labor strikes surrounding the nation's railroads occurred in a dozen cities across the United States, putting the protest-policing strategy of use of force on display for the entire nation—and the world. The Railroad Strikes of 1877 took place at a time when the

United States was in the midst of an economic depression. The railroads responded to the depression by issuing wage cuts for workers who already received paltry wages while working jobs with high rates of injury and death. Of course, the railroads, whose owners had amassed much wealth, owed their success largely to government handouts of free land and million-dollar bonds—a fact not lost on the workers. Upon notification of the wage cuts, workers across the country quickly brought the trains to a halt, in essence shutting down much commerce in the United States. In response, police used force against protesters; only this time, the strategy backfired.

In Martinsburg, West Virginia, local police were unable to handle the sizeable crowd gathering to support the railroad workers. The state militia was called, but as it turned out, the militia itself was composed largely of striking railroad workers, who refused to serve. So federal troops were sent. In Baltimore, the National Guard responded to rocks thrown from the crowd with gunfire, resulting in ten deaths and many wounded. By day's end, fifteen thousand people had turned out to support the striking railroad workers. At that point, the use of force was simply not a realistic option. In Pittsburgh, a unit of Philadelphia Guardsmen that was deployed to provide assistance reportedly "fired indiscriminately into the crowd, among who were many women and children."[13] The *New York Times* reported that the Guardsmen had been "terribly mismanaged" in their efforts, and other area newspapers opined similarly.[14] Meanwhile, in Chicago, six thousand people took to the streets to demand the nationalization of the railroads. When police responded by attacking the crowd, the press reported that "the sound of the clubs falling on skulls was sickening. . . . A rioter dropped at every whack."[15] It seems that far from dispersing the crowd, the use of force against workers was attracting public sympathy for the labor movement.

The Railroad Strikes of 1877 mark a pivotal point in U.S. history, as they represent among the first large-scale domestic disturbances in which common citizens took to the streets to demand social justice. They also caused police to question whether a strategy calling for the swift and certain use of violence against protesters was truly an effective approach, though much of their questioning was predicated more on concern over public relations than concern for the rights or well-being of the crowds. By the 1920s, both politicians and the public had adopted a new rhetoric of progressive reform. In time, protests were no longer viewed monolithically by authorities (or by the public) as purely revolutionary forces, and protest policing had little choice but to adapt to the changing political climate.

In response to these changing times, police began to confront large gatherings in a manner that attempted to discriminate between "crowds" and "mobs." According to one policing manual at the time, a crowd was defined as a group that had yet to resort to unruly or violent behavior, whereas a mob had "lost all sense of fear of the law" and could only be controlled "by an overpowering demonstration of force."[16] The revised goal of protest policing therefore advocated the *display of force* over its actual use. Just as the NYPD had reasoned by inviting media to Floyd Bennett Field, one police manual argued that "a strong display of a well-disciplined and skillfully handled force will in most instances be sufficient to suppress the mob."[17] Or still better, in the best of all cases, a display of force can be used to prevent crowds from becoming mobs at all.

Apart from the civil liberties concerns over the violation of protesters' right to speech and assembly, the use-of-force approach to policing simply does not work against individuals who are deeply committed to their principles of social justice. In fact, the use of force against a nonviolent crowd can garner public sympathy for protesters and their causes. That proved to be the lesson of the 1960s, when the use of force against civil rights organizers who were intent on denouncing the violence of war and racism only proved their point when they endured water cannons, attack dogs, and police batons while an entire nation watched. Quickly, protesters not familiar with the philosophy of bearing witness soon discovered that activists actually benefit from the police use of force, since it renders them martyrs and helps communicate the violence inherent in law. In fact, Martin Luther King's Birmingham organization considered canceling a planned demonstration if no mob turned up to attack the marchers or if no television cameras were in evidence to capture either the crowd or the police response.[18] Simply put, even the mere display of force that stops short of its actual use can ignite a crowd rather than quell it. After all, police represent the very agents of State to which protesters and even the public writ large are often opposed.

By the early 1970s, then, police and policymakers alike were acutely aware of the need for a reformed approach to crowd control and protest policing—an approach that allowed the right of speech and assembly without granting protesters the upper hand. A series of government commissions investigating unrest at political events and on college campuses concluded that "authorities often bear a major part of the responsibility" for protest-related violence.[19] In many instances, the nature of the government response to protesters "was unrestrained and indiscriminate police violence," a situation made all the more shocking by the fact that "it was often inflicted upon persons who had broken no law."[20] Noting that dissent is a valued part of contemporary governance, these commissions admonished law enforcement for using "unnecessary harshness and illegal violence" against protesters.[21] To replace the use of force, these commissions called for an approach to protest-policing that employed only the minimum force necessary to ensure that protesters' First Amendment rights are protected. This new policy came to be known as *negotiated management*.

Negotiated Management: "Normalizing" Dissent

In a landmark study of the history of punishment, Michel Foucault documented a shift in the nature of punitive practices during the seventeenth and eighteenth centuries, one in which punishments "lost some of their intensity, but at the cost of greater intervention" by the State into our daily lives.[22] Thus, over the span of mere decades, the infliction of pain on the body was replaced by the discipline of the mind. Under this new model, State actions were not designed to seek revenge on troublesome individuals; rather, the goal was to exert control over behaviors. For Foucault, this new approach to punishment entailed the use of various practices that when used effectively yield a highly disciplined citizenry. These techniques include total monitoring and surveillance (a technique that Foucault compared to Jeremy Bentham's idea of the panoptic prison, which creates the perception that prisoners are constantly under watch); the distribution of individuals into their own space so that they self-consciously feel different from others and wish to gravitate toward the norm (Foucault referred to this technique as "enclosure" or "partitioning"); and finally for our purposes, the control of activity through a highly regimented schedule, which allows for the maintenance of time-structured behavior.

For Foucault, the net result of these disciplinary techniques is that they allow for incidents of nonconformity to be readily identified and addressed. Interestingly, the application of these techniques has not been limited to the penitentiary but has become the method of social control on which all social relations are based, including—as we shall see—police-protester relations. Discipline, then, entails the practice of "normalizing judgments," a process by which behaviors are constantly assessed according to an assumed norm. Perhaps most important for Foucault, because the normalizing judgments that constitute discipline have become so central to our culture, discipline seldom requires enforcement from any State official. Instead, it is the fear of being perceived as abnormal or nonconforming that is sufficient to foster personal discipline and self-policing. Thus, what appears to be a shift in punishment toward a more lenient machinery of punishment is in fact a movement toward a much broader application of power.[23] This new application of power has resulted in a highly obedient and disciplined populace—even during times when the populace is confronted with gross injustices.

In many ways, the shift in the nature of protest policing that began in the 1970s and continued through the 1990s is one that closely resembles the type of qualitative change described by Foucault. Known as a strategy of *negotiated management*, this new model of crowd control substituted the application of force against protesters with a highly monitored public-order management system (POMS).[24] Under POMS, riot gear is replaced with a series of permits and policies designed to regulate the time, place, and even the manner of political dissent. Gone is some of the intensity of the type of police behavior on display during the Railroad Strikes and again during the days of civil rights and Vietnam; but as was the case with punishment, this reduction in the use of force comes at the cost of greater police intervention into the nature and content of political marches and rallies. Thus, although many observers may credit negotiated management as a more disciplined and humane policing strategy, one must recognize this change as indicative of tighter control by police over popular protest.

To be sure, with negotiated management, police are under orders to protect the First Amendment rights of protesters. Even the most provocative of speakers are granted permits to hold a demonstration, and police must protect the speakers' right to free speech by ensuring that counter-protesters do not infringe on these rights. The job of the police, then, is to steer demonstrations to times and places where community disruption is minimized without having to prevent the protest from occurring. Even civil disobedience—which is disruptive by design—is not problematic for police under negotiated management because police often cooperate with activists "when their civil disobedience is *intentionally symbolic.*"[25] Under negotiated management, police and city officials issue demonstration permits to regulate dissent, and they may assist protesters in securing parade routes and access to parking. In return, demonstrators appoint among themselves protest marshals or peacekeepers, who in essence police their group to ensure that demonstrators adhere to the terms established with the police. In the case that protesters deviate from the terms of the permit or the dictates of protest marshals, arrests are secured only as a last resort, with the use of force against demonstrators held to a minimum. What results is a highly disciplined street protest.

When assessing the application of negotiated management from a law-enforcement perspective, this model of protest policing has proven successful in allowing sizeable demonstrations to occur without widespread community disruption or confusion. Increased communication between police and protesters has dramatically reduced the level of violence displayed by law enforcement in previous decades. Indeed, in cities such as Washington, D.C., San Francisco, and New York, even large-scale rallies, marches, and demonstrations are now commonplace and occur without police resorting to mass arrests or the use of force. In this regard, then, negotiated management has worked well for law enforcement, for its success in negotiating the terms of dissent reflects positively on its ability to maintain law and order.

Yet when viewed from the activists' perspective, the negotiated management model ultimately serves the function of disciplining groups working for radical change, because the POMS established to regulate the manner of protest is closely aligned with the techniques of disciplinary power identified by Foucault as means of control that in their totality have the effect of pacifying dissent. For example, the requirement that protesters obtain a permit specifying the time, manner, and location of protest embodies precisely the disciplinary devices of observation, enclosure, and timetables mentioned earlier, thus providing the State with leverage over protest groups to enact limitations and restrictions on certain forms of political speech. Further, because a permit system brings into play "the binary opposition of the permitted and the forbidden," POMS ultimately normalizes dissent by suppressing certain forms of political speech.[26] Indeed, it is not uncommon for permits to be awarded and denied based on the criterion of the normalcy of the political message.

The denial of a permit on ideological grounds is precisely what happened in 1976 when a neo-Nazi group calling itself the National Socialist Party of America (NSPA) sought a permit to parade in the village of Skokie, Illinois. With one of every six Skokie residents being Jewish, village officials were determined to prevent NSPA from marching. First, the village required NSPA to post a $350,000 bond. Later, village attorneys obtained an injunction preventing NSPA from holding a demonstration on the day in question. Finally, the village passed three ordinances, each designed to prevent the neo-Nazi group from ever holding an event within its borders. Two years later, the U.S. Supreme Court finally denied Skokie's appeal of an Illinois Supreme Court decision ruling the injunction a violation of NSPA's rights. Throughout this legal battle, the village of Skokie never raised policing concerns when denying NSPA a permit. In fact, Skokie's police chief was not even called as a witness during the initial legal hearings to obtain the injunction.[27] With the ability to grant or deny demonstration permits, the city simply exercised its disciplinary power and denied a group its right to public demonstration based solely on NSPA's ideology—however distasteful that ideology may have been. And therein lies the normalizing function of the permit system, for it shifts public concern away from the State's power to "allow" speech and instead focuses public attention on the "deviant" aspects of the speech itself. Quite simply, with the Skokie case, even the most ardent supporters of free speech found themselves playing a role in the normalizing process of ideology by desperately attempting to make a distinction between acceptable speech and "hate" speech.

Critics of negotiated management also contend that protesters' cooperation and communication with the police regarding the nature of protest has the effect of placing protest completely within a Statist context: "The role of the police, whose function is to support state policy by minimizing disruption of its procedures, should be in natural conflict with that of a movement purporting to challenge these very same policies and, indeed, to transform the state itself."[28] Under negotiated management, however, conflict with the police is replaced by cooperation, rendering most gatherings hardly protests at all. Meanwhile, within the demonstration are the protest marshals, who in effect take over the responsibility of policing. Thus, as Ward Churchill and other critics of negotiated management have opined, under negotiated management "the police find themselves serving as mere backups (or props) to self policing."[29] And it is this self-policing function that renders the discipline and control of dissent nearly total, for when protesters willingly abide by the rules of dissent established by the State to satisfy State interests, the possibility for radical social change all but vanishes.

Militarized Policing: "The Look of a War Zone"

Practically speaking, the negotiated management model of policing requires "a certain kind of cop and a certain kind of protest."[30] As noted earlier, it works well when dissent is manifest as a purely symbolic action that does not disrupt the day-to-day mechanism of the government or corporate structure. Under such circumstances, police feel little need to intervene physically in the carrying out of the protest, since protesters have already communicated their protest strategy and their policy of restraint. Negotiated management breaks down when protesters engage in strategies of active resistance or direct action. With direct action, the goal is to prevent, close, or interfere with business or politics as usual. Because direct action entails taking *over* the streets rather than simply taking *to* the streets, it often catches law enforcement off guard. Kristian Williams provides a clear summation of the limits of negotiated management: "The danger for activists is that they might permanently limit themselves to tactics that are predictable, non-disruptive, and ultimately ineffective." Meanwhile, "police . . . may come to rely on this cooperative arrangement. If the police assume that activists will conduct themselves within the bounds set by this approach, they leave themselves open for some nasty surprises." Williams observes, "Essentially, this is what happened to the Seattle police in 1999," when both protesters and police abandoned their tacit agreement about the nature of and response to political dissent.[31] Symbolic actions gave way to direct actions, and negotiated management gave way to a more militarized display and use of strategies of force.

To be sure, the road to the Seattle protests had been long in coming. Since the emergence of negotiated management in the 1970s, many activists had become increasingly uncomfortable with the air of paternalism inherent in the new model of policing. It is no wonder that corporate media were portraying activists as relics of the past. In response, from the mid-1980s through the 1990s and into the new millennium, a new tenor of activism was emerging on the changing political and social landscape that would be unshackled from the ghosts of negotiated management, in which dissent was never spontaneous and always orderly. The catalyst for this new activism was corporate globalization.

The championing of the North American Free Trade Agreement (NAFTA) by the "liberal" political establishment during the early 1990s had the effect of uniting aspects of the political Left and Right. In Seattle, conservative blue-collar workers marched alongside liberal conservationists, both of whom were feared to become a dying breed in the United States, what with manufacturing jobs being outsourced and with environment regulations being rolled back. Moreover, people suffering from AIDS and other health issues were especially affected by the growth in corporate power and the expansion of a health-care industry that placed profits over people. The AIDS activist network Aids Coalition to Unleash

Power (ACT UP) emerged as a significant factor in the resurgence of aggressive, though nonviolent, dissent on the Left. According to one source, the members of ACT UP "pioneered a punk-inflected style" of nonviolent direct action that relied heavily on the visuals of theater, spectacle, and confrontation.[32] Thus, less than a month before Christmas 1991 and on the busiest shopping day of the year, twenty-two ACT UP activists who were dressed in Santa Claus costumes chained themselves together inside New York City's famous Macy's department store in Herald Square to protest the store's refusal to rehire a store Santa who tested positive for the virus that causes AIDS. That act represents just one of the many dramaturgical displays of direct action performed by ACT UP throughout the 1990s.[33]

In short, by the end of the millennium, people upset about the outsourcing of jobs and environmental degradation joined forces with those concerned about the lack of generic pharmaceuticals and the AIDS pandemic in a new campaign to stem the tide of corporate globalization. To the surprise of everyone, the changing political landscape that developed with globalization brought about a resurgence in the willingness to risk arrest without prior negotiation with the police. This new tenor of activism was met with a return to the use-of-force police response, only with a new military and technological bent. During the weeklong demonstrations marking the 1999 Ministerial Conference of the WTO, then, it was not uncommon for news reporters to describe the streets of Seattle as having "the look of a war zone" as activists from an array of movements took to the streets in direct action.[34] Gone was any hint of negotiation between police and protesters. Law enforcement donned riot gear and discharged tear gas, pepper spray, and rubber bullets while patrolling in roving police tanks or armored personnel carriers. Meanwhile, protesters participated in large demonstrations and rallies; some took part in acts of nonviolent civil disobedience, such as blocking street intersections and forming human chains to block delegates' access to the trade negotiations. Elsewhere, a handful of protesters from the Black Bloc contingency caused property damage to such downtown chain stores as Starbucks Coffee and Niketown—both corporations with poor workers'-rights records that stood to benefit further from the WTO trade negotiations.

By midweek, the city had erected a militarized "no protest" zone with entry controlled by police and with people barred from expressing views critical of the WTO. On Tuesday, November 30, the mayor issued a proclamation of civil emergency and established a nighttime curfew for downtown Seattle. He also asked the governor to send in the National Guard.

Seattle police even used the old Sand Point naval base to process the hundreds of protesters who were arrested. By the end of the week, the events that unfolded around the WTO had come to be known as the "Battle for Seattle," with most media accounts suggesting that the protesters were winning the battle, if not the war.[35]

The problem that confronted the Seattle police was one of strategy, not gadgetry—as officers had at their disposal some of the most sophisticated tools for crowd control ever on display. In fact, the years preceding the Battle for Seattle witnessed a blurring of the distinction between police and military functions. With the collapse of the Soviet Union, weapons manufacturers contracting with the U.S. military sought new markets for their products. So they turned to the Department of Justice for support. In the seminal book *Crime Control as Industry*, Nils Christie describes how in 1993 then Attorney General Janet Reno presented a challenge to the defense and intelligence communities and to the industrial sector that were gathered at a university seminar: "turn your skills that served us so well in the cold war to helping us with the war we're now fighting daily in the streets of our towns and cities across the nation." The goal, Reno said, was to find ways to adapt their military technology for domestic use. Weapons manufacturers did not have to think very hard, since among the themes of the seminar was "Emphasize Opportunities for Industry in the Law Enforcement Marketplace."[36] Ironically, this militarization of the police occurred at the same time that policing scholars were proclaiming the triumph of community policing.

The protests in Seattle provided many people with their first glimpse of the militarization of municipal police, but it was certainly not their last. Virtually every major demonstration since Seattle has been met with the application of this more militarized approach to protest policing. That is especially the case in the wake of the terrorist attacks of 9/11, after which the threat of terrorism has served as a default response to critics who charge the police with suppressing civil liberties. Gone today is the practice of ceding partial control of the streets to demonstrators. Instead, the creation of police-enforced "free speech" zones and the containment of demonstrations within so-called protest pens (or again, what Foucault referred to as "enclosure" and "partitioning") is now commonplace, a practice that all but guarantees police-citizen tussles over physical space, since "spatial dynamics" are a major topic of contestation between protesters and the police (hence the often heard protest chant "Whose streets? *Our* streets!").[37] Meanwhile, just as the panoptic gaze became a

In riot gear, New York City police officers watch protesters behind a row of metal barricades during the 2004 Republican National Convention. These barricades are often used by police to create protest pens or "free speech" zones. (AP Images)

chief disciplinary strategy of the prison, total surveillance has become a primary component of protest policing, with law-enforcement agencies using hand-held cameras, cameras mounted on poles, and even blimps to monitor individuals exercising their free-speech rights. Finally, seemingly borrowing a page from history, the current use of pepper spray, tear gas, and rubber bullets signifies a new means of applying escalated force against a crowd that—at least from a police perspective—runs the risk of quickly becoming an unruly mob.

In sum, it is hard for even the most ardent supporter of law and its enforcement to overlook the fact that the State has increased its law-enforcement powers and tactics in the age of corporate globalization and, now, in the age of terrorism. The end of the Cold War allowed for the expansion of capitalism around the world and the consolidation of power among a handful of very powerful corporate conglomerates wielding an unparalleled level of influence on a range of issues, from the economy to the environment to war and militarism. These changes in the allocation of resources and in the distribution of political power were coupled with changes in law-enforcement strategies and tactics that witnessed an increased use of force, military-style weapons, and surveillance in order to quell the growing opposition to war and corporate rule. Community policing may have been the dominant paradigm during the early 1990s, but the new political climate has brought a new fervor of activism and, with it, a new approach to crowd control.

Individuals and Institutions

When taking to the streets in protest, many activists risk both the denial of liberty and physical injury for their performance of illegal dissent. Historically, reformers who have sought an end to such injustices as slavery, segregation, the exploitation of labor, and militarism have had to endure police batons, attack dogs, water cannons, and tear gas when conventional means of redress have failed—during even the most peaceful and passive forms of dissent. Although police officers justify their actions as necessary to maintain order and prevent chaos, activists often come to view police as "the enemy's foot soldiers," who protect the very individuals and institutions that propagate injustice.[38] Given the conflicting nature of police and protester objectives, as well as the violence that befalls people working for change, it is understandable that attitudes of open hostility by activists toward police should periodically become manifest.

During the early years of the twentieth century, relations between police and labor organizers were particularly hostile, especially following an unprecedented effort by government municipalities to suppress collective action among the nation's labor force. Beginning in 1905, a labor union known as the Industrial Workers of the World (IWW), or "Wobblies," began to organize around the principle that efforts at social change must be more than merely symbolic. Wobblies therefore advocated strategies of direct action and intervention in the pursuit of workers' rights, and they stood on soap boxes at street corners to appeal to the laboring class to join the movement. When city officials placated business owners by banning the practice of "soap boxing," Wobblies naturally defied these laws in mass numbers, which triggered a sizeable and brutal response from police.

On one such occasion, the *Portland Oregonian* reported that the police had been "armed with wagon spokes and axe handles for use as clubs, and these weapons have proved most effective."[39] In San Diego, law enforcement likewise initiated a violent crackdown on labor organizers who engaged in soap boxing. One worker apprehended while riding into San Diego on a freight train filled with labor organizers described the "police" they encountered as a makeshift militia of violent hooligans:

The vigilantes all wore constable badges and a white handkerchief around their left arms. They were all drunk and hollering and cursing the rest of the night. In the morning they took us out four or five at a time and marched us up the track to the county line . . . where we were forced to kiss the flag and run a gauntlet of 106 men, every one of which was striking at us hard as they could with their pick axe handles.[40]

In response to the police violence, IWW publications began to speak disparagingly about the police, calling law enforcement a violent and unrestrained government entity that served the interests of the propertied class. The *Industrial Worker* proclaimed police to be "a gang of sluggers."[41] The labor newspaper *Solidarity* wrote that workers should begin to "actively protect themselves from these thugs."[42] Soon, Wobblies began to recite the tale of the San Diego Free Speech Fights in verse:

> In that town of San Diego
> When the workers try to talk
> The cops will smash them with a say
> And tell 'em "Take a Walk."
>
> They throw them in the bull pen,
> And they feed them rotten beans,
> And they call that "law and order"
> In that city, so it seems.
>
> They're clubbing fellow working men
> Who dare their thoughts express
> And if [the Man] has his way
> There's sure to be a mess.[43]

As the labor movement gave way to the civil-rights and antiwar movements, it was common to hear revolutionary groups such as the Weather Underground and the Black Liberation Army refer to city cops as "pigs." The actual origin of this now-familiar epithet remains disputed. One explanation links the term to the 1968 Democratic National Convention in Chicago, where the activist group known as the Yippies had been running a pig as their presidential candidate. When police moved in to disrupt their rally, protesters began referring to the cops as pigs.[44] Since then, the term has been adopted at various times by activist groups among the political Left. At the close of the 1960s, the Black Panther Party announced to its members that the "revolution has come" and that it was time to "off the pigs—time to pick up the gun!"[45] Meanwhile, in New York City, a cop responding to the 1969 Stonewall Riots (which resulted from a police crackdown at a gay bar in Greenwich Village) had his badge stolen. It was found by police the following day stuck in a string of pickled pig's feet hanging from a tree in Washington Square Park.[46] The insult was undeniably clear.

Today, many new and emerging anarchist groups adopt a militant approach toward social change, one specifically designed to trigger an escalation of tension between activists and law enforcement. Specifically, the Black Bloc anarchists that played a prominent role in the WTO Battle for Seattle and the property destruction that ensued describe this new militancy as necessary to unmask the brutal nature of the State by exposing the brutality of the opposing police/military force. "Simply by resisting arrest, refusing to remain on sanctioned parade routes, challenging police barricades and by actively directing its anger at corporate targets, the Bloc ensured that such an escalation would ensue."[47] They contended that by showing the public the means by which the status quo is maintained, more people will become radicalized and join in the struggle for social change. The goal of this new wave of anarchists, though, was not to render oneself a martyr through deliberate apprehension and arrest. Instead, the goal was to "punch Cops in the face . . . and get away with it!" as one anarchist journal boldly suggested.[48]

These examples notwithstanding, the activists interviewed for this book contend that their interaction with and, therefore, opinion of police is far from universally negative; rather, it is more nuanced and complex. To be sure, they identified police as street-corner bureaucrats who receive directives from the institutions of government and who have as their mandate the carrying out and enforcement of orders. They recognized that individual officers have limited on-the-job discretion and are actually trained to suppress their individualistic tendencies in favor of official policy. It is this unwavering protection of policy that serves as a source of frustration among the activists interviewed, who feel that police too often protect and serve the interests of government and business and not those of the people. New York City activist Benjamin Shepard raised the behavior of the NYPD during the RNC to describe his impression of the police function in contemporary society:

[Police are] sort of becoming the Roman guards of the Empire right now. They're really all about protecting capital. I don't think they're about protecting citizens, and I'm a taxpayer. I pay a lot of money to live in New York. . . . I mean, during the RNC, [police] were so interested in protecting corporate classes above everyone else.

An antiwar protester from the Midwest echoed this belief that police serve the interests of the wealthy, but he believed this to be less indicative of one city agency's response to one event and more indicative of a broader police mandate. In that regard, the police are mere players in a larger political struggle that pits some members of the working class—like cops—against others in the working class: "It's really important to me not to demonize the police. . . . for the most part, the police [officer] finds himself victimized in the [political] process as well, because [police] are charged with protecting property or protecting the interests of the moneyed class." Still another protester referenced the RNC to explain his sense of a police bias toward the rights of the rich and politically powerful. Specifically, he expressed frustration that antiwar protesters were denied their right to free speech in the proximity of Madison Square Garden, the site where the Republican Party platform was being discussed. At the same time, he too reserved his criticism for the government itself and *not* for the individual officers:

The RNC was an example of when the police overreacted. But I think that in part was because of the instructions they'd gotten. "Don't let them get near Madison Square Garden! Don't let them do this! Don't let them do that." But part of the problem was the orders they had gotten, . . . and I think they felt in a pinch. They were being put between the government and demonstrators. I have a certain sympathy for the average cop. I don't have a lot of sympathy for the higher-ups that make the decisions. But for the average cop, I think by and large they're decent, regular-old folks just like us.

Actually, many of the protesters I have encountered during my research make an important distinction between police as individuals and the institution of "the police," and they save their animus for the latter. Ellen Barfield, who is organizer with the War Resisters League among other organizations, explained to me the importance of distinguishing individuals from institutions:

[When interacting with police] I try to be calm and respectful and know that they are just doing their job. Even when they are a little over the top, I try to recognize what they are doing and what they've been told to do and know that it's not the person who's the problem—it's the system that's the problem.

She continued to argue that her training in nonviolent resistance *requires* that she distinguish between individuals and institutions: "Regardless of who it is you're facing, disrespect is not a good thing from either side, and that's part of learning to be nonviolent: to respect the individual regardless of what they're doing and regardless of what system they're participating in."

This distinction between officers as individuals and the broader government institution is an important one. The story of twentieth-century governance is that of the increasing prestige of the official position coupled with the diminution of the position holder. Today, the modern State is synonymous with the bureaucratic structure in which rules are the work product of organizations and the singular foot soldier is, as Max Weber wrote, but a "cog in an ever-moving mechanism."[49] It is therefore naive for the modern citizen to view governance as simply the product of individuals; it is astute to recognize that we are all ruled by institutions. The activists I encountered during my several years of research seemed acutely aware of this reality.

This ability and willingness to distinguish individuals from institutions has allowed some of the activists to form friendships of sorts with individual officers, especially since many of the protesters I interviewed have repeatedly been arrested at the same location (e.g., a military base, a family-planning clinic) and often by the very same officers as on previous occasions. Antinuclear activist "Veronica," who has been arrested over fifty times since the 1970s (and often at the same location), explained her relationship with the police:

I've been arrested by an officer who says, "Hi Veronica. How are you doing? I see you're back again. Can you please come with me?" I say, "No, I'm not going to get up. I'm just going to be on the floor." And he says, "Oh please, I don't want to drag you," and then they'll come with a couple other people and drag you away. . . . [Sometimes] you can have some kind of dialogue with them. . . . They're not our enemy.

Police respond in riot gear to protests outside a women's health organization in Hinds County, Mississippi. (Operation Save America)

Occasionally, individual officers find subtle ways to reveal their sympathy—if not solidarity—with the cause of the protesters, whether the cause is to the left or the right on the political spectrum. One woman active with a pro-life/anti-abortion organization gave the following description of her interaction with individual officers: "To be perfectly honest, [officers] try to remain neutral, but it's very obvious the ones that are sympathetic to our cause and the ones that are very anti- or opposed to what we do." She told of a scenario in which sympathetic police allowed protesters who were blocking access to a clinic (including her husband) to take "baby steps" as the police carried them away to the patrol cars.

The police actually allowed them to very slowly just put one foot in front of the other and very slowly get on the bus. So you might have two to three hundred people sitting down [in front of the clinic], and it would take a long time, literally more than an hour, for them to clear the driveway. [This] gave us more time to counsel [incoming women and to block access].

James Tracy, an advocate for the homeless who was once arrested while trying to prevent an eviction, told of a rather unique encounter with the police when—upon arrest—the arresting officer turned to him and said, "Hey, my cousin's getting evicted. Where can I get her some help?" Still another protester I met told of being arrested along with the wife of a big-city police chief, who accompanied protesters in an act of civil disobedience against militarism. With news reporters present, the police chief personally administered the arrest. Clearly, not all police-protester encounters are hostile.

None of this should suggest that contemporary police-protester interaction is never hostile. Although he conceded that most of his interaction with law enforcement has been uneventful, Ed Hedemann has nevertheless had some negative encounters, as he explained to me:

> I've been kicked by police. I've had my hair pulled by police. I've had my arms twisted around in unnatural positions. [I've been] dragged and walked on. A cop walked over my stomach as I was lying on the ground. I've been threatened verbally while things were happening to me physically any number of times by police.

James Tracy, the housing advocate, took a practical stance when characterizing the overall quality of his encounters with police by conceding that he had never received anything from police that he "certainly didn't ask for." In that respect, he had never been "beaten down to a pulp or anything like that."

> My contact with police—the actual arrests has been eight out of ten times okay. . . . And then two out of ten the cops were just real assholes. The booking stuff is where I've experienced the most trouble. You know, cops in San Francisco are pretty smart to know that most of the time, if you beat an activist, it's going to make the news sooner or later. But losing your booking papers or getting you lost for a little while is plausible deniability.

Of course, there are also times when a police response to dissent is wholly inappropriate to the events at hand, as was the case at the WTO protests in Seattle. Although there were elements within the larger demonstrations, such as the Black Bloc anarchists, who were intent on creating violent altercations with police, the overwhelming majority of attendees

ing on and off their gas masks and such. All of a sudden we got pepper
spray, tear gas, rubber bullets in the back and concussion grenades all at
once. And it worked. It scattered us. But people kept coming back again
and again.

The Seattle Police Department's (SPD) own *After Action Report* conceded
that there existed "critical flaws in command and control," which lacked "a
detailed, well-rehearsed plan" for dealing with that type of protest. Those
problems occurred because the SPD, like most law-enforcement agencies,
"gets few opportunities to train and practice execution of special events of
the scope and complexity of the WTO conference."[50] On this point, Delgado is in agreement:

> Police officers are often trained for riots, as my friend—a Park Ranger—
> was trained. But they're not trained for nonviolent direct action, . . . and
> they get scared. I've seen so much fear among them. They're taught that it
> can turn into a riot at any time. So police officers need better training.

As a result of the lack of police training in dealing with nonviolent resisters, seasoned activists simply go into an action accepting that "there's always the threat of police violence." Recognizing this fact, Tracy proffered
the following advice to readers who may wish to become fellow demonstrators: "Keep the 'fuck you's' to the cops to a minimum. You don't want
to piss them off."

Privileged Protesters

Any further discussion of police-protester interaction must address the
fact that in the United States and other industrialized democracies, activists seldom reflect the constituencies that find themselves on the receiving end of police misconduct. Instead, those who take to the streets
often qualify as privileged protesters in that they tend to be white, well
educated, and of middle-class (or upper-middle-class) economic status.

Although this statement is somewhat of an oversimplification and should not be interpreted to imply that all protesters are either demographically or experientially privileged, social-science data nevertheless highlights a somewhat inorganic aspect to the composition of the activist class. Simply put, the people who demand change are often those least likely to require immediate change to their social standing.

To understand the abundance of the privileged among the protester class, it is important to recognize that activism requires three key components: a vision of hope, a sense of empowerment, and access to resources. Financially, people who lack resources do not have the luxury of time or money to develop a strategy for change, and they therefore feel utterly powerless to effect any lasting social transformation. At the same time, constituencies who have to worry about racial and ethnic profiling on a daily basis are not likely to be quick to encourage a confrontation with police, even a confrontation that is nonviolent and designed as an expression of protest. By necessity, then, poorer classes, which often include minorities, must live purposeful lives and limit themselves to goals that are concrete, immediate, and certain.

If the economically or racially disenfranchised are without the means or the will to agitate for change, then those who live comfortably and who avoid racial or ethnic discrimination are free to mobilize politically should their standard of life ever be threatened or should their pursuit of achieving more ever appear stymied. Eric Hoffer has referred to this pool of potential agitators as "the new poor," because the people who are most easily recruited to the ranks of mass movements are the individuals whose comfortable existence is precarious at best, namely, those who compose the middle class.[51] Thus, Hoffer hypothesizes that participation in mass movements is greatest among constituents whose misery (if any) is bearable and whose hopes for improved conditions appear attainable and within reach, and social-science research appears to bear out this hypothesis.

In a qualitative study of individuals who were actively working to oppose the Vietnam War, Kenneth Keniston noted that all the radicals he interviewed were white and came from the middle class. In fact, he noted more broadly that those who belonged to the New Left came from advantaged sectors of American society, had parents within the upper middle class, and attended prestigious colleges and universities.[52] Other studies of anti-Vietnam movements have also highlighted the large role played by college and university students (and particularly by wealthy Ivy League students) in initiating political agitation. Even the civil rights movement "was greatly helped by a student movement of the North, but probably not more than 5,000 students—or fewer than one out of every hundred—were involved."[53] Examining more recent events, political scientist Russell J. Dalton has examined data from the World Values Survey/European Values Survey to predict participation in protest activity. He concludes that distrust in government has "only a modest impact" on the willingness to engage in protest. Moreover, "protest in advanced industrial democracies is not simply an outlet for the alienated and deprived: often, just the opposite appears."[54]

That the people who willingly tussle with police at protests are often among the privileged class can certainly influence their assessments of law enforcement when engaging in crimes of dissent. That is especially likely given the extensive research on citizens' attitudes toward police, which reveals that race, ethnicity, and neighborhood characteristics (such as socioeconomic status) greatly predict citizens' assessments of law enforcement, with whites predictably holding more favorable opinions than nonwhites.[55] Even if we acknowledge the antiauthoritarian leanings of many of the protesters interviewed for this book, it simply remains a possibility that activists' assessments of police-protester relations are likely to be more favorable today than if protesters largely came from the racially or economically disenfranchised classes. That observation was readily conceded by the individuals I met. "Once I'm arrested, I always try to have a good conversation [with the arresting officers] so they know I'm a person [and] can't dehumanize me. . . . And I get a lot of good results. But it's a privilege. I'm a white, educated guy, and the police always recognize [that]." Another protester—a twenty-four-year-old white male active with the Los Angels Catholic Worker—noted the latent racism (to his benefit) that takes place whenever he is arrested and taken to county jail: "[Police] realize you're a protester, you're not exactly a drug dealer or pimp. . . . I remember in county jail they would just look at me and realize I didn't belong there. In county jail, it's staffed by the Sheriff's Department, and they would look at me like, 'What are you in here for?'"

Sometimes, however, being a white and wealthy protester can actually be an aggravating—rather than a mitigating—factor when it comes to the quality of interaction with police, at least when the interaction is at a protest. Sharon Delgado described some of her more harsh experiences with cops and jail officials:

When we're treated harshly and crudely, it isn't happening in a vacuum. It happens all of the time to people of color and to people who don't have the white privilege and the class privilege. And so when a bunch of us are arrested for protesting, the police are pissed off at us because we are making their job harder. . . . So they start threatening us and saying, "Nobody can see you in here. There are no cameras. We can do whatever we want."

Only one of the activists who sat down with me for a formal interview is a racial or ethnic minority. Not surprisingly, she spent much of our interview discussing civil disobedience as "something for the privileged." As a Latina, Sharon Lungo is acutely aware of the symbolism inherent in each act of dissent. It is for this reason that she works hard to ensure that the racial and ethnic composition of the participants in an action in which she engages is reflective of the constituency affected, namely, the people in her community—Los Angeles.

Who lives in Los Angeles? What do our faces look like? It will definitely make me stop if I see brown faces in that crowd [of arrestees]. It will definitely make me stop and say, you know, "Who are you? And where do you come from? And how did you get into this?" And I think it makes things look more real to me, versus, you know, there are a bunch of white dudes who are [just] going to get off.

At the same time, Lungo readily acknowledged that it is difficult for the disadvantaged to engage in acts of dissent, such as civil disobedience.

In poorer communities it's harder to pull off civil disobedience because of the imminent threat of police on the communities. People react to those kinds of things in different ways. I certainly wouldn't want to use civil disobedience around a group of people, say, who had been prone to a lot of [police] violence in their life, because I can see that being a very uncomfortable situation for them.

So although Sharon grappled with the image communicated by "a bunch of white dudes" engaged in protest, she conceded that it is much easier for the privileged to engage in dissent. Therefore, the onus is somewhat on them to forsake their privilege and be among those arrested.

It's very appropriate for white dudes—to speak of them as a group—to put themselves on the line, because white dudes have the most privilege, and they should do that. They should put their asses out there for everybody. . . . One of the biggest issues that we're dealing with in the community is issues of privilege. We know white people are going to get off a little bit easier [for their acts of dissent], but as a person of color, I don't let that stop me.

Policing beyond the Streets

In 1950, Yale Law School professor Harold Lasswell joined several other scholars of public policy to study the impact of the Cold War on American customs and practices. Acknowledging the real threats to American culture posed by a nuclear-armaments race and the encroachment of communist ideology, Lasswell and his associates were perhaps more concerned about the threat to individual freedom posed by the United States' own national-security measures. Reminding readers of James Madison's words that "it is a universal truth that the loss of liberty at home is to be charged to provisions against danger, real or pretended, from abroad," Lasswell identified several policy trends that were having a deleterious effect on cherished civil liberties.[56] Top on the list was concern over the expansion of government. "When we divert resources to large-scale arms and other defense programs, we automatically enlarge the scope of government in industry, in politics, in science and education, and in every sphere of life." Next on the list was the "withholding of information," since a concern for national security creates a reluctance to disclose facts relevant to the machinations of State. National-security measures also create an "atmosphere of suspicion" in which government officials begin to compile lists of individuals and organizations deemed threatening to the State and in which secretly obtained evidence may be used to prosecute individuals deemed national-security threats. All these measures have led legal scholars to observe that during times of national crisis, the greatest threat to a political system is not the failure to provide national security; it is the failure to appraise "the extent of the danger and then to test proposed measures of security by the yardstick of long-established guarantees of the freedom of the individual."[57]

It is an unfortunate fact that the history of U.S. concern over national security has indeed been met by the formation of policies and practices that threaten long-established freedoms. During World War I, Congress passed an encroachment on the freedom of speech, the Sedition Act of 1918, which in essence made it a crime to speak disparagingly of the United States, the Constitution, and even the flag. It is estimated that some two thousand persons were prosecuted under this law, primarily for speaking out against the war. During the Cold War, the Smith Act of 1940 criminalized membership in or affiliation with the Communist Party or any group organized to overthrow the government. In 1950. the office of the attorney general of the United States had a list of two hundred groups it deemed subversive. Congress even formed the House Un-American Activities Committee, which was charged with the mandate of investigating the activities of members of these groups.[58] During the social-justice movements of the 1950s and 1960s, the FBI initiated its Counter-Intelligence Program (also known as COINTELPRO), through which federal law enforcement not only spied and kept files on individuals it considered dangerous or un-American (such as Martin Luther King, Jr., John Lennon, and John Steinbeck) but also authorized agents to infiltrate social groups and act as provocateurs for the purpose of disrupting and neutralizing their activities.[59]

In the aftermath of the terrorist attacks of September 11, 2001, the United States again appeared to be placing national-security concerns above those of the freedom to dissent. Signed into law just forty-five days after the attacks on the Pentagon and the World Trade Center and adopting a clever acronym, the USA PATRIOT Act—among other provisions—authorized the attorney general to expand telephone and Internet surveillance, to extend the reach of wiretaps, to monitor library usage, and to conduct secret searches without first obtaining a warrant. It also gave the attorney general broad powers to define certain "alien" individuals and organizations as terrorists and allows for them to be detained for periods up to six months while limiting judicial review on grounds of habeas corpus. Perhaps of most concern to the activist community, Section 802 of the act amended the federal criminal code to include in its definition of terrorism a new classification of "domestic terrorism" defined as

> activities that occur primarily within the U.S. jurisdiction, that involve criminal acts dangerous to human life, and that appear to be intended to intimidate or coerce a civilian population, to influence government policy by intimidation or coercion, or to affect government conduct by mass destruction, assassination, or kidnapping.[60]

The USA PATRIOT Act

CHECK IT OUT
BEFORE
YOU CHECK OUT!

SECTION 215:

allows the FBI to monitor the type of books you read and the kinds of web sites you visit.

SECTION 216:

gives law enforcement authority to secretly monitor all electronic communication, including Library Internet use.

KNOW YOUR RIGHTS!

Created by the Orange County Peace Coalition upon the passage of the USA PATRIOT Act, this bookmark was distributed to Southern California libraries as part of a grassroots information campaign. (Artwork by Spacious Mind Art & Graphic Design)

Although it is certainly reasonable to expect government to incorporate such activities as mass destruction, assassination, and kidnapping under the rubric of terrorism, language discussing "criminal acts" that may be "dangerous" and intended to "influence government policy" is clouded in vagaries, since activities such as tax resistance or the burning of draft cards can be deemed acts that impede the war on terror and therefore are dangerous to human life. As one legal scholar has observed, "The vagaries in the USA PATRIOT Act's definition of domestic terrorism grant the government license to lump non-violent civil disobedience in the tradition of Henry David Thoreau, Gandhi, and Martin Luther King, Jr. together with the Al Qaeda network's ruthless murders."[61]

Concern about the application of antiterror legislation is not merely academic. Indeed, it has made its way into the editorial pages of U.S. newspapers. As the Senate was preparing to vote on the Patriot Act in October 2001, Nadine Strossen of the American Civil Liberties Union was among the few public figures arguing against the legislation: "If this bill passes as written, it will affect absolutely everybody in this country who uses a telephone or a computer." She continued: "It will threaten our most basic constitutional rights against unreasonable search and seizure, and it will have a chilling effect on our rights to free speech and free association."[62] The bill passed by a vote of ninety-eight to one. Yet it did not take long for people to begin to question whether the law handed the government too much authority.

Only months after the bill was signed, on January 1, 2002, the *New York Times* began reporting about a government "dragnet" whereby hundreds of Middle Eastern immigrants deemed security threats were being detained indefinitely on charges of immigration violations, all under the auspices of the Patriot Act.[63] Three days later, an editorial in the *Oakland Tribune* warned readers that the act threatened the First, Fourth, Fifth, and Sixth Amendments to the Constitution. It therefore called on its readers to "resist these encroachments on our fundamental rights."[64] Over the following few years, newspapers across the country reported instances in which animal-rights activists, environmentalists, antiwar groups, religious communities, and other so-called extremists were being secretly monitored by the federal government under suspicion of domestic terrorism. Consider just the following examples:

- Through the enhanced powers of domestic intelligence surveillance authorized under the Patriot Act, in the years following the attacks of September 11, 2001, the FBI attempted to establish a connection between the animal-rights advocacy group People for the Ethical Treatment of Animals (PETA) and other groups that the government deemed domestic terrorist organizations. As one newspaper reported about federal law enforcement's policing of PETA, "Records were seized, phone calls were traced, undercover agents infiltrated PETA and disgruntled former PETA workers were enlisted in the case." Despite the investigation, no charges were ever filed, and obtained records provide no proof that PETA was involved in any terrorist activities.[65]

- In early 2004, a federal judge ordered officials at Drake University in Iowa to hand over all documents relating to an on-campus antiwar group. The Associated Press called the order "the first subpoena of its kind since the Communist-hunting days of the 1950s." Several months earlier, Drake University had been the site of a student-led antiwar forum. In addition to records about forum attendees, the university was also ordered to provide all records relating to the local chapter of the National Lawyer's Guild, a legal-activist organization that sponsored the forum.[66]

- In late 2005, the Associated Press revealed that government documents obtained by the American Civil Liberties Union through a Freedom of Information Act request revealed widespread domestic spying on various domestic organizations by federal law-enforcement agencies. According to the documents, not only was the government monitoring such groups as PETA, but federal terrorism investigators had infiltrated the Washington-based American-Arab Anti-Discrimination Committee. Moreover, other documents revealed government monitoring of such groups as Greenpeace and the Catholic Worker for their protests against missle testing in California.[67]

Despite the growing national debate over the threats to civil liberties posed by law-enforcement efforts against terrorism, after a sunset clause threatened renewal of the Patriot Act in February 2006, Congress renewed the act, making only minor revisions to the bill. Yet that did not prove to be end of the controversy. In March 2007, the U.S. Senate Judiciary Committee conducted hearings on the misuse of Patriot Act powers after it was revealed that national intelligence agencies were secretly spying on U.S. citizens through telephone records seized under false pretenses. This revelation all but confirmed Nadine Strossen's predictions about the threat to civil liberties posed by the Patriot Act. According to Senate testimony, in the year prior to the enactment of the Patriot Act, the FBI had issued approximately eighty-five hundred requests for National Security Letters (NSLs), which allow the government to obtain personal information (e.g., emails, bank and phone records, credit card information) without

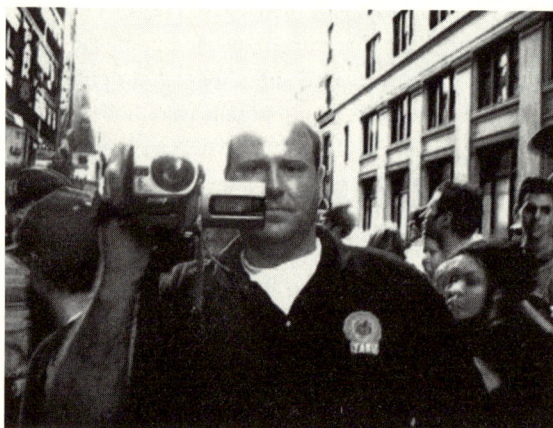

As part of the new strategy of surveillance, a New York
City police officer films peaceful protesters at the 2004
Republican National Convention.

judicial or grand-jury oversight. By 2003, the annual number of NSL requests jumped to thirty-nine thousand. By 2005, the number was as high
as forty-seven thousand, which illustrates the growth of domestic spying.
Moreover, the testimony revealed widespread violations in the manner
in which personal information was obtained. In a sample of just seventy-
seven cases, the inspector general found twenty-six procedural violations,
with documentation missing or inadequate in 60 percent of the files examined. One senator concluded that even with the expanded powers provided by the Patriot Act, the government had been acting "with total disregard for the law."[68]

It is difficult to determine the impact that the Patriot Act and other
antiterrorism measures have had on the level of domestic dissent. One
possibility is that new legislation has done little to suppress dissent among
people already active within protest communities. Yet it is equally likely
that individuals concerned about one issue or another have thought twice
about participating in public displays of dissent after 9/11. Still a third
possibility is that government efforts to crack down on dissent have only
made protesters more determined in their campaigns. One activist I met
told me that the events of September 11 made him "more deliberate in
seeking out opportunities to stand in solidarity with marginalized communities, especially Muslims." Moreover, new antiterror legislation seems
to have only increased his level of activism. In fact, as the United States

was preparing for war in Iraq, in December 2002 this activist joined the Iraq Peace Team and flew to Iraq to serve as one of many human shields in an effort to stave off war. As he explained it, "9/11 did prompt me to consider taking new risks."

Ben Shepard responded to the events of 9/11 by helping to organize events designed to express opposition to the Patriot Act through local city council resolutions. Working with the activist network Reclaim the Streets, area activists created what they called a "Patriot Act Free Zone," wherein some three hundred people converted a major intersection in the city into a party zone, complete with music, fire dancing, and cyclists. Only a handful of arrests were made while the party continued unabated.

Not all activists were as brazen as the preceding examples suggest: "I think that 9/11 has made us who favor direct action much more mindful of the consequences of our actions. It takes much more to convince people to take action outside of accepted electoral means when the stakes are this high." At the same time, this longtime activist conceded that "the stakes have always been high." For him, "the Patriot Act is only one part of a larger agenda and overall push to expand State power and regulate dissent." As he sees it, the only difference with the Patriot Act is that with the legislation on the books, "law enforcement feel emboldened to be as punitive as possible." The question of whether the judicial process proves to be equally punitive or preventive toward people who engage in nonviolent—though illegal—dissent is the subject of the next chapter.

5

Working the System

The system is really constipated.
                    —Ellen Barfield, War Resisters League

They called it "Guantánamo on the Hudson," but on any given day Pier 57 was an otherwise nondescript three-story building located along New York City's West Side. Extending some seven hundred feet into the murky Hudson River, the facility normally served as a parking garage for the buses of New York's public transit system. Yet just as Brooklyn's Floyd Bennett Field functioned as a counterprotest training camp during the 2004 Republican National Convention (RNC), Pier 57 was likewise converted into a large makeshift detention center whose sole purpose was to house individuals arrested for protesting the policies of the Republican Party. Sparse benches and scarce portable toilets took the place of speed bumps and tire cinder blocks. Chain-link fences adorned with razor wire snaked throughout the concrete structure and created a series of holding cells through which each arrestee had to traverse before finally being transported—by bus, of course—to the Manhattan Criminal Court for booking.

Consider it a sign of the times that in a country already known for having the most expansive criminal justice system, government officials deem it necessary to build additional detention facilities to house its discontented during times of politically significant events. But even open-access and democratic states experience paroxysms of dissent, proving that even in the most free of societies there exist large pockets of dissatisfaction among the masses. Thus, Seattle city officials deemed it necessary to use the old Sand Point naval base as a holding center for people arrested while protesting the World Trade Organization. Hundreds of activists were transported by buses approximately half an hour outside the

Protesters at the 2004 Republican National Convention were detained
and warehoused at Pier 57, an abandoned bus depot that quickly became
known as "Guantánamo on the Hudson." (Photo by Jacob Richards and
Connie Murillo)

city—first to the naval base, where they reportedly were given no food or
water and were denied access to lawyers, then on to the King County Jail
and the Kent Regional Justice Center.[1]

Five years later, war, torture, domestic spying, and the curtailment of
civil liberties were among the issues protested outside the RNC. So great
was the level of dissent that New York City officials deemed it necessary to
convert an old bus garage into a mysterious detention center, that "Guantánamo on the Hudson," where conditions were far from idyllic even for
the most seasoned of protesters, though the conditions hardly compared
to those within the real Guantánamo Prison Camp, which housed people
caught up in the U.S.-led war on terror. Still, during the week of protests
surrounding the RNC, law enforcement arrested nearly two thousand
persons, and all of them were sent to the abandoned bus depot known
as Pier 57, where they sat for hours on end. On just one day, the NYPD
arrested nearly twelve hundred persons, the largest number of arrests on
a single day in any of New York's five boroughs.[2] All these arrests created
a backlog of arrestees to be processed. It was not uncommon, then, for

persons to be held in excess of thirty hours before finally receiving an arraignment or desk-appearance ticket. During this time, protesters were unable to meet with lawyers or to call family or friends to notify them of their detention—much like the detainees being held at the real Guantánamo Camp.

Midweek during the RNC, news reports began to surface highlighting the negative conditions at Pier 57. On August 30, the *New York Times* described the pier as an "aging" and "dingy" facility, and it quoted sources who questioned whether the pier was appropriate as a detention center. The next day, the paper reported that arrestees were suffering from mysterious skin rashes that probably resulted from having to sleep on the chemically laced floor of the depot, where unknown substances (perhaps oil slicks, perhaps antifreeze) blanketed the concrete.[3] Meanwhile, the backlog of persons to be processed continued. Responding to a motion filed by the Legal Aid Society, on September 1 a judge of the New York State Supreme Court ordered the city to release within twenty-four hours the five hundred defendants still in custody, or the city itself would face punishment. Despite the ruling, little changed to expedite case processing. The day after the judge's ruling, the negative press reports continued. Reporting from Manhattan's Criminal Court, a *New York Times* reporter noted that even as late as eleven in the morning, "there were no judges on the bench in three arraignment rooms, and a fourth room was locked." The article continued, "Frustration was building for everyone. By late afternoon, the scene was much the same."[4] Twenty-four hours later, the same judge held the City of New York in contempt of court for failing to adhere to his ruling calling for the timely release of arrestees, and he fined the city one thousand dollars for each individual detained longer than the twenty-four-hour limit. The judge was later quoted as saying that the city's delay in releasing the arrestees was "willful and intentional."[5]

One of the most noteworthy facts to emerge during the arrests at the RNC was that among those arrested at RNC-related protests were innocent bystanders, legal observers, members of the press, and other nonparticipants in the various acts of dissent, who were nevertheless swept up in the mass arrests that ensued. Also among the many arrestees were novice activists, who likely received their first taste of civil disobedience and the criminal justice system during the high-profile event. Thus, the duration and conditions of confinement were rather unusual, considering that most of the people were arrested for such offenses as marching without a permit. Indeed, although over 80 percent of those arrested faced only minor charges (that is, charges that are characterized as "violations," or the equivalent of a parking ticket, rather than "crimes"), they nevertheless faced unnecessary (and lengthy) detention, some for as long as forty hours. According to a post-RNC investigation launched by the New York Civil Liberties Union, nearly a year after the 2004 convention over 90 percent of the RNC-related cases resulted in dismissals, conditional dismissals, or acquittals.[6]

Going to Jail for Justice

For the budding activist thinking about lending a voice of dissent at the next big march or rally, news reports emanating from either the WTO or the RNC can make the idea of going to jail for justice rather off-putting. Certainly, the justice system's response to the activism surrounding the Seattle trade negotiations and the renomination of George W. Bush as the Republican presidential candidate was extraordinary; thus, it would be an error to consider the conditions of confinement and the system's machinations as either typical or representative of all responses to crimes of dissent. Nevertheless, little is known about how the system responds to persons who deliberately and publicly transgress a law, however nonviolently the transgression may have been performed. What happens postarrest? What are the conditions of confinement? How are people arrested for dissent treated by jail officials and by other inmates? Do judges recognize civil disobedience and nonviolent resistance as legitimate means of political communication, or do they consider such cases a waste of the court's time? Do activists attempt to work the system to maximize exposure of their cause, or do they cease to protest postarrest? Finally, does the experience of traversing the system change activists' perspective on the meaning of justice?

In the sections that follow, I attempt to answer these questions. I begin by examining some protesters' experiences in jail and their assessments of the conditions of confinement. Although it is common to think of confinement as occurring postadjudication, the fact is that, contrary to criminal justice organizational flowcharts, many protesters experience jail *only* during the pretrial stages of the system. In fact, some protesters are quite adept at avoiding the trial phase altogether by engaging in postarrest/ pretrial protests of noncooperation in a strategy known as *jail solidarity.* Moreover, many municipalities decide against charging protesters with offenses because of the cost of a trial as measured in both time and human resources. That is particularly the case when arrests ensue during large political events, such as the WTO negotiations or the 2004 RNC, where the goal of city officials is often little more than to remove protesters from the streets until the conclusion of the high-profile event. Therefore, this chapter breaks with tradition and explores confinement first, followed by an examination of court procedures for the political protesters who do proceed to trial.

"A Killing Institution"

In Fyodor Dostoevsky's *Memoirs from the House of the Dead*, a semiautobiographical telling of the author's four-year incarceration for illegal political activities, the prisoner-narrator describes the penitentiary that confines him as an institution that "sucks the living sap out of a man" by wearing down his spirit and weakening him to the point that the average prisoner resembles a "shriveled, half-demented mummy."[7] It is a sentiment shared by many contemporaries of Dostoevsky's prisoner-narrator. Eugene V. Debs was another political prisoner whose writings have become celebrated for the insight they provide into the politics and conditions of confinement. A longtime agitator, Debs was incarcerated for speaking out against the U.S draft at the time of the First World War. Although his case ultimately made its way to the U.S. Supreme Court, the justices ruled against him, and he ended up serving nearly three years behind bars for his political speech. While in prison, not only did he run for president of the United States on the 1920 Socialist Party ticket as "Convict No. 9653 For President," but he also wrote *Walls and Bars: Prisons and Prison Life in the "Land of the Free."* In the book, Debs described the penitentiary as "a killing institution in a moral as well as in a physical sense," because penitentiaries are "designed to break men and not to make them."[8] He argued that if prisoners enter institutions of confinement already half broken, then they depart them utterly powerless and without hope.

With the United States leading the world in incarceration, there is certainly no shortage of writings providing insight into the impact of criminal detention on the human spirit. During the 1960s, Eldridge Cleaver wrote that prisons produce "a sense of ultimate defeat" in the souls of prisoners.[9] More recently, and writing from death row, Mumia Abu-Jamal called incarceration "a psychic cocoon of negativity" in which the most damaging aspects of confinement are not the outbursts of violence that occasionally occur but the "second-by-second assault on the soul" that comes from being locked away in a cage.[10] There is even an academic journal of sorts devoted to the experiences of prisoners. The *Journal of Prisoners on Prisons* provides inmates with an opportunity to use the craft of writing both as a tool of advocacy and perhaps even as therapy.[11] Many of the essays within the journal tell of injustices inside prisons that echo those of the outside world—tales of violence, racism, and sexism.

It is in the context of this legacy of emotional cruelty and psychological control that I turn to activists' perceptions of the conditions of confinement, for not surprisingly the activists interviewed for this study provided tales of incarceration similar to those of their prisoner-narrator brethren. Of course, activists are not likely to experience the conditions on death row of which Mumia Abu-Jamal wrote or those within a maximum-security prison as told by Eldridge Cleaver. Instead, they are more typically housed in county jails or in makeshift holding facilities such as the Sand Point naval base or Pier 57. At the same time, many of the nations' county jails suffer from overcrowding, unsanitary conditions, and violence. In 2006, the Commission on Safety and Abuse in America's Prisons issued a report that exposed evidence of assaults and other acts of violence taking place in both prisons and jails. Former prisoners testified to having endured gang violence, beatings by correctional officers, and "illegal and humiliating strip-searches."[12] The report noted with irony that at the time of the commission's seating in Los Angeles, the county jail in that very city (and the largest jail system in the United States) was experiencing a massive outbreak of inmate violence. On February 6, the *Daily News of Los Angeles* reported that more than two hundred inmates were involved in rioting that led to one death and twenty serious injuries.[13] By the end of the week, the number of participants involved in the jail violence increased tenfold. The *Christian Science Monitor* told of an inmate having been beaten to death and of inmates throwing beds off balconies. To quell the rioting, authorities transferred hundreds of jail inmates to state prisons in what the paper called "a bid to separate the most violent offenders from the general jail population."[14]

Like maximum-security prisons, then, jails too can be brutal and violent places. This violence no doubt stems from the fact that jails are often overcrowded and overburdened institutions. According to the Bureau of Justice Statistics, midyear 2006 jails in the United States operated at 94 percent capacity, though the number rose to 100 percent capacity when factoring in "the peak number of inmates incarcerated on any given day."[15] With overcrowding often comes violence, especially when jails are burdened to the point that officials are unable to segregate violent offenders from the general inmate population. Among the conclusions of the Commission on Safety and Abuse in America's Prisons was the rather axiomatic observation that crowding contributes to violence, but the prevention of violence requires an appropriate classification and segregation system of inmates within jails and prisons—something that due to overcrowding is frequently not possible.[16] As a case in point, one activist I interviewed told me, "[In] county jail, I was thrown in with everybody, some who had already been convicted of murder and were there on appeal, some who were facing charges of murder, rape, assault, etc. . . . Why would you put a nonviolent offender in with a violent offender?" It is worth noting, though, that during our conversation about jail, this activist argued, "For me, the people in for murder were much easier to get along with than the people who were in for burglary. The people in for burglary had made a lifestyle choice of criminal deviance. . . . the people in for murder—generally it was a crime of passion, a one-time thing."

These already overcrowded conditions within county jails can be exacerbated during large-scale political demonstrations when law enforcement secures mass arrests. Picked up by police for civil disobedience at the antiglobalization protests surrounding the WTO, Sharon Delgado told of widespread evidence of violence while in custody. According to her, activists were pepper sprayed at close range, one woman in holding suffered from a broken nose (which Delgado presumed occurred while the woman was in holding), and her "fifty-nine-year-old friend was abused in jail":

> She was given pain compliance techniques in jail. [Jail officials] pushed her down to the floor and put their knees into her back and twisted and did things to her feet and arms, because when we were being booked—she and I—a woman guard had run her hand up my friend's crotch really hard, and my friend jumped and protested and just spontaneously said, "Ouch!" It wasn't like she yelled at her or anything. Then the woman grabbed her by the hair. My friend had long hair, and she was taking it out by the handful, because the officers had pulled her hair so badly and did pain compliance techniques on her even though she's completely nonviolent.

Concluding her story about the violence in custody, Delgado added the following disclaimer: "Remember, we weren't just booked into jail. We were booked at Sand Point naval base first, and we were there for a long time."

With this context established, and with the acknowledgment that jails are unwelcoming and even violent environments, both for hardened criminals and for activists alike, we must also take a step back and acknowledge that although the threat of jail violence is always present, more often than not the violence that activists encounter while in confinement is primarily psychological. Indeed, quite a few activist handbooks caution protesters about the psychological violence that they are choosing to face through their illegal activism. For example, the *Handbook for Nonviolent Action* (which is copublished by the War Resisters League) warns readers that jails function to completely "alienate and isolate the accused, to destroy one's power and purposefulness."[17] Author/activist Starhawk advises dissenters to be aware that jails are "designed on every level to make you feel bad, wrong, inadequate and powerless." As if borrowing a page from Michel Foucault's *Discipline and Punish*, she notes that the jail "controls us . . . by controlling the space we inhabit, the way our time is structured, and the information we can send and receive."[18]

The near complete level of control that defines correctional confinement stands in stark contrast to the pleasures of resistance that immediately precede incarceration, when the chains that bind the conscience of activists are finally removed. After all, if what passes for society is little more than a labyrinth of social controls, then dissent is not merely the act of finding one's way through the maze; it is to abandon the maze altogether. Yet even when incarceration is anticipated as an end result, jail still proves to be an immediate buzz kill, as one activist told me:

> It's fun to do civil disobedience. It's fun to get . . . arrested. I think that's part of the fun. Maybe it's a little bit of that shadow side coming out. You get to defy your parents or something—that Robin Hood quality, maybe. [But] I don't enjoy jail that much. I probably don't do as well as some people do in jail.

Similarly, another activist described civil disobedience in terms of highs and lows:

> [W]hen you get arrested, [it] is great for the first five minutes. . . . But afterwards, you know, when you're by yourself and you realize how stupid it is and your fellow inmates remind you how stupid it is, you're not feeling too good about what you did. When I was in L.A. County Jail, I actually felt really threatened, and I thought, "What the fuck?" I thought,

"I don't need to be here. I've been to college. I'm supposed to have a good job and be comfortable right now."

So although Starhawk cautions her readers against becoming dispirited, holding back feelings of disillusionment can prove to be somewhat of a difficult task.

Jails, therefore, are places that attempt to exert control not only over inmates' actions but also over their emotions. To accomplish this control, humiliation is essential, and tales of humiliation were all but universal among the various activists interviewed for this book. Sometimes, the humiliation is generalized and simply comes from being treated as "an inmate." It is the humiliation that comes from having to be handcuffed and chained to other inmates, from having to be fingerprinted, then strip-searched, then showered in cold water in front of guards, then finally warehoused. All of these things I experienced firsthand upon my arrest at the RNC, and I have experienced less humiliating variations of this procedure upon my subsequent arrests. One handbook notes that some

Actor Martin Sheen (right) is among the people held in a makeshift detention center, where treatment is rather lax, after performing civil disobedience at the Nevada Nuclear Test Site. (Nevada Desert Experience)

facilities even "spray new inmates for vermin."[19] Fortunately, that was not something I had to endure.

As if the generalized humiliations of booking are not bad enough, the activists I encountered invariably told of specific instances when jail officials behaved in a manner that was less than professional. One protester told of corrections officers playing football over activists' heads. Another told of guards taunting and even threatening activists by reminding them that they were no longer in the public eye. The implication was clear: jail officials have free rein over how they treat protesters. Still another activist told of a guard who turned off all the cold water when inmates were showering, an action he claimed would have scalded him had he not pressed up against the opposite wall. These and similar behaviors by jail employees explains why an antinuclear activist told me that guards "can be meaner than the prisoners themselves."

Perhaps one of the most candid assessments I received regarding the professionalism (or lack thereof) among jail officials came from Flip Benham, the abortion protester we met earlier in the text. Benham told me that "as far as the guards in jail [are concerned], you find that they desperately need help. A lot of the time they're more needy than some of the guys that are in jail." He continued, "A lot of the guards—you have to know—are really messed up. It breaks my heart to see it. Listening to all of that stuff that you [have to] listen to—the lewd jokes. It's just hard. Abu Ghraib—you look at these things and you can understand how they go down that way." Hearing Benham's description, I was reminded of a bitter memory relayed to me by Catherine Morris, who had been active with the United Farm Workers during its heyday. When I met her, she was a longtime member of the Los Angeles Catholic Worker. She told of her experience in Los Angeles County Jail following a protest when she was arrested with a fellow Catholic Worker:

> At County Jail, I found it very insulting. We had a forty-five-day sentence, and [my friend] said, "Let's work, and we'll get more good time and we'll get out faster." And so I was working in the laundry and folding big, blue shirts for days. And every day when we came back from work, we were strip-searched by this set of women [guards]. I was just appalled by them making jokes. We're all standing there naked, and they're making jokes [about our age, about our bodies] about old women's *whatever*. I just felt so bad for [these female guards]. I thought, "God, get out of jail [so you

don't] lose your soul. You know, go work at McDonald's. Go do anything, but don't keep doing what you're doing." That was the most insulting and saddening experience—having to go through those [strip] searches.

The harsh treatment and humiliation of jail notwithstanding, the activists I interviewed were quick to acknowledge that this type of degradation probably "happens all of the time to people of color and to people who don't have the white privilege and the class privilege" that they do. That is, they were acutely aware of the fact that they can (and often do) receive favorable differential treatment from other inmates and even guards. Sometimes they benefit by deliberately making their personal politics known to people within the jail. As a Free Methodist missionary and abortion protester, Flip Benham told me that when he is in jail after performing an abortion "rescue," other inmates constantly seek him out for spiritual guidance once they discover his profession. In that respect, he usually finds that jail can be rewarding, because "the truth gets into their hearts. . . . a lot of them meet the Lord in jail." "Veronica," the antinuclear activist mentioned in previous chapters, noted that when she goes to jail, there is typically a "motherly type" among the inmates who watches out for her. And although she found most of the guards to have bad attitudes, she conceded that some looked at her more favorably because she was doing time for a political action. As a final example, during my travels through the Midwest, I met two activists who served time in a federal penitentiary for an action at the School of the Americas (SOA) in which they trespassed onto the grounds of the military camp at Fort Benning, Georgia, in protest of the training in terrorist and torture tactics that the United States provides. One of the SOA activists I interviewed was of the opinion that he received preferential treatment from other inmates while in prison: "They recognized that I was in this for three months, that I trespassed to try and stop terrorist training from going on. I got treated differently than someone who was in there for snitching on someone to a prosecutor to get a reduced sentence." He concluded by adding, "Moral systems still find a manifestation in the prison system."

Political ideology nevertheless can negatively affect the conditions of confinement. That was especially the case in the period after 9/11 (and thus during the lead-up to the wars in both Afghanistan and Iraq), when dissent was often considered traitorous.[20] One antiwar activist explained, "[if jail officials] ever talked to me and figured out what I was in there for, they [would be] pissed." Animal-rights activist Freeman Wicklund acknowledged that his political lifestyle played a prominent role in how he was treated behind bars both by staff and by other inmates. Sentenced to ninety days for protesting primate drug-addiction experiments taking place at a major university, once in custody he always had to explain to the nurses and the staff the meaning of *vegan* so they could provide an appropriate diet and toiletries for him. When they (surprisingly) accommodated, the special treatment he received caught the attention of other inmates, to his detriment:

> I had to shower with the general population. And one guy *gooses* me—he pinches my ass. . . . I'm like, "Shit! What the fuck?! Get me out of here!" And this guy gooses me, and he's like, "Your shampoo smells so good and so nice," because I got special soap and shampoo that wasn't tested on animals. So I just ended up staying in my cell.

Another time, Wicklund found himself incarcerated in what he called "a very conservative town." This time, he was one of nearly one hundred animal-rights activists arrested while protesting a local charity that used a hunting contest to raise money for its cause. Not only were the activists strip-searched and put into isolation for three days "purely for intimidation"—as he viewed it—but they were also verbally abused by the other inmates, who viewed people committed to animal rights as "a bunch of effeminate animal lovers." When one of the activists was almost sexually assaulted by another inmate in the general population, "the jail guards turned away"; "The jail guards didn't like us. Nobody liked us in that community."

Despite the harshness of conditions and the emotional humiliation that comes with confinement, activists can find the jail experience both personally and politically transformative and therefore somewhat rewarding, since the experience can often serve to sustain one's commitment to social change. If going to jail for justice serves as a badge of honor within activist circles (and it does), then going to jail for a social cause also becomes a wonderful opportunity to discuss concerns with people who otherwise would not be open to hearing activists' concerns. Steve Clemens used his three months in federal prison for protesting the SOA to write articles, opinion pieces, and personal logs. Even when these writings merely circled among his friends and neighbors back home, he found that they made a difference in their receptiveness to his views. "They listen a lot more closely when you're writing from prison then when you're on the streets with signs." Similarly, Benham admitted that some of the most rewarding times in his life have been times spent in jail because, as mentioned earlier, other inmates seek guidance from him and are eager to listen to his sermons. At the same time, activists may be eager to listen to the stories of inmates. Veronica told me that she finds jail "fascinating" because the inmates she has met provided her with a glimpse of social reality rarely seen on the evening news. When I asked her for an example, she told me about the reality of poverty and motherhood that one encounters when in custody. "Some women [I've met] were so poor that the only way that they could feed their children was to . . . do a trick. They were arrested and left in jail for three days without anyone checking on their children at home."

These little glimpses of reality can provide activists with a sense of legitimacy for their crimes of dissent. In that regard, they find that the jail experience often sustains their commitment to activism. In *Prison Literature in America*, H. Bruce Franklin wrote about a common theme within the genre of inmate narratives that finds the prisoner undergoing a radical transformation from being someone who views his captivity as a concern solely of the individual to being someone who views his captivity as symbolic of flaws in the social structure. From this common theme, Franklin identified two categories of prisoner-narrators: the *activist-turned-prisoner* and the *prisoner-turned-activist*. Ultimately, the two categories become indistinguishable as both sets of narratives tackle issues that are inextricably rooted in the social structure.[21] So although not every activist I met necessarily felt energized or radicalized by their jail experiences, jail as a transformative experience nevertheless remained a possibility.

Perhaps no other activist I met exemplified the possibility of a transformative jail experience more than Marv Davidov, who in 1961 took part in a series of crimes known as the "freedom rides." The crimes that constituted the freedom rides involved little more than boarding buses headed south. In the spring of 1961, more than four hundred activists from across the United States were incarcerated for challenging the Jim Crow laws that institutionalized racial segregation. History records the beginning of what became known as the Freedom Rider Movement as occurring on May 4, 1961. On that day, thirteen activists boarded buses in Washington, D.C., headed for New Orleans, intent on challenging existing segregation practices in interstate transportation. The response from segregationists was intense. In Anniston, Alabama, one of the buses was stopped and set afire, and activists who ran from the scene were chased by local residents.

In Birmingham, another bus was stopped, and the activists were pulled from the vehicle and severely beaten. All this violence was documented by members of the press; so the freedom rides instantly became a media event, and the publicity they generated helped to spark a broader campaign. By the end of the year, more than sixty separate freedom rides were undertaken. The civil rights movement was then in full swing.[22]

In his midseventies, freedom rider Marv Davidov has spent his life dedicated to social justice. Born and raised in a working-class Detroit neighborhood, today he teaches nonviolence at St. Thomas University in St. Paul, Minnesota. A white Jewish male, in 1961 he was an undergraduate at the University of Indiana living with a black roommate in the dormitory. One night, his roommate came back to their room bloodied; he had been beaten by the cops merely for being a black man alone on the streets after dark. Davidov stayed up all night talking to his roommate about what had happened. Shortly thereafter, he was presented with an opportunity to go on a freedom ride, and he decided that he needed to seize the opportunity. So on June 9, 1961, Davidov was one of six white students who headed to Nashville for an orientation given by John Lewis and Diane Nash. There, he learned the principles of nonviolence and received words of encouragement for the protest in which he was about to engage. Next, it was on to Jackson, Mississippi, where he and the other freedom riders deliberately violated a Jim Crow law by sitting in a "colored only" section of a Mississippi bus station. The punishment was four months of incarceration in a state prison, of which Davidov ended up serving forty-five days.

Listening to Davidov tell the story of his experience on the freedom ride, I was struck by the importance he afforded his time in a Mississippi cell. Certainly, the events preceding the incarceration—his roommate's victimization, the training in nonviolence, the challenging of an unjust law—featured prominently in the development of his political life, so much so that more than forty years later he is still protesting. (I met Davidov in 2006 at a Minneapolis protest, where he coordinated an act of civil disobedience involving some seventy-eight protesters.) Still, he identified his experience in a Mississippi cell with dozens of other freedom riders as perhaps the most formative event in his political life.

> That first night in the Mississippi penitentiary, people were singing freedom songs. The freedom singers were born there. And I was listening to the songs and crying—not because the bastards were punishing us but

because of the nobility of everybody in that cell block. That night as I lay in my bunk and listening to the people sing freedom songs, I thought to myself that there's no other place I should be but right there in the cell block with those people. I felt human solidarity with people I didn't know and couldn't see, and we all felt the same thing. Anyone who was there would tell you the same thing.

It is this experience, Davidov noted, that sustained his level of activism over the course of decades.

People ask me why I keep doing what I'm doing at my age. After all, there's no money in it, you get a big FBI file, you get death threats on the phone, you get beaten up, and you get jailed. I always say that I'm looking for that feeling again, that feeling of human solidarity that comes from taking a real risk to make social change.

Considering all that has been spoken to me about going to jail for justice, and factoring in my own experiences, three conclusions about activists' experience in confinement become apparent. The first is that jail officials "can be a little bit nastier than the cops," as one activist put it. Even when speaking somewhat favorably about specific guards in specific facilities, the activists I have encountered were uniform in their position that if jails are indeed killing institutions in a moral sense—as Eugene Debs suggested—then jail officials are the ones who orchestrate the metaphorical killing. Ed Hedemann, the war tax resister, offered an opinion as to why jail guards are "nastier" than cops. Although both cops and jail employees have to encounter difficult people in difficult situations, those who work in jails "don't have to deal with the public so much, whereas regular beat cops. . . . deal with the public and they have to have a little more finesse." To that explanation he added, "Plus, you are behind bars, and jail employees figure you're guilty. And that's that."

The second conclusion we can form about the jail experience is that, the horrors of confinement notwithstanding, by and large the jail experience does not necessarily cause activists who are prepared for confinement to become emotionally beaten down or dispirited. Finally, we can conclude that the jail experience ultimately resembles "a game," as one activist put it, and it is a game that is "highly choreographed to a large extent." This game is one that we have seen is primarily psychological, whether through generalized humiliation or through taunting. Perhaps one activist put it best when he said that while in custody, his biggest issue was "the inconsistency of enforcement of the rules." While he was in federal prison, he "never knew which rules were going to be enforced, [and] when."

If incarceration following a protest is little more than a game, then one solution to this problem of learning its rules is simply to avoid abiding by them altogether. After all, if activists have come so far by breaking the rules, why stop there? Certainly, for many activists the only thing more odious than an injustice is graciously accepting punishment for speaking out against it. Of course, a strategy of noncompliance with the rules of a jail can potentially result in worse treatment and harsher punishments. It is therefore important for activists to know what they are doing if they continue their noncooperation postarrest.

Jail Solidarity and Noncooperation

What possible rationale can exist for continued protest behind bars? Should not an arrest mark the end of the protest phase and the beginning of cooperation to secure a better sentence? Once caught up in the system, will a strategy of noncooperation not just lead to additional punishment? Most of the time, the answer to these questions is yes. Cooperation with criminal justice officials is often the most prudent strategy available when one is arrested for dissent. That is especially true for protesters who simply cannot risk additional time away from work, from family, or from other obligations. If getting out of jail quickly is a necessity, then cooperation with officials serves as the most expedient means of achieving this end. Cooperation is also practical for protests involving a small number of arrestees. In that case, noncooperation is not likely to produce a sizeable impact (if any), since one of its goals is to fill the jails, to clog court dockets, and thus to pressure the prosecutor to dismiss all charges. Moreover, when jail solidarity and noncooperation involve only a small number of participants, jail officials can more easily single out noncompliant inmates. A third reason activists may choose to cooperate with jail officials is because they feel they have achieved their mission of using the visible display of dissent to educate the public about a perceived injustice. For all practical purposes, the public phase of dissent has been brought to closure. When that is the case, cooperation is the most prudent postarrest strategy.

Yet once we recognize that the criminal justice system functions to exacerbate existent racial and class biases while punishing protesters who act out against these injustices, we can begin to understand the rationalizations underlying strategies of *jail solidarity* and *noncooperation*. Some activists feel that to cooperate with the State even postarrest is to take part in a legal process that merely sustains the status quo. Worse, they feel that cooperation communicates a message that they concede the State's authority to act against people who dissent. As they see it, it is one thing to accept the reality of arrest and punishment; it is another matter altogether to assist the State in the carrying out of punishment. Jail solidarity and other acts of noncooperation are therefore strategies of dissent in which to varying degrees arrestees refuse to cooperate with, or refuse to take part in, the State's capacity to punish political dissent.

So how does jail solidarity work? The strategy, which begins after arrests are made, marks a concerted effort among people in an affinity group to hold out for equal treatment by the justice system. Specifically, the members of an affinity group may choose to withhold their names and other identifying information. They may also refuse to accept a citation or court appearance or to post bail, and they may collectively refuse to accept a plea until they receive a guarantee from authorities that *all* members of the group receive similar case dispositions. The purpose of the strategy is to prevent the legal system from engaging in a tactic of "divide and conquer" by treating organizers, minorities, the poor, or youth more harshly than others within the group.[23] With an understanding that the criminal justice system acts on varying demographics differently, the purpose of jail solidarity is to protect the less fortunate and differentially positioned within a given affinity group.

An example of how jail solidarity works can be seen in an incident that occurred when the media began to shed light on alleged links between officers within the Los Angeles Police Department's Rampart Division and gang members and drug dealers in the late 1990s. In response to the allegations, about fifty activists staged an illegal protest in front of the Rampart station. Prior to the protest action, all fifty members of the affinity group had agreed to participate in an act of jail solidarity, as one member explained:

> We [agreed that we] would not give our names, and some of us would not eat until [police] agreed that we were all going to get the same consequences, that they weren't going to pick out anybody who had previous arrests or target any one person. We would all have the same consequences. It would be a misdemeanor and it would be time served, because we didn't want to drive back and forth to Los Angeles for court.

The strategy proved successful. The LAPD conceded to all demands made by the affinity group.

As a second example, Veronica told me that, with an excess of fifty arrests to her name, she typically conceals her identity upon arrest. When questioned, she will tell the authorities that her name is "Every Child," "Outraged Citizen," or "Ms. Future Generations." She gives these names until she can guarantee for herself treatment that is equal to that received by other arrestees within her affinity group. On those occasions when she does provide her real name, she is rarely treated equitably or with leniency, as she explained to me:

> They'll put my name into a computer and out will come my [rap] sheet. Like my last arrest, I was protesting this Iraqi War and I had six pages of a computer printout with maybe twelve or fifteen arrests, and that wasn't even half of it. They said, "You're worse then everybody else." So everybody else got a sixty-dollar fine. . . . They ended up giving me one hundred hours of community service and probation for ten months.

As Veronica continued to explain, she decided to provide her real name on that occasion because she wanted to go to court and have a forum to talk about the reasons for her dissent.

Many times people who engage in jail solidarity do so as an act of solidarity with other inmates within the criminal justice system who cannot afford to pay their way out of jail. Activists may refuse to pay fines and may decline any opportunities for bail, opting instead to stay in jail until arraignment and be "in solidarity" with other, less fortunate arrestees. As an example, members of the Los Angeles Catholic Worker invariably refuse all fines and monetary payments. As they have dedicated their lives to serving the poor, it is their belief that it is not enough merely to feel sorry for, or to sympathize with, the disadvantaged, because feelings of sympathy are fleeting and are rather inorganic—that is, they are emotions that are one step removed from the real experience of suffering. Instead, Catholic Workers believe that one must come to empathize with the disadvantaged by situating oneself with those who suffer. When in jail, then, members of the Los Angeles Catholic Worker decline any opportunity for early release resulting from economic advantage.

When performed in sizeable numbers, jail solidarity can yield many advantages for protesters, such as reduced or even dropped charges, because strategies of solidarity can rapidly fill the jails and clog the justice system. Prosecutors are therefore pressured to dispose of these case files quickly in order to concentrate resources on what they probably consider to be cases of real criminals.[24] That is what occurred in Seattle at the protests surrounding the WTO. With approximately six hundred demonstrators arrested in just two days, countless activists refused to disclose their names to authorities, thereby making it difficult for officials to process the arrestees. After several days in custody, many activists deliberated collectively and agreed to provide their names, yet they also collectively agreed to plead not guilty and decline any plea bargain. Finally, they collectively refused to waive the right to a speedy or to a jury trial and instead requested court-appointed attorneys. This placed the prosecutor at risk of violating the mandated timely processing of defendants, so the city ended up dropping charges on 92 percent of the cases to be processed.[25]

Less than a year after Seattle, approximately thirteen hundred people were arrested protesting the meeting of the World Bank in Washington, D.C. There, about 150 activists engaged in jail solidarity. The strategy proved effective since the jail warden risked monetary fines if conditions of overcrowding persisted. When it came time for the demonstrators to appear before a judge, they refused to appear in court, in a strategy designed to keep the jail cells full. The bottom line was that by refusing to cooperate with the criminal justice system, these 150 activists were able to negotiate an agreement in which they would face only civil infractions (i.e., no misdemeanor or felony charges) and would have to pay only a five-dollar fine. Even better, the negotiated agreement applied not only to the select population of 150 activists but also to the activists who had already accepted a separate plea bargain.[26] Once again, jail solidarity worked.

Postsentencing, jail solidarity gives way to a pledge of noncooperation with any institutional rules, such as work-related programs, exercise time, and meal time, or with any sentences of community service or probation. The objective of protesters is to continue to push their message forward while illustrating both the illegitimacy of State authority and its inability to extinguish the passion of conscience through punishment. To use Veronica as an example again, not only does she conceal her identity while in jail, but she also refuses to eat. She does so, she explained, so that jail guards will look at her differently from other prisoners and view her postarrest behavior as a continuation of her political action. Freeman Wicklund, the animal-rights activist mentioned earlier in the chapter, once refused to eat for the first fourteen days of his ninety-day sentence. And he did so even though the jail staff provided him with vegan meals. "I was still trying to move the message," he told me. Apparently, it worked. Not only did he receive numerous letters of support while fasting, but reporters from National Public Radio also visited him while he was in custody to conduct an interview with him for broadcast. Although he estimates that he lost about a pound a day while fasting, for him it was a very powerful postarrest strategy that took his message beyond the confines of the barbed wire.

The decision to engage in noncooperation of any kind is one that requires much deliberation and preparation, for it does not always prove successful and it can even greatly exacerbate the length and conditions of confinement. Sanderson Beck was sentenced to a prison camp, where he was required to spend his first weekend washing government trucks. He refused to do so because he considered himself a political prisoner and therefore felt that he "reserved the right not to work and waste . . . time doing some piddly thing for them." As a result, he was placed in what he called "a punishment cell" in an adjacent maximum-security prison for about a month. As another case in point, David Gardner of the Los Angeles Catholic Worker was arrested at an antiwar protest where he engaged in a mock exorcism of a downtown federal building to rid the government of its evil. Upon sentencing, the judge offered him community service, but he refused this offer, explaining to the court that as a member of the Catholic Worker Movement, he considered it "an honor" to serve the poor and needy of his community. He added that he resented the court's attempt to convert an otherwise honorable service such as helping the community into a form of punishment. Instead of simply being released, he was given additional jail time.

Clearly, when performed strategically, jail solidarity can prove immensely effective, but it requires a sizeable number of people. Precisely how many people are required varies according to the circumstances, but from the preceding case studies it appears that jail solidarity is most effective when the arrests are of a number that threatens to clog the system if individuals are not processed in a timely manner. Activists considering jail solidarity need to be willing to spend time in jail while carrying out the strategy, and they need to consider the possibility of additional time tacked onto a sentence should the strategy of solidarity backfire. All the same, for demonstrators wishing to stand as one with other, less fortunate inmates or for demonstrators wishing to avoid the tedium of a trial, solidarity may be worth the time and risk. Of course, for quite a few activists, going to court is the sine qua non of activism since it affords a much-sought-after opportunity to put the offending policies of State on trial.

Contempt of Court: The State on Trial

It had to be one of the most peculiar criminal trials in American history. Nearly a year after chaos broke out in the streets of Chicago, eight activists were put on trial by the federal government for allegedly conspiring to incite a riot at the 1968 Democratic National Convention (DNC). To be sure, the unrest surrounding the DNC occurred entirely within the limits of the Windy City. Still, the Justice Department argued that it had jurisdiction, since the defendants crossed state lines in order to demonstrate outside the DNC. To even the most casual of legal observers, the case could have had a chilling effect on the right to dissent. If successfully prosecuted, it would have set a dangerous precedent, since protest organizers would risk conspiracy charges if their marches or rallies sparked political disruption. Moreover, the threat of federal charges for crossing state lines would inhibit the formation of future grassroots campaigns that would be national in scope. But these potential effects were of little concern to the federal government. On September 24, 1969, the trial of the Chicago Eight began.

Why would the Justice Department (and one operating under the Republican Nixon administration) want to prosecute activists who were mucking things up for the Democratic Party? The answer was rather simple. The antiwar movement was gaining in popularity; the government therefore had to discredit the movement outright by putting some of its most prominent spokespersons on trial. So they targeted eight of the counterculture's most recognizable figures to make an example of them. It is this point that constitutes the essence of historian Jon Wiener's introduction to the published transcripts of this unique trial.[27] As Wiener notes, the case of the Chicago Eight was less about convicting the eight activists and more about indicting the antiwar movement en masse. But if the Department of Justice wanted to put the antiwar movement on trial, then the Chicago Eight were ready with a strategy of their own: put American history *itself* on trial. What followed, then, was more a competition of wits and wisdom than of testimony or evidence. And if the verdict was on wits alone, then the defense would win hand down. After all, the people on trial were legendary Yippies Abbie Hoffman and Jerry Rubin, as well as the ever militant Black Panther Bobby Seale, ready to attack the State head-on, with Tom Hayden, Dave Dellinger, Lee Weiner, John Froines, and Rennie Davis providing balance with reasoned arguments about the facts of the case, but only when absolutely necessary. With a witness list for the defense that included poet Allen Ginsberg, musicians Phil Ochs and Judy Collins, former attorney general Ramsey Clark, and author Norman Mailer, to name a few, such a trial today would need to have a witness list including Jon Stewart of *The Daily Show* or Steven Colbert of *The Colbert Report*, musicians Rage Against the Machine and the Dixie Chicks, filmmaker Michael Moore, and former ambassador Joseph Wilson.

The trial was little more than justice as public spectacle, or else it was a public spectacle masking as justice. Consider the following: a little more than a month into the proceedings, Judge Julius Hoffman ordered Bobby Seale bound and gagged after he repeatedly asserted his right either to have an attorney of his choosing or to defend himself. Or this: from the witness stand, Allen Ginsberg began leading the courtroom in a meditative chant of "O-o-m-m-m-m" after some legal squabbling. Or even this: at one point in the trial, Judge Hoffman actually admonished defense attorney William Kunstler for attempting to read from the Declaration of Independence to make an argument. Other examples of justice as spectacle: when defendant Dave Dellinger shouted "Oh bullshit" in response to government testimony, the judge asked the court clerk to be sure that the outburst was reflected in the court transcript; one morning, defendants Jerry Rubin and Abbie Hoffman appeared in court wearing black judicial robes, to ridicule the authority of the court; meanwhile, throughout the trial, spectators in the gallery cheered on the Chicago Eight with chants of "Right On, Right On!"

After nearly five months, the case of the Chicago Eight ended with the defendants acquitted on the conspiracy charges. Four of the defendants were convicted of crossing state lines to incite violence, though these convictions—and countless contempt-of-court charges levied against Kunstler and the defense—were later reversed upon appeal. The most spectacular legal farce of recent years was finally over. Still, for all its theatrics and political grandstanding, the case presented activists with a valuable lesson on courtroom strategy. Although issues of guilt and innocence were certainly of concern to the defendants, who, if convicted, would have received lengthy prison sentences, the trial itself afforded them an opportunity to present an antiwar argument to the national media and thus to a national audience. They therefore used the proceedings "to assert an American 'right of resistance'" and, in the words of defendant Tom Hayden, reflecting back on the trial, to provide Americans with insight into "what was going on in America that motivated [the defendants] to take a stand in Chicago."²⁸ They did this by bringing the rationale for protest in front of both judge and jury. In this regard, it was the crimes of government that were really on trial. And though these crimes may have been serious, nothing plays better than a little humor and theater when one is up against the odds.

Like the trial of the Chicago Eight, court proceedings stemming from crimes of dissent provide contemporary activists with a socially acceptable and politically sanctioned venue to air their grievances with State policy or practice. In fact, one of the primary motivations for civil disobedience and other strategies of dissent is that they afford activists an opportunity to challenge the legality or constitutionality of State law and practice.²⁹ Suppose politicians in a particular jurisdiction are hell-bent on passing a law that makes it a crime to burn the American flag. A grassroots campaign to block the legislation fails, and the law passes. Ironically, people opposed to flag-burning legislation can still challenge the State's action in court—but *only* after deliberately (and publicly) burning the flag, for it is when criminal charges for the behavior in question are brought against the activists that they have legal standing in a court of law. Illegal actions, then, sometimes provide people who compose a political minority—and who were stymied in all previous legal means of redress—with an opportunity to gain access to legitimate channels of redress (i.e., the courts) after all previous attempts have failed. Once there, activists are free not only to challenge the offending law or practice but also to challenge the characterization of their own actions as illegal by raising the Nuremberg Principles and the Necessity Defense, common defenses among people who engage in crimes of dissent.

The Nuremberg and Necessity Defense

Without acknowledging guilt, Steve Clemens stipulated to the facts presented by the State during his January 2006 trial in a U.S. federal court. Yes, the previous November he was indeed one of some nineteen thousand concerned citizens who marched to the military base at Fort Benning in Columbus, Georgia, to picket the School of the Americas (SOA). The SOA is a U.S. training camp that over the years has provided instruction in counterinsurgency tactics to more than sixty thousand Latin American military and police officers. Some of these tactics include the use of torture, false imprisonment, and the targeting of civilians as a means to achieve political ends. The *Washington Post* has reported that graduates of the SOA have included some of Latin America's "most notorious human rights abusers."[30] Specifically, the paper linked graduates of the school to the killings of students and a professor by six Peruvian officers, and it linked SOA graduates to the death of an American innkeeper living in Guatemala. When six Jesuit priests, their housekeeper, and her daughter were murdered in El Salvador during its 1989 civil war, a United Nations Truth Commission concluded that the people responsible for their assassinations received training in assassination at the SOA. Each November, activists march to the SOA at Fort Benning, since renamed the Western Hemisphere Institute for Security Cooperation (WHINSEC), on the anniversary of the El Salvador murders. The demand of the protesters: shut down the SOA.

As the procession approached the front gate of Fort Benning that November day in 2006, Steve Clemens and a handful of others took a few additional steps and, perhaps scaling a fence, entered the military installation, whereupon they were arrested. Appearing before a judge during sentencing the following January, Clemens did not deny his actions. Instead, he issued the following statement:

> The U.S. Government as a signatory to the Convention Against Torture and the Universal Declaration of Human Rights has legally committed itself to forgo the activities [that] I believe have been taught and encouraged by the School of the Americas and its successor, WHINSEC. As such, I feel I have a moral and legal obligation under the Nuremberg Principles not to be complicit by remaining silent in the face of the atrocities committed by graduates of this military school which has promoted torture, rape, assassination, and repression.

It was a powerful statement. Not only did it highlight the illegality of his government's actions, it also argued that as a citizen, he would be complicit in those illegalities had he *not* attempted to intervene in the actions of his government. Thus, by raising the issue of the Nuremberg Principles at his trial, Clemens sought to justify his actions with two legal arguments. First, he attempted to argue that because the SOA violated international law, it also violated U.S. law, because Article VI of the U.S. Constitution makes no distinction between domestic laws and international treaties ratified by the government. Second, because his country was in violation of international law, as a citizen of that country he had no choice *but* to prevent the continued illegality of his government.

If the Nuremberg Principles can be said to contain a central theme, it surely is one that has been addressed throughout the pages of this book, namely, that when individual morality is at odds with State authority, it is the conscience of the individual that must reign supreme. Indeed, when the Allied Powers brought twenty of the major Nazi war criminals to trial in 1945 and 1946 in Nuremberg, they sought to discredit the ideology of the Third Reich that "the individual must submit totally to the collectivity."[31] The various articles that today compose the Nuremberg Principles hold an individual accountable for his or her actions when these actions violate international law and even when the person acted under the authority of State. Stated simply, under the Nuremberg Principles the policies of government cannot relieve an individual of his or her responsibility under international law, "provided *a moral choice* was in fact possible to him [or her]."[32] As Clemens saw it, knowing that his government was in violation of international law, he had the moral choice of doing nothing (a crime of omission) or of intervening by trespassing (a crime of commission, at least according to his own government). Morally speaking, what else *could* he do but intervene?

An appeal to the Nuremberg Principles is certainly a sensible defense, though it is one that judges seldom allow during trial. As Clemens explained to me about his SOA trial, "I entered a plea of nolo contendere [no contest] because the judge previously ruled before the trial [that] we were not allowed to use international law or necessity as a defense." Nevertheless, appeals to international law or to necessity are common among protesters at trial. In fact, many activists deliberately plead not guilty and pursue a trial simply so that they can raise issues of international law in a public forum. Another SOA protester I met pled not guilty at his trial, as he explained: "I chose to plead not guilty, and I argued that I was morally obliged to take the action I did. And that was why I felt I was not guilty, and that at no time in the process was I guilty." Similarly, an antiwar organizer active with the War Resisters League told me that whenever facing criminal charges she always pleads not guilty. Doing so allows her to raise the Nuremberg Principles in an open court. For her, part of an antiwar action involves taking it to court and raising issues of international law. Unfortunately, as in Clemens's case, activists find that judges are often reluctant to allow a defense based on international law. That has also been the case for Sanderson Beck, whose antiwar and antinuclear actions are invariably based on his commitment to international law.

One judge at my arraignment said, "What's your defense?" And I said, "Well, it's international law." And he said, "Well, I'm not going to allow any arguments of international law." And I said, "Excuse me, but I think I should have another judge because you don't know anything about this case and already you are saying you aren't going to allow international law. I think that shows you are prejudiced." And he slams down the gavel and says, "Motion denied!"

Related to a defense based on the Nuremberg Principles or international law is the necessity defense. But whereas the former defense is limited to actions that protest the government's foreign policy (e.g., war, torture, nuclear proliferation), the latter can be used either in conjunction with an appeal to international law or separately to challenge domestic policies or practices. Like defendants who rely on a defense of international law, those who argue necessity do not deny their participation in what the State had deemed to be a criminal offense. Rather, they attempt to make the case that a far *greater* offense would have occurred had they not taken action. That is, when weighed against the actions of State (or against the actions of corporations, as is often the case), the behaviors of protesters constitute the lesser harm. Like appeals to the Nuremberg Principles, then, an appeal to necessity is often referred to as an "affirmative defense" since defendants affirm that they engaged in the alleged behavior but offer as a defense the need to act.[33]

Freeman Wicklund typically pleads not guilty and raises the necessity defense at trial. Whether the issue is the trapping of animals for fur or the use of primates to test drug addiction, the argument he presents is that animals are suffering needlessly and would have continued to suffer had he not attempted to intervene by blocking the entrance to a department store that trades in fur or to a university laboratory needlessly testing the effects of narcotics. For him, the advantage of the necessity defense is not its likelihood of being met with success. "[T]hat's the hardest [message] to get through to people outside of the movement—that I'm not going to trial in an attempt to get off. I don't care about that." Instead, Wicklund takes his case to trial so he can use the necessity defense and appeal directly to the jury. "Our goal is to get the message out there, even if only to the jurists in my trial. I typically want a jury trial because then you're dealing with people." He explained that unlike judges, prosecutors, and district attorneys, who see the law as black and white, juries may be more inclined to sympathize with a necessity defense.

For the necessity defense to be successful, five elements must be proven: (1) there is danger or harm, (2) the danger is imminent, (3) other attempts to block the danger have failed, (4) the behavior taken by the defendant was less harmful than the imminent danger, (5) a reasonable person would view the defendant's actions are capable of removing the danger.[34] Before a judge will even allow such a defense, the court must first be swayed that the defense stands a reasonable chance of proving all five elements. With such a high threshold, judges are reluctant to allow this line of defense. At the same time, the necessity defense raises the specter of jury nullification. Judges may therefore be quick to exclude the necessity defense on the grounds that it encourages juries to ignore breaches of the law. Again, Steve Clemens's experiences in his dozen or so criminal cases provide insight:

> For the most part judges will not allow juries to even be aware of jury nullification, which is an absolutely crucial question when it comes to civil resistance and civil disobedience because juries need to have the understanding that they have the ability to rule with their hearts and not just with the legal technicalities prescribed to them.

Clemens told me that once, when he was on trial for an action at Pantex, a factory in Texas that assembles nuclear weapons, the judge

> basically said to the jury [to] ignore everything the defendants said. "It's not relevant because the question is 'Did they trespass?' 'Did they knowingly trespass?' If so, they violated the law, and you must find them guilty." So basically, any explanation we gave about nuclear weapons, nuclear power, U.S. foreign policy, or our religious convictions [was dismissed].

To punctuate the point, Clemens provided me with a copy of the judge's instructions to the jury in a similar case. In that instance, Clemens was on trial (along with seventy-eight codefendants) for criminal trespass at the Minnesota headquarters of Alliant Techsystems, which manufactures antipersonnel landmines for the U.S. military. Because landmines are considered weapons that cause indiscriminate injury or death, the International Committee of the Red Cross notes that their use is "restricted by the general principles of international humanitarian law and more specifically by the Convention on Certain Conventional Weapons."[35] Nevertheless, landmines continue to be manufactured in the United States for use or sale by the U.S. government, an action that the defendants argued necessitated their trespass. Unfortunately, the judge did not see it that way, as can be seen in the instructions provided to the jury:

> If the evidence proves that defendants intentionally violated the law, they are guilty even though it appears the violation was undertaken to advance or accomplish an otherwise lawful or praiseworthy end. In other words, the ends do not justify the means if the means are proven to be criminal.

This judicial raising of the means/ends equation is rather curious since the central principle of nonviolent resistance is that the means must always be strictly nonviolent, even when working to prevent violent ends. This is because, as Gandhi famously argued, the only thing we have control over is means. Since we can never guarantee the ends, we need to take steps to ensure that our actions always minimize harm. Nonviolence meets this requirement. In Clemens's landmine case, the judge was not concerned with violence and nonviolence, only with criminal and noncriminal behavior irrespective of the potential violence that could ensue from inaction. That is, the means (i.e., trespassing) were nonviolent, whereas the ends (i.e., the manufacture and sale of landmines) were violent. Yet the judicial instructions explicitly directed the jury away from considering this moral calculation.

> It is not necessary [for you to] decide whether the manufacture of use of [*sic*] landmines is actually lawful or unlawful, or good or bad. . . . The only question for you, to repeat, is whether the prosecution proved beyond a reasonable doubt that these defendants on this occasion were on the property and at the time alleged and refused to leave without claim of right.

Ironically, the defendants were acquitted of the trespassing charges not in spite of the judge's strict instructions but because of them. After carefully considering whether the defendants had a "claim of right" to be on the property of Alliant Techsystems, the jury found that the protesters lacked the requisite criminal intent. Their reasoning was that Minnesota's trespass statute provided exemption for persons who in good faith believed that another law, rule, or statute granted them permission to be on another's property. As it turned out, the jury considered the appeal to international law after all.

Sanderson Beck, in March 1988, just acquitted by the jury in Concord, California, for blocking access to a train transporting weapons to Central America. Although the judge did not allow the use of the Nuremberg Defense, Sanderson was able to recite the Principles during his closing arguments over the prosecutor's objections.

Pro Se, Pleas, and Penalties

Even when the issues before the court are serious, and even when the potential punishment is severe, criminal proceedings against protesters can nevertheless have moments of levity and absurdity. In that regard, dissent on trial is not wholly unlike the trial of the Chicago Eight, where the theater of the absurd sometimes takes center stage. Like Bobby Seale, whose attempt to represent himself sparked a series of bizarre courtroom displays, activists who choose to represent themselves in court (pro se) can provide some of the more absurd aspects of dissent on trial. In those cases, one begins to see the legal arena as a terrain of the privileged, where experts speak legal discourse to construct subjective truths of guilt and innocence; meanwhile, people who defend themselves by speaking plainly and simply without the legal cover of statutes and jargon are deemed to be fools. There is, then, some relevance to the postmodern critique of crime that views the legal process as an exercise in the construction of a subjective truth defined by the few.[36]

The rationale for self-representation is simple. Some activists do not wish to downplay their actions by allowing an attorney to speak for them, to try to find a loophole, or to coerce them to accept a plea bargain. Activists who proceed pro se have the opportunity to speak for themselves, and they can confront the politics of conscience head-on. And though defendants may be serious about the issue at hand, there nevertheless may be some moments of awkwardness in such cases when activists expose the pedantry of the legal bureaucracy. Freeman Wicklund told of a time when he represented himself in court:

> I got a book on how to represent yourself in court for a criminal trial. I thought, "Screw it!" I subpoenaed all of these people. I had a blast with it [*laughs*]. The judge would often be like, "What are you doing?" And I'd say, "I'm submitting evidence." And he'd say, "You can't do that. You need a sticker." [Meanwhile,] I'm showing these big pictures of monkeys with screws drilled into their heads. I laugh about it now, but at the time I was very serious and was respectful and was trying to do it appropriately. But at the same time, I was just using [the court] as a platform for my cause. I went into it not being too concerned about what happened. I actually had an enjoyable time.

Steve Clemens, too, usually proceeds pro se when appearing in court. He said that with attorneys speaking for defendants, "you end up with a kind of judicial game where it's kind of a wink and a nod" among the legal experts in the courtroom. That is, "you can't say this, but obviously it means this, and all of that. So for the most part when possible we [i.e., members of the affinity group] try to defend ourselves." Along with speaking for oneself, the benefit of this strategy is that it allows activists possibly to circumvent some of the cumbersome rules of evidence. "Some judges will give you a little more leeway in what you say because you're not a trained legal counsel and maybe you don't know that you shouldn't be saying this."

Thus, although there is always a fear that judges will view with derision and as a waste of time activists who decide to plead not guilty and proceed pro se, it is sometimes the case that judges evidence respect for activist-defendants who wish to present a defense for their actions. In fact, judges may even sympathize with activists' cause or at least welcome the novelty of the case. One antiwar activist told of a New York City judge who flashed a peace sign to the defendants as she approached the bench. During the trial, one member of the group realized that he actually knew the judge and once had dinner with her. He chose not to call attention to this fact because this "lefty judge" might have had to remove herself from the trial. Another lefty activist was once assigned a judge who confessed in court to having helped raise the Pentagon with Abbie Hoffman and the Yippies during the 1960s. Still another activist—Jeff Dietrich from the Los Angeles Catholic Worker—told of a judge in Southern California who viewed a case involving nonviolent civil resistance as a welcome break from his usual docket:

> In the morning, the judge did traffic court, petty stuff. In the afternoon, he did . . . our trial. I think he was kind of having fun, because at the end of the day he would ask me [and my codefendant] to come into his chambers, and he'd ask, "How do you think it's going today?" And we'd be sitting there with the judge and looking at all of these pictures of him standing there with Ronald Reagan and other prominent Republicans. But he was really just devoted to the whole process, and I think he really enjoyed the whole kind of sense that somebody was doing something a little more significant than traffic tickets. But I'm sure it drove the prosecutor crazy.

To show gratitude, on the last day of the trial, Dietrich brought homemade bread he had baked at the Skid Row soup kitchen as a gift for both the judge and the prosecutor. Still, he said, "the prosecutor was not pleased."

Why do defendants plead not guilty when they deliberately and publicly violated the law and often in the presence of a sizeable audience composed of reporters and news cameras? There are, of course, several ways to answer this question, one of which rests on purely idealistic reasons. In a handbook titled *Questions and Answers about Civil Disobedience and the Legal Process,* published by the National Lawyers Guild (NLG), activists are asked to consider the following question: "do you feel guilty and ashamed of what you did, or are you proud of your action?"[37] The implicit message in this question is that guilt is little more than a state of mind. At the same time, by entering a plea of not guilty, defendants can proceed to trial and use the courtroom as a platform to raise political issues. A second reason proffered by the NLG is purely

legalistic: irrespective of what activists might have done, the law requires a presumption of innocence, so why assist the State in securing
one's own conviction? A final reason for refusing to plead guilty is strategic. Prosecutors almost invariably overcharge defendants with violations so they can later use these allegations as leverage to secure a plea
bargain. (Indeed, I was initially charged with a felony upon my arrest
at the 2004 RNC. At arraignment, the prosecutor offered to reduce the
charges to a misdemeanor if I accepted a guilty plea. When I rejected
the plea, the prosecutor subsequently agreed to dismiss all charges upon
proof of a day's worth of community service. Naturally, I chose to work
in the soup kitchen run by the local Catholic Worker).

To be sure, protesters are most often charged with what are called *infractions*.[38] An infraction (or *violation*) is the equivalent of a traffic citation, carries with it no possibility of jail time, and is therefore not considered to be a "crime" in a meaningful sense. Above infractions on the scale
of criminal severity are *misdemeanors,* crimes punishable by up to a year
in jail, such as trespassing or resisting an officer. At the top of the scale
are *felonies,* which are punishable by over a year in jail. Although these
greater charges rarely stick, they are often used by prosecutors as leverage during possible plea negotiations. When I asked Benjamin Shepard
about his strategy in entering a plea, he told me that he holds out until the charges are no longer "criminal" in nature because he is a social
worker by profession and cannot have a criminal record. "The longest I've
stayed in jail I think was forty hours. I've never had anything stick. I've always had charges reduced, reduced, reduced. . . . Once it's a violation and
not a crime, I plead guilty and pay ninety-five dollars and get the hell out
of there and get Chinese food."

Sitting in a makeshift holding cell in the parking structure that services
Alliant Techsystems after one of my own arrests, I had an opportunity to
chat with a prominent grassroots organizer and activist who has made it
her career to engage in antiwar civil disobedience since the attacks of 9/11.
She told me that when given the option, she always accepts an infraction as a disposition and simply pays the required fine. The reasons are
obvious. For one, the organization she cofounded has a well-established
reputation for performing numerous acts of nonviolent direct action in
opposition to war, torture, and the curtailment of civil liberties. To be
bogged down in court cases for each of her arrests would cripple the organization and bring her public appearances to a standstill. For another,
the cost of the fine pales in comparison to the cost of her organization's

taking out an advertisement in a national publication. But with the publicity that her arrests receive, she considers the cost of a fine a promotional bargain. Finally, she feels that the State does not really profit from her having to pay a fine, so paying one allows her to continue on with her various campaigns.

Finally, there are activists who refuse to bargain with the State at all, even if they can get off with a small fine or probation. Like Henry David Thoreau, who expressed disgust at having been released from jail upon the payment of a fine on his behalf, many activists likewise refuse to make any payment. Veronica takes this position. "I don't pay a fine. I'd rather stay in jail. I don't pay a fine because I identify with the poor people who can't pay a fine. [Further,] I would never ask anybody to pay my fine for me. I would just do the jail time. Everybody has a different style of activism. My style is, I like to do the action and I like to go to jail immediately" without paying a fine and without posting bail. This approach tends to be the one taken by some Catholic Workers, too, who purposefully refuse bail and will not accept being released on recognizance, since these options are seldom available to the poor and the homeless. Although people who refuse to pay infraction fines or accept bail are guaranteed to spend a couple nights in jail, the benefit is that it renders the need for a trial moot, since the punishment already outweighs the "crime" for which they have been charged. When they appear before a judge, they are typically released.

Along with overcharging defendants, prosecutors often use a punishment of probation in lieu of jail time as a form of leverage with activists. The prospect of avoiding jail time can seem appealing, but probation has a catch: for all practical purposes, it may require activists to avoid attending any marches, rallies, or demonstrations if there is even a small possibility that an arrest could ensue. Wicklund refuses to accept probation: "[it] stifles free speech because to violate the terms of probation means greater consequences, and just going to a protest puts me at risk of getting arrested." Arguing that probation has a chilling effect, he said, "I'd rather just serve my time and be done with it." That option, however, is not always available, as he explained:

I was [once] sentenced to ninety days. . . . Actually, I wasn't sentenced per se. The judge said, "We're going to give you probation." And I said, "I won't do probation. I don't want to do probation. I'd rather just serve time." At the time, she was like, "Okay, you have a right to do that." And

I was like, "Okay, let's do that." And she was like, "Well, no. Let's let you think about that for two weeks, then come back." When I came back, I was like, "Okay, bring it on!" So they threw me in jail. . . . And then the judge called me back into her chambers [after serving two weeks]. . . . She said, ". . . I've reviewed the laws, and you do not have the option to go to jail if you want to." So she booted me! [*Laughs*] So I was booted with probation. It was kind of bizarre, the whole thing.

Another activist told of a similar scenario. Given a sixty-day jail sentence *plus* probation, he refused the probation and instead had his jail time doubled—that is, until the case was sent back to the trial judge. This time, the strategy worked. After serving only thirty days, he was released *without* probation. He was trying to work the system. Apparently, he was successful.

Conclusion: Disorder in the Court

If the entire justice system appears to be little more than a game, it is probably because it *is* little more than a game. Worse, it is one in which the rich and white are at a strategic advantage, while the indigent and nonwhite play with a handicap, if they get to play at all. Most of the time, they are relegated to the sidelines, where they watch as others play the game on their behalf. Consider the following observation related to me by a white, middle-class female who is also a seasoned activist:

[T]he lawyers and prosecutors and also the public defender, they're all in cahoots. They all work together every single day. They all have lunch together every single day. The person who got arrested can be on the sidelines with no one talking to them, no one asking what they want. Those three—the judge, prosecutor, public defender—they're going to decide what's going to happen to you without even asking you.

She added that this working relationship is particularly problematic for the homeless women she has encountered while in jail. Another activist concurred, noting that "the whole system is crazy. . . . And it's obviously skewed against poor people and people of color."

So when asked to provide an overall assessment of how "justice" works, the activists I interviewed could not help but plead guilty to possession of the privilege they embody. Given that the courts and the jails are filled with defendants who are economically poor and are among those considered to be racial or ethnic minorities, the demographically privileged protesters I have met do admit to feeling guilty about the pleasure they derive from working the system, especially since the cases of protesters serve to further clog the system. As Ellen Barfield sharply observes in the epigraph to this chapter, the justice system is already "constipated," so much so that justice "has nothing to do with guilt or innocence," as another activist put it. Instead, "it's all about expediency for the courts." In that regard, the actions of a bunch of privileged activist do-gooders will only make it worse. Because of this situation, at least one woman acknowledged feeling "a little guilty" blocking up the system: "because of this little minor thing I did and making them try me for it." But she added that "perhaps that extra little bit of pressure will help some elected official see that we have to work on this, that the system is a problem."

It is one of the central ironies of contemporary activism that people who work on behalf of the wretched of the earth—as Franz Fanon put it—often feel uneasy about the fact that they cannot fully shed their privilege and be as one with the disadvantaged, even when they refuse bail and probation. As one activist put it, "I'm white and privileged, so I feel [the system] has been a cakewalk for me, generally. I see [the system] not from the side of somebody facing the brunt of it but as somebody who faces a slap on the wrist." His recommendation: "I think everybody should get arrested and go through a trial just to see how messed up our court system is. It's atrocious, not so much from my experiences of it as much as having to sit through so many other court cases waiting for mine to get called and watching what transpires. . . . It's so awful."

6

The Impact of Dissent

No one who wields greater power in the political mainstream is likely to voluntarily acknowledge our impact as activists on the important issues of our time. In many ways, that just leaves us the victories to claim.

—Kate Donnelly, *Handbook for Nonviolent Action* (1995)

The letter began as follows:

Dear Friends: Today I resigned from Honeywell Marine Systems where I have worked as a Marketing Writer since 1981. To mark the good day, I am enclosing a contribution to your organization. It's a small contribution, I'm afraid. When I find a new job, I will do better.

Sent to the activist group the Honeywell Project in the summer of 1984, the letter represents a small success in a decades-long campaign to end war profiteering, or the practice wherein businesses capitalize on international conflict by selling the tools and services that make war easier to wage. In the letter, the employee describes his work at Honeywell as having been that of a "weapons promoter." More specifically, his job was to create advertisements, video tapes, brochures, and other materials that hype Honeywell's line of munitions to the Pentagon and to others in the international arms market. Always careful to present a benign corporate image, he tells of having made frequent use of buzz words like "effective," "high performance," and "state of the art" while avoiding language describing how these torpedoes, submarines, and mines are actually used for destructive ends. And he was good at his job. Midway into his letter he confesses, "I can make the Mk 50 torpedo as bland as a microwave oven."

At the time the letter was drafted, its author was stationed some sixteen hundred miles west of Honeywell corporate headquarters in Minnesota. Still, it was known throughout the company that picket lines, human blockades, and other acts of dissent were commonplace outside its Minneapolis office, all courtesy of the activist group the Honeywell Project. Founded in 1968 by Twin City activists, the Honeywell Project was one of the most unique and high-profile antiwar campaigns to emerge from the anti–Vietnam War era. Not only did its membership call for an end to the war outright; it also had the goal of dismantling war profiteering and the war-based economy. With regard to war profiteering, Honeywell was considered particularly egregious. During Vietnam, it manufactured, marketed, and profited from the sale of such weapons as antipersonnel landmines and cluster bombs, which are notoriously indiscriminate in their killing capabilities. In protest, the Honeywell Project organized rallies and demonstrations and picketed outside Honeywell headquarters. Its membership also participated in acts of civil disobedience by blocking access to the building or by trespassing onto Honeywell property. These acts continued for years. Then, in 1971, the Honeywell Project received a boost in national publicity when Chicago Eight defendant Jerry Rubin and antiwar poet Robert Bly joined protesters in their efforts outside Honeywell headquarters.

In time, of course, the Vietnam War ended. Yet unlike many other campaigns that dissipated when headlines of troop casualties disappeared, the Honeywell Project had enormous staying power. Its membership understood the long-term inevitability of war so long as it remains a profitable enterprise. Therefore, people in the campaign were determined not to give up their efforts until Honeywell (which was already a profitable manufacturer of innocuous household products) opted out of the munitions business. To that end, activists kept the heat on the company by speaking out at shareholder meetings, by staging vigils outside Honeywell plants and sales offices worldwide, and by continuing to protest in front of Honeywell's Minneapolis headquarters.

The high visibility of dissent staged by the Honeywell Project was ultimately what pushed the former weapons promoter to resign. It seems that the protests, shareholder actions, and arrests were making a difference in damaging the company's reputation. Indeed, in an attempt to offset the negative publicity, Honeywell began to take out full-page advertisements in Twin City newspapers. But when one advertisement boasting of the company's work with nuclear weaponry crossed the desk of the weapons promoter, he finally decided it was time to quit. "Odd as it may seem," he wrote, employees at the Marine Systems division had not known about the company's involvement in nuclear weapons. "It came as some shock, even among us torpedo builders." And with that admission, the letter concluded as follows:

> By your protests of Honeywell, and [by] Honeywell's nervous response, you make the company acknowledge that their business may be considered morally repugnant, work that should best be done hidden. And in the hiding, they daily cause their employees to consider the type of work they are doing. I have quit for this reason; others have quit for the same; more will, for I have never talked closely with anyone at Honeywell who hasn't volunteered that he or she found the work sordid, sustained only by some mesh of rationalization—this from people, who, like me, knew what Honeywell did before they hired on. Your voice has a profound effect. I think it's important that you know that, and important that you continue to protest.

Five years later and over two decades after the Honeywell Project campaign began, Honeywell management finally announced that it had decided to sell off its weapons division. Marv Davidov was a founder of the Honeywell Project and one of its most recognizable leaders. A garrulous personality with a gritty sense of humor, he knew firsthand that sustained acts of protest can yield amazing successes. As discussed in the previous chapter, in 1961 Davidov joined the historic Freedom Rider Movement and traveled to the Deep South to challenge racial segregation. Today, the freedom rides are credited as having had a tremendous impact on the successful campaign for civil rights. So when asked whether the actions of the Honeywell Project *really* factored into Honeywell's decision to sell its weapons division, Davidov's opinion ought to carry some weight. But rather than proffer a lengthy defense outlining the effectiveness of civil disobedience, nonviolence, and grassroots organizing, Davidov simply scoffs, all the while displaying his brand of in-your-face humor:

> The day Honeywell made its announcement that it was selling its weapons division, the Honeywell Project held a news conference, and twelve news sources came to interview me. Every one of them said, "Well, this was a business decision. Your people didn't have much to do with it." And I responded by saying to them, "Tell me. Are you in the habit of interviewing marginal radicals? Why the fuck are ya'll here today if we had nothing to do with it?!"

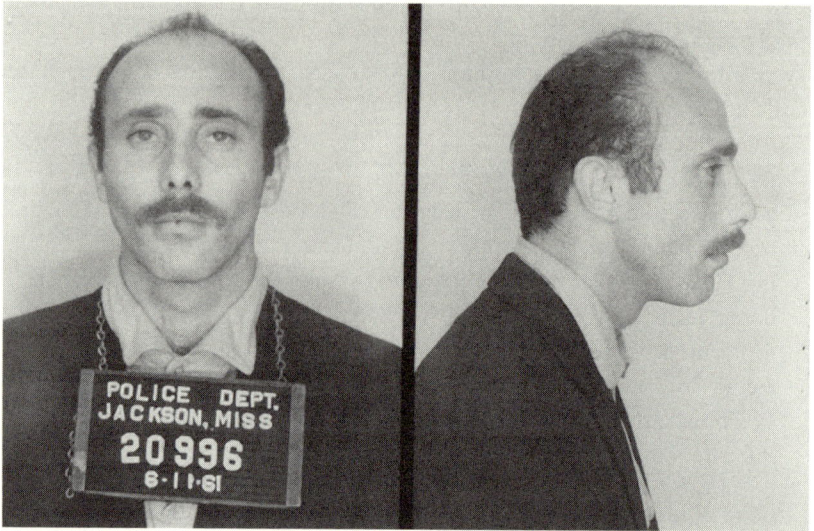

Marv Davidov upon his arrest in Jackson, Mississippi, for violating Jim Crow laws against segregation as part of the Freedom Rider Movement. He later founded the Honeywell Project to oppose war profiteering. (Courtesy of Mississippi Department of Archives and History)

The Meaning of Success

There are few tasks more difficult for social movement scholars than assessing whether a given grassroots campaign had any impact in hastening social change. Indeed, a sampling of just a few scholarly texts examining mass movements seems to bear out this difficulty. For example, an anthology with the title *How Social Movements Matter* begins with a rather candid admission that the ability of researchers to ascertain the outcomes and successes of protest efforts remains among the "neglected areas of inquiry."[1] Too often, the book's editors argue, researchers focus attention on the etiology of social movements while overlooking their long-term impact on policy and social practice. Elsewhere, the editors of a volume titled *Methods of Social Movement Research* introduce the readings with an acknowledgment that social movement research falls victim to what has been called "theory bashing," the dismissal of any assertion of a causal link between a protest and a policy reaction.[2] And in the book *The Strategy of Social Protest,* author William Gamson begins a chapter titled "The Meaning of Success" with the confession that with regard to protest, "success is an elusive idea."[3]

Handbooks written for an activist audience also concede that attempts to ascertain the success of a strategy do not yield clear-cut, straightforward, or even objective answers. One such book cautions its readers that "influences, pressures and forces" surrounding particular campaigns can never be replicated. Therefore, absent uniformity in conditions, determinations of what— if any—particular strategies prove successful become difficult. Another handbook tells its readers to accept the fact that "no one who wields greater power in the political mainstream is likely to voluntarily acknowledge our impact as activists on the important issues of our time."[4]

To be sure, the problems inherent in the assessment of social movement effectiveness are varied. For one, it is clear that activism never exists in a historical vacuum. Any statement of a protest's impact must therefore always account for the historical context in which dissent occurs. Given that it is impossible to isolate the contributions of history or to subject the conditions underlying social movements to replication, one simply can never truly come to know the relative contribution of a grassroots campaign to policy or social practice. Another problem is that protest strategies are often carried out concurrently with the mainstream strategies of politics as usual such as lobbying, letter writing, and petitioning. Should a change in social policy or practice result, practitioners of both conventional and less-conventional politicking can claim success without any proof to the contrary. Finally, there is the problem of the institutional bias against unconventional means of realizing social justice. Unlike legal battles, in which jurisprudential decisions are rendered, explicated, and justified, and unlike the ballot box, which yields numerical measures of success, there simply exists no objective measure readily available to people who participate in crimes of dissent with which to ascertain success. And few politicians are brave enough to acknowledge having been influenced by what Marv Davidov referred to as "marginal radicals."

In addition to the textbooks and how-to guides, the activists I interviewed too are often hesitant to declare a measurable success. Although they often do so publicly, among their inner circles they are more cautious in their assessments, for it is rare that a success is not quickly offset by some related setback. Consider one activist's assessment of an action for nuclear disarmament that called for activists to block a train from delivering nuclear weapons to a military base:

[I]n one way, you could say I was effective when we blocked the nuclear train because another group [followed our lead and] blocked the train the next year. After those two actions, the government never shipped nuclear weapons through Georgia again. That's a success on a microscale. On the macroscale, they are still getting those warheads to [the military] base by trucks or by air or by some other way. But at least they're not bringing them by train through communities.

Here, the activist vacillates between the appropriate units of analysis in measuring success: should one consider the success of the immediate action, or should one assess the action in light of the long-term campaign? "Obviously, civil disobedience is not completely successful because we've [still] got all of these weapons," said another activist, who similarly placed his body in front of a train. "But," he continued, "it's a movement, and it took the suffragettes sixty-two years, okay?"

As another example of the murkiness of measuring impact or determining success, consider the victory of the Honeywell Project. Although decades of protests against Honeywell pressured the weapons manufacturer to opt out of the munitions industry, in truth Honeywell faced difficulty finding a buyer for its conventional-weapons division so it simply spun it off as a separate legal entity. Known today as Alliant Techsystems, the company generates over a billion dollars of business manufacturing—you guessed it—landmines and cluster bombs, the very forms of weaponry targeted during the decades-long campaign against Honeywell. So nearly twenty years after it proclaimed success, the Honeywell Project is now called AlliantACTION, and its membership—including Marv Davidov—can once again be found protesting outside the Minneapolis headquarters of Alliant.

With myriad affinity groups, multiple factions, and overlapping philosophies, the fact is that the structure of contemporary protest movements does not readily allow for the type of analysis that is typical when assessing other types of organizations. In a book on the methodology of evaluation, Carol Weiss outlines the conditions under which formal process and outcome evaluations are ideal. More to the point, she also itemizes the circumstances under which such evaluation can prove problematic. Topping the list is a description that almost certainly applies to protest groups, namely, whenever the actors being studied must by necessity "improvise activities from day to day" and choose their course of action sometimes

ON THE TENTH ANNIVERSARY OF NONVIOLENT CIVIL RESISTANCE AT ATK JOIN ALLIANTACTION IN

CELEBRATING THE BIRTH OF

CONNECTIONS SYMBOLIZED BY THE SPOKES OF

MAHATMA MOHANDAS GANDHI

THE SPINNING WHEEL AND THE WEB WE WILL WEAVE

WHILE DEMONSTRATING

THE POWER OF NONVIOLENCE IN

STOPPING THE MERCHANT$ OF DEATH

AT THE LARGEST MINNESOTA-BASED MILITARY CONTRACTOR

ALLIANT TECHSYSTEMS (ATK)

DU MUNITIONS · LANDMINES · CLUSTER BOMBS · TRIDENT II

MONDAY OCTOBER 2ND – 7 AM
ATK HQ · 5050 LINCOLN DRIVE, EDINA

SUPPORT OR PARTICIPATE IN THE
GANDHIAN SPIRIT OF NONVIOLENT DIRECT ACTION
DIRECTIONS TO ATK: HOPKINS 5TH STREET EXIT FROM HIGHWAY 169, TURN EAST.

LEARN MORE OR CONTACT US ONLINE
ALLIANTACTION.ORG

PRE-ACTION CONCERT AND RALLY
SUNDAY EVENING, OCTOBER 1ST - 7 PM
COLLEGE OF ST. CATHERINE, O'SHAUGHNESSY AUDITORIUM

ACTION INFO: 612 701 5227. RALLY INFO: 612 874 7715.

WAR RESISTERS LEAGUE
A COALITION ACTION

Continuing the movement against war profiteering and the production of illegal munitions, members of AlliantACTION hold protests outside Alliant Techsystems, manufacturer of landmines and cluster bombs.

with "little thought and less theory."[5] This characterization does not suggest that protest groups are all action and no theory or that they lack any long-term vision for change. Instead, it merely highlights the extent to which actors and organizations that rely on civil disobedience and direct action must be flexible enough to act quickly and with little organizational restraint in order to meet the demands of a changing political environment. Nor should that characterization be interpreted to suggest that the evaluation of protests cannot be accomplished or that the people who participate in such street-level actions do not perform self-assessments. Even when the challenges are difficult, Weiss tells readers, evaluation can always "produce something of value, some glimmering of insight that will light a candle for the future."[6] The remainder of this chapter focuses on the ways in which protesters themselves choose to evaluate the impact of their dissent, beginning with a discussion of whether the protest is able to generate mass publicity about an existing injustice, followed by a discussion of whether the protest generates new interest and fosters solidarity, and concluding with a discussion of whether protest movements effect real change as measured by a shift in public policy or social practice.

(Media) Publicity

Among the defining features of civil disobedience, direct action, and other forms of nonviolent resistance is the fact that these legal transgressions are deliberately public. Not only does the visibility of dissent call the public's attention to the existence of what is perceived to be a prevailing injustice; it also adds legitimacy to the activist's actions by distinguishing them from common crime, in which violations of law are staged to be hidden and do not serve the broader social interest. The amount of publicity generated from the staging of dissent is therefore a crucial measure of success for many of the activists I interviewed for this book. One activist in particular described civil disobedience and direct action as "a great moment of public education." Another explained, "I don't want to do a civil disobedience in my backyard and nobody pays attention. If nobody knows about it, then what's the point? . . . I think it's very important that the government know that I'm doing this and why I'm doing this. . . . I want to be in their face."

One of the most expedient ways to generate publicity for an issue or grassroots campaign is to capture the attention of the news media. In our news-driven society in which conflict is a reigning theme and spectacle a marketable commodity, the demands of media often work to the advantage of protesters, whose crimes of dissent provide reporters with visual drama and arresting imagery (pun intended). "Revolution," says the Situationist scholar Guy Debord, "is not 'showing' life to people, but bringing them to life" through the creation of spectacle and drama.[7] Activists know that stories of individuals publicly violating laws and being carried away in handcuffs constitute acts of spectacle and that they are all but certain to make the evening news. To that end, protesters are incredibly sensitive to the visual biases of media formats when planning an action. As an example of the effective use of media to garner publicity for a political position, consider the actions of the New York chapter of the antiwar group the Raging Grannies, which emerged in the wake of the war against Iraq. Its membership consists of women who dress in old-fashioned, stereotypical "grannie" attire and who converge on military recruiting stations determined to enlist for war in an effort to save America's youth and, in the process, the people of Iraq. Among the group's main goals, as one member explained, is to use the visual bias of media to speak out against war.

The New York Grannies actually set out to get arrested, because arrests make the news. They arrange for arrests. And it's [all] about media. The irony of [police] arresting Grannies is really funny when they're trying to say, "Stop recruiting our young people!" . . . the thing about the Raging Grannies is that we like to get our message out through the media, because a few people seeing us as they pass by is great, but there's a certain power in the media. And civil disobedience will get news coverage when a regular demonstration has not. And it shows a sense of seriousness, too, that you're willing to go to jail for justice. That's what civil disobedience is all about.

Many of the affinity groups that gathered in Seattle to protest the WTO were also sensitive to the importance of media in gaining publicity for their concerns over international trade policy. Among these groups was the Black Bloc anarchists, whose destruction of a Starbucks or Niketown storefront helped garner the media's attention. Although many of the labor unions and other groups assembled in Seattle were not sympathetic to the tactic of vandalism, today many activists nevertheless acknowledge that this tactic—along with the human blockades that prevented WTO delegates from gaining access to the trade talks—proved pivotal in gaining public awareness of activists' causes. One activist explained:

Part of why Seattle was successful in some ways—it was brilliant in lots of ways and historical [how] things came together—but there was a little P.T. Barnum moment there; there was something to write about. You know, I think if the media decided to write about the issues [and asked] substantive questions about corporations, trade, access to AIDS drugs, democracy, and money in politics without [people] doing direct action, that'd be great! But they don't. The only reason they write about it, the [reason] we know about the IMF or the World Bank, is because of people doing civil disobedience, including breaking some windows in Seattle. And when there isn't somebody doing something crazy, they just don't write about it. You haven't heard about it recently, you know?

In making his point, this activist liked to contrast media coverage of the protests against the WTO with the coverage of the protests coinciding with the meeting of the World Economic Forum, which convened just a few years later in New York City and which received scant media coverage despite protest crowds numbering in the tens of thousands: "Ted Koppel [formerly of the ABC News program *Nightline*] was going to do a big thing on the World Economic Forum, a big show. And we were all good boys and girls and did our march and got our permits and put our outfits on and didn't break shit, and they didn't do a twenty-minute thing on anybody!"

Aside from merely drawing attention to a perceived injustice, media attention can also yield tangible and perhaps even objective measures of success through its ability to shame people holding positions of power. For example, several years ago a coalition of advocates for affordable housing staged a sit-in at the office of a realtor that was in the process of evicting an elderly woman. Because of the media publicity the action received, it resulted in what can only be described as a strategic success, as explained by James Tracy, who was one of the sit-in participants:

> [W]e got so much press over it, and it was actually a really good thing in changing the tone [of the] debate around evictions because up until that point, the press had portrayed all evictions as simply an unfortunate thing. . . . it wasn't portrayed as a massive class struggle where the consolidation of property by large management corporations and a multi-million-dollar real estate industry was actively flipping property, and—yes!—they'd kick out your grandma. You know, so it changed the whole debate. We were able to keep the woman [in her home]. . . . as far as a demonstration to the general public, it was perfect.

When measuring the success of protest, then, publicity is crucial to ensure that knowledge about an existing injustice can reach the public and can pressure the people capable of bringing about change. Illegal forms of dissent play a key role in generating publicity because, unlike conventional political strategies that often lack the drama and visuals that media require, civil disobedience and direct action can readily play into the hands of newsroom editors and work to the advantage of grassroots organizers. For some activists, the ability to generate media coverage of an existing injustice is the only justification for staging crimes of dissent. For example, one member of the Los Angeles Catholic Worker told of having been raised in a politically conservative family that generally treated the law as sacrosanct. Although his father often agreed with his politics, it was difficult for his father to accept his tactic of civil disobedience:

He'd say [to me], "Well, I understand that sometimes you have to get arrested just to get on TV. You know, it's hard for you guys to get your message out. I'm not happy about it, but I understand why you're doing it."
And he was content until I told him that the media didn't [always] show
up but that we do it anyway without the media. And then he couldn't
understand it. He was against the war and supported the idea of civil disobedience, but only to get the message of dissent out there. So in theory
he supported the idea of civil disobedience. He just didn't like [that] . . .
we did it [without media]. And it was hard to argue against that, because
he was making sense.

Despite the media's ability to generate publicity, it is important to note
that not all activists court the media. Some activists prefer to play to an
audience unencumbered by a middleman. Indeed, as outlined in chapter
2, many activists view corporate media as obstacles to justice. Ellen Barfield with the War Resisters League, Veterans for Peace, and other antiwar
organizations observed that "mainstream media is corporately controlled,
and their vested interest is not to publicize the people questioning war,
especially the people nonviolently questioning." She added that when the
news does decide to focus on protesters, they are frequently characterized in a less-than-flattering manner. "They try to imply that, 'Well, okay,
maybe they didn't crack police heads—but they were about to! . . . I get
really tired of the media always doing that—saying 'They're just hippies'
or something like that." Another antiwar protester agreed: "most of the
media is in the hand of [corporations]. . . . I don't expect them to come
and cover us with any sense of objectivity." Unlike the Raging Grannies,
who feel that humor allows their antiwar message to be readily conveyed
(i.e., their message of "let the old enlist; they're going to die soon anyway!"), one activist pointed out that many issues require lengthy explica-
tion, something corporate media simply do not allow:

They want a sound bite, and I cannot condense my feelings about the
illegality of depleted uranium [weapons] into a sound bite, because you
need to explain what depleted uranium is and how it's affecting U.S.
troops and enemies and civilians. . . . and you can't do it in a blurb that
they can put on the TV.

Notwithstanding some activists' reluctance to communicate to corporate media, they nevertheless acknowledge that the public curiosity

generated by news footage of their willingness to get arrested and to render themselves martyrs can work to their advantage in the long run by
building support for the activist community. An action by a Catholic
Worker community against the military contractor Rockwell is a rather
telling account of how to measure success.

> It was years ago in the eighties when someone responded to an article
> in the newspaper about our protest outside of Rockwell. This man drove
> down to our soup kitchen—he was a Rockwell employee—and a whole
> group of us had just been arrested and in jail for our action. And he came
> and he said, "Well what is it you want us to do?" And, you know, we
> talked to him for a long time, and he said, "Well, I can't quit my job. I
> have to take care of my family." And so it's pushing twenty-five years now,
> but every month that man still sends us a check, [all because he learned
> about us] in the newspaper.

In conclusion, publicity helps draw attention to a perceived injustice
and can sometimes pressure or—as in the case of the pending eviction—
shame the people responsible to change their ways. The visual bias of contemporary media works to the advantage of activists who use civil disobedience and direct action, because even when they are denied a sound bite,
curiosity about their willingness to suffer can generate interest in their
cause and can help expand the number of the activist community.

Community and Solidarity

Although activism is often associated with such actions as "tearing down
the streets,"[8] even the people who use this expression (whether as a playful
metaphor or more seriously) are nevertheless quick to point out that, ultimately, activism is about building things up. When the Russian anarchist
Mikhail Bakunin wrote that the destructive force is also a creative one,
he was not only addressing the dialectic nature of social movements (i.e.,
the end of one era marks the beginning of another); he was also reminding revolutionaries that the real work of activism begins *after* an action,
through the building of community, solidarity, and social networks to help
sustain the cause into the future. One measure of the success of an action,
therefore, is not only whether a staged protest has produced cracks in the
prevailing and offending social structure but also whether new forms of
community and solidarity have emerged from the staging of the event.

Whether or not one risks arrest, publicly expressing dissent can be an intimidating endeavor in a culture that measures success according to the level of conformity and ability to keep up with the Joneses. Aside from the risks of arrest by police and judgment from the courts, activists also face the potential judgment that can come from family and friends who might disapprove of their loved ones' public dissent. For years, academics have studied the deleterious and stigmatizing effects that can come from having been labeled "deviant" or "criminal." For example, in the book *Outsiders,* sociologist Howard Becker notes that people who have been socially labeled for participation in even just one deviant activity are often "cut off" from participation in conventional social gatherings and activities.[9] It is therefore possible that for many activists, the true punishment begins upon release from police custody, when they must face family, friends, and co-workers.

The activists interviewed for this book have certainly experienced stigmatization and isolation. One abortion protester told me that as a result of her participation in actions in front of clinics, she and her husband's friendship circle "has shrunk."

> [We've lost] a lot of people that used to be our really good friends as long as we were [sticking to] the status quo and we weren't making waves. I'm not going to say we don't have friends. We have a lot of people who support what we do. But you cannot be concerned with how you appear to people when you are following conviction.

Because this activist has often appeared on television as a spokesperson for her cause, her public persona is especially heightened, which influences not only how people treat her but also how they treat her children. "My kids go to a private Christian school, and there are a lot of people who think that . . ." After trailing off, she simply added that the treatment her family receives is not "deliberately offensive." Flip Benham of Operation Save America has even received scrutiny from members of the congregation for which he serves as pastor. Their concern is that his activism might damage the reputation of the church. "Some of the people in my church have said, 'You love the babies more than you love us!' And those are some of the daggers that really hurt."

In addition to losing friends, some of the activists I interviewed risk intense judgment from their own families. This proved to be the case with two members of the Los Angeles Catholic Worker. One woman admitted that her family finds her "embarrassing." David Gardner joined the Catholic Worker house after graduating from a university with a degree in computer science. When I asked him about his family, he told me, "My mom is pissed and doesn't want to talk about it. [She says] I'm throwing my life away, no woman's going to want to marry me, that kind of stuff." He continued:

> My grandmother is a little more supportive, but she worries about me. My grandfather, you know, both of them cry a lot. . . . My grandfather showed up to one of my sentencing dates, and it was good to have him there because he met all of the other people who were there supporting me. And a lot of these people . . . told my grandfather what a great guy I was, and it was good for him to see that. But ultimately when [the proceedings began], he just cried and [walked] around the court hallway.

Of course, even if and when activists attempt to conceal some of their actions from loved ones, modern technology does not allow protesters to pick and choose with whom they go public. As one activist told me, "My dad did a web search on me. He didn't like that very much." As another example, in the aftermath of the attacks on September 11, I was inadvertently photographed by an Associated Press photographer while I was protesting the pending war on Afghanistan on the streets in front of Capitol Hill. When the picture hit the newspapers, I heard a mouthful from some friends and even from family who were unaware that I made a special trip to Washington, D.C., to voice my dissent. Many people found my actions less than patriotic. Finally, it is important to note that stigmatization aside, some activists risk their personal or professional relationships every time they risk a jail sentence, as a lengthy stint behind bars can prove disruptive to everyday relationships. An activist who met his wife within the peace movement discovered that going to jail hastened the end of his marriage:

> [My wife] was very active in the peace movement, so it wasn't that she disagreed with me going to jail or prison. . . . But as it turned out, me being in jail for six months was big. We had only been married for six months before I went to jail for six months, and her old boyfriend came by. He had tried to talk her out of marrying me for a whole day before we got married. Anyway, he came and started living with her while I was in jail. I didn't know this. So by the time I got out of jail she wanted to get a divorce. But it turns out she didn't want to be with him either.

With the risk to families and friendships posed by crimes of dissent, it follows that an important measure of activist success is whether grass-roots campaigns can ultimately cultivate new relationships and sources of social support. The formation of activist communities and social networks increases individuals' chances to go against the grain of the mainstream, and they can strengthen activists' commitment to their causes.[10] They provide protesters with a sense of trust and of real companionship, and when protesters are risking arrest, they provide a legal support network that can help ease the process of being handled by the system. One activist talked about the importance of community:

> Whenever we are working with someone who's new in the group, and they've gotten arrested, we really always reach out and make sure they get a lot of support. You just don't want someone to feel like once they've gone through an arrest situation, the rules change. You really need to take care of a person. . . . I want to make sure that people have a community backing them up, because it can be scary.

Another protester, who was active with School of the Americas (SOA) Watch, which stages protests in opposition to the SOA, floated in an out of various activist communities until he found "the right group," which he defined as one having both the same values and—equally important—the same level of commitment. "[I'm] serious about standing up, and sometimes that's a quality that can make or break a community for a specific individual. . . . I don't want to say that there are people who attend groups because they think it's a fad or because they're bored. I don't think that's realistic, but maybe a little bit." When he found SOA Watch, he discovered a group of like-minded individuals whose opposition to U.S. foreign policy and whose commitment to nonviolence resonated with his own. A year after attending his first protest at the gates of Fort Benning in Georgia and attending SOA Watch meetings, he realized that he had an affinity with the group and that it provided him with a level of support and community. This feeling of support and community convinced him to face arrest and time in federal prison, where he ultimately served three months.

> [There was a] meeting where you get information about doing the direct action [i.e., trespassing onto the military base]. . . . The people from SOA Watch made it a point to see me the next day before I was going

to get arrested. I filled out a whole press release [justifying my actions]. I met some of my best friends [through SOA Watch], and they all gave me support.

Steve Clemens, who also served three months in prison for his protest at the SOA, echoed these sentiments about the importance of community:

> I had a wonderful support network for the last three months when I was in federal prison. It was embarrassing how many letters I got and how many visitors. Most prisoners don't have that at all. It's almost a disadvantage, because you really can't be in solidarity with other prisoners the way you really want to be.

As this statement indicates, community (or perhaps, more appropriately, solidarity) extends beyond immediate activist circles and may include the moral or even financial support of family, neighbors, and friends. People who may not have the ability or desire to risk arrest can nevertheless stand in solidarity with more-seasoned activists by lending a hand whenever needed, thus freeing up those who have committed to step across the line.

> Before I went to prison [for three months], we had a fund-raiser here to help with any extra expenses we had. [I had] just a wonderful group of people and support, so that makes a huge difference for people who are facing longer times. I think it's much harder for a spouse or partner or family member who is left behind. . . . but having the support of the community was absolutely essential. That has really given me a lot of freedom and [an] ability to take some risks.

Community building is therefore a crucial phase of any staged act of dissent, and the extent to which new friendships are forged and networks are extended constitutes an important measure of success. Clemens concluded, "I think about community building, and I think direct action contributes to community building. And I think you always have to build something, even if we're opposed to something else. [Otherwise] you are just doing direct action in a void."

Of course, when it comes to community building, the old adage stands: there is strength in numbers. An expanding number of participants or supporters provides activists with a sense that theirs is not a futile endeavor. As one activist-writer told me, "If there was a lot of people, even a substantial number and a growing number especially willing to do this, I'd be willing to do this full-time for the rest of my life." More numbers in solidarity also translates to more financial, legal, and logistical resources, allowing for future action to occur. Finally, growing numbers send a message to the targets of dissent that public opinion is changing, forcing them to reconsider politics (or business) as usual. Still, there exists within the activist (and, in particular, anarchist) literature an ongoing debate over the importance of movements' reaching "a critical mass." Proponents of strategies calling for direct action note that unlike more-symbolic gestures, which are designed to persuade onlookers, "direct action need not be popular to be effective. The point of direct action is the action itself, not pandering to supposed public opinion or anticipated media coverage."[11]

There is a truism to the assertion that too much is often made of the numbers game, and it is common to hear event organizers arguing with police or the press over the true numbers in attendance at a particular rally or event. In reality, sometimes it simply takes the action of one person to make a difference. "Let's go back to Thoreau," said Ed Hedemann, the war tax resister. Recall that Thoreau was just one person who refused to pay his poll tax, was jailed, and subsequently published his essay on the experience. He was only one person engaging in direct action, but as Hedemann noted, even despite Thoreau's star power as one of America's most celebrated writers, he had no idea of the impact that essay would have on future generations. There is therefore a certain danger in assuming that the effectiveness of an action requires large numbers or a vast network of support.

Effecting Change

Although publicity and solidarity are important signposts on the road to success, ultimately it is the ability of an action or campaign to effect change that historians document as the true impact of dissent. But how can one ever come to know the true contribution of (illegal) dissent to changing social policy or practice, especially given the methodological dilemmas posed at the introduction to this chapter? It would appear that there exist few—if any—"objective" measures of the impact of dissent on social policy or practice. At the same time, an important question to ask is whether an objective assessment of success is really necessary. The fact is injustice is not something that is experienced objectively or distributed equitably, nor is it something that can be (or should be) neutralized through dispassionate scientific analysis. Because I believe that what is of most importance in a book about the people who fight injustice (and who risk arrest in the process) is their opinions—however subjective they may be—about whether their efforts are "worth it," my focus is on their own assessments.

Notwithstanding my disclaimer about the subjectivity of activists' assessments, the activists I interviewed did not deceive themselves into thinking that their protests would bring about immediate change to official policy or social practice. To the contrary, they were acutely aware of the lengthy process that is ahead of them. For example, Sanderson Beck pointed out that although the modern civil rights movement took flight during the 1950s and 1960s, initial acts of dissent began during the 1940s, "but they didn't have the impact that they did ten, fifteen years later." He added, "when you do something, you never know the impact it's going to have" on future generations. Although acknowledging the significant gains made by the activists who fought for civil rights, another activist also emphasized the slow pace of social change: "It's amazing what King and the civil rights movement did in this country in the South—not that there's no racism in this country anymore, but they certainly got rid of Jim Crow and segregation." Pointing out that racism and segregation were entrenched in our country for hundreds of years, he turned to the problem of nuclear weapons for a parallel: "We've had nuclear weapons for sixty years now. [Advocates of nuclear disarmament] have a long way to go, because it's a huge problem."

It is important to note that some activists, though they acknowledge the slow pace of success resulting from their efforts, do not really concern themselves with questions of whether their campaigns will prove victorious in the political realm. For them, concern about protests' success has the unfortunate effect of converting their principled positions into what feels like their unwilling participation in a game of odds or chance. So when questioned about protest "successes," most of the activists I interviewed prefaced their assessments with brief disclaimers. That was especially the practice among protesters of faith. Consider the response of Flip Benham of Operation Save America, who began his assessment of the effectiveness of his abortion "rescues" at family-planning clinics with his insistence that he is not on a mission to be successful. "I'm called to be faithful. . . . I don't go to an abortion clinic so babies may be saved, as noble as that is. I go to honor my Lord Jesus and give a voice for those children. . . . God requires my faithfulness, not my success." Expressing a similar sentiment, another activist within the rescue movement prefaced her assessment of success by reminding me that she is a Christian: "So when you know what you're really called to do, then it's a spiritual thing."

Members of the Los Angeles Catholic Worker also initially dismiss the notion of protest success. "Dorothy Day [cofounder of the Catholic Worker Movement] says we are not called to be successful; we are called to be faithful, and so if we don't pull something off as well as we have hoped, there's [still] a great deal to be said for trying." Of course, one need not be religious to share this perspective, as the antinuclear activist Veronica pointed out to me. "You know, Gandhi says you can never look for success in what you do. You just have to do something because it's the right thing to do. And that's how I feel."

None of these qualified statements about the pace of change or about the lack of preoccupation with protest outcome should suggest that the protesters I met did not maintain a preoccupation with, or a sense of accomplishment at, having effected change. For some of them, meaningful change occurs whenever a campaign can alter public opinion, even if that does not readily translate into a change of policy or practice. "If we also change the hearts and minds around [a policy], change public debate, those are things that are successful as well." As a case in point, recall from the beginning of the chapter that the "success" of the Honeywell Project was quickly offset by the formation of Alliant Techsystems, which allegedly not only continued to profit from the manufacture of antipersonnel landmines and cluster bombs but which activists claim in recent years has also profited from the manufacture of weapons laced with the carcinogenic substance known as depleted uranium. Although protesters have not been successful in convincing Alliant Techsystems to end the sale of that controversial weapon, there is evidence that their campaign against the manufacturer is having an impact on public opinion.

> Alliant Tech is still making depleted uranium, but they've taken it off of their website. They used to brag about it. Now they call it "kinetic energy weapons" because it's become a controversial issue. So at least they're defensive about it. I think we've brought it to some people's awareness, which is good. It's the first step.

When we think about the ability of dissent to spark measurable change to social policy, success is most recognizable when we examine the impact of dissent at the microlevel. After all, to be grassroots is to begin from the ground up and at the local level. Consider the work of James Tracy and his efforts to offset the rising cost of housing in San Francisco during the dot-com bubble of the late 1990s. Although the efforts of his affinity group alone (and those of likeminded activists) have not reversed the practice of flipping property and the subsequent rise in housing costs that come with it, he measures success one house at a time: "Normally what you're doing is getting a landlord to back off an eviction." So for him and for those with whom he works, success is measured one blocked eviction at a time. Activists who perform what they call abortion rescues similarly measure success at the microlevel, one procedure prevented at a time—a number that adds up, as one activist told me: "If [my action] saves one life, [then] civil disobedience is effective. . . . in 1991, there were over 2,000 abortion clinics. Today there is 738." She continued: "The average age of an abortionist is fifty-nine years old. We know that it's only a matter of time—not that abortion will ever totally end, but legally we believe that in time it will become [difficult to perform]." Although Flip Benham's numbers differed slightly, he agreed with this assessment of success, adding the important point that the decline in access to abortions over the years has occurred without a dependency on the Supreme Court's reversal of *Roe v. Wade*.

Tax resisters likewise measure the success of their activism at the microlevel, one dollar at a time. Certainly, the size of the federal budget is so large that it would take millions of Americans to withhold taxes before officials become worried. But that does not negate the claim by Ed Hedemann and Bob that they are having an impact. As Bob told me,

When people say that "you're not going to have any effect," that's total hogwash, because the stuff that myself and others were doing decades ago has grown. . . . We've been out there sowing the seeds and sowing the seeds. Some of them take root. Some of them never take root. But some of them will. Some will be on worthless soil, some on fertile soil.

Similarly, Hedemann said,

The modern war tax resistance movement basically began in 1941. It was very small until the Vietnam War, but nevertheless there was a core group of people refusing war taxes and writing about it. When Vietnam hit, [tax resistance] exploded into something terrific, when there was something like five hundred thousand refusing to pay their telephone tax and twenty-thousand refusing some or all of their income tax. But the people who had been [keeping the movement alive all those years] didn't know

[Vietnam] was going to happen. They kept plugging away until the right historical moment happened.

The point made by Bob and Hedemann is an important one, namely, that when beginning a campaign, one can never predict how the confluence of history and public opinion will convert the lone voice into a sizeable mass. However immeasurable success may be in the short term, activists are often content to view their actions as the seeds of a measurable success in the long term. That being said, it is sometimes possible to gauge the impact of even the lone voice speaking out against power. Never mind the impact of Thoreau's singular act of resistance or of countless other acts that history often erroneously portrays as singular acts absent a sizeable network of support. Instead, consider the actions of one unknown individual who Hedemann told me used to picket outside the Johnson administration's White House every day with a sign declaring that the very thought of the Vietnam War made him sick.

> There was this lone picketer in front of the White House every day. This *one* person, every day! And you think, "Oh man, this is kind of useless. The war is going on, people are getting massacred, [yet this guy just pickets every day]." But it turns out that we found out from FBI files and reports that the president was so annoyed by this guy, it was driving him crazy. But the guy didn't know it when he was out there picketing every single day. It wasn't civil disobedience; it was legal, but it annoyed the hell out of the president and . . . [it] had an impact. And this [guy], he had no idea. So there is a danger in saying, "We can't do this because it isn't going to be successful," or saying afterward, "it failed," because you never know.

In sum, the meaning of success seems rather elastic, for success can be defined both spiritually and philosophically and therefore both personally and politically. Moreover, in the immediate term, the successes of grassroots campaigns are best measured at the microlevel, with an eye always looking to the future, when history may suggest that the lone dissenter has led by example. There are, however, those rare occasions when success is achieved in the immediate term, when the actions of a relative handful of people can yield meaningful and measurable results. We see it when James Tracy and the Coalition for Affordable Housing successfully prevent a poor, elderly woman from being evicted. We see it when activists within a local chapter of Food Not Bombs feed the homeless in defiance of public ordinances.

And we see it when union organizers and environmental activists unite and bring a halt to the undemocratic practices of corporate globalization.

One last example of a measurable success can be seen in a campaign from the early 1970s. At that time, a convention center in Orange County, California, played host to what was called an annual arms bazaar. As surprising as it may seem, each year a group of military arms merchants would display their wares to members of the public, who were free to purchase various products of their choosing. So it was only a matter of time before area activists campaigned against the use of the city's convention center to promote militarism, as Jeff Dietrich of the Los Angeles Catholic Worker explained to me: "The first year there were just four of us. . . . So the next year we really did it up. I went down four months before and organized a petition drive, and we got ten thousand petitions, which at that time was about a tenth of the population, and we turned it in to the city council." When the petition failed to persuade city officials to reconsider the convention center's hosting of the bazaar, Dietrich and others organized an act of civil disobedience. Forty people were arrested. Most of the protesters simply spent the night in jail, but Dietrich and a fellow activist received six months because they had been arrested outside the bazaar the previous year. But the judge offered them a proviso, and here is where the story gets really interesting:

> The proviso was that if we would write the judge a letter within thirty days saying that we would never do it again [i.e., perform civil disobedience outside the convention center], then he would let us out. Well, of course, we didn't write the letter. But because he put that little twist in it, it made the case interesting. There were about two thousand protesting outside the convention center, so it was a pretty significant event, and the press continued to cover it. The *Los Angeles Times* came down and interviewed us in jail about the whole aspect of the letter: would we write it, would we not write the letter. So there was a big article in the *Times*. The inmates in jail were saying, "You stupid motherfuckers! You better write that letter! You get your ass out of here!" Then, when the article in the paper came out, they said, "Man! Now you can't write that letter. You better not write that letter. You'll look like a fucking pussy if you write that letter." Of course, we weren't going to write the letter, but now we looked pretty cool.

Not only did Dietrich and his codefendant not write the letter, but he received so much community support that the Catholic Worker was able

Used by a neighborhood peace group on fliers and publications, this image symbolizes the endurance needed to realize peace and social justice. (Artwork by Spacious Mind Art & Graphic Design)

to organize a letter-writing campaign to the judge—though they were not the kind of letters the judge had in mind. After receiving some seven hundred letters opposed to the jailing of nonviolent protesters, the judge brought Dietrich and his codefendant into the court, along with the news media.

> We didn't want the news media there because we didn't know what the judge was going to do. But he actually apologized to us, and he said that he'd gotten seven hundred letters, and he explained the whole philosophy of sentencing. And he said, "I was wrong to do this, and I want to apologize to you." And we said, "You know, we're going to do it again next year." And he said, "I don't think so. I have a letter here from the convention center saying that the arms bazaar is not coming back."

It was a victory for the protest's organizers, to be sure, and one that allowed them to witness the achievement of their goals firsthand. It is the type of victory that Dietrich called "one of those classic examples of a successful campaign that almost never happens in our experience."

Counterculture or Just Culture?

As the legacy of the civil rights era, as the successes of the Vietnam-era antiwar actions, and even as the apex of the antiglobalization movement recede further into our collective past, it is easy to become disillusioned about the prospect of realizing social justice anytime in the near future. In this post-9/11 and, more broadly, postmodern cultural climate, dissent simply is not what it used to be. Today, when dissent approaches relevance through strategies of direct action, it is quickly branded as "terrorism" by the State. That has particularly been the case with animal-rights activists and, in particular, with environmental activists, who have been dubbed "eco-terrorists" by federal law-enforcement agencies.[12] When strategies are limited to more symbolic actions, dissent can be wholly managed, contained, and therefore pacified by persons in power. Not only does this management of protest diminish the pleasures of resistance and subversion (since nothing is really being subverted), but it can even serve as political fodder to illustrate the professionalism of the State in its ability to address and contain minor political disruptions. It seems as though the very idea of a meaningful oppositional movement that can realize social change is becoming merely a relic of our cultural past.

Part of the reason for dissent's apparent ineffectuality no doubt stems from history's fetishism of the mass movements of the 1960s and the myriad protest strategies that were ultimately met by social and political gains. Because of these historic successes, activists by and large have been employing these same protest tactics for more than four decades. As one commenter in the *Utne Reader* has noted, "A generation of rabble-rousers, schooled in the 1960s-style dissent, have adopted nonviolent civil disobedience not only as a default tactic, but in later years as a profession, a lifestyle, and most disappointingly, an end in itself."[13] This opinion is shared by Sharon Lungo, whose first exposure to civil disobedience was through her work with Greenpeace. For Lungo, nonviolent civil disobedience has become such a natural component of what many protest organizations do that the very strategy itself "loses some of its power." As she sees it, this overdependence is the natural result of civil disobedience having become historically "romanticized." Indeed, activists composing the Critical Art Ensemble (CAE) have argued that in our current postmodern climate marked by the end of imagination, social movements are imprisoned by history. The problem is that nostalgia for sixties-era activism "endlessly replays the past as the present" and leaves activists with little reason to believe that new strategies are necessary. Without dismissing civil disobedience outright, the CAE nevertheless contends that its efficacy "fades with each passing decade" because the targets of its strategies have come to anticipate disruptions and thus make adjustments accordingly.[14]

Other observers of contemporary mass movements have made the case that the lack of a truly oppositional countervailing grassroots force is not due to the strategies of choice so much as it is the result of a political system itself that has become immune to radical change, thus leaving activists with no viable protest options. This argument has been made rather pointedly by such scholars as Herbert Marcuse and Theodore Roszak, both of whom describe life in a late capitalist system as one that is wholly resistant to radical social transformation. In the books *One-Dimensional Man* and *Counter-Revolution and Revolt,* which became cornerstones of the New Left, Marcuse describes the United States as a political system in which dissent has become fully integrated (or incorporated) into the mainstream of social and economic life, rendering it no longer a threat to the system at all. As Marcuse observes, the Marxist prediction that the continued growth of capitalism would cause the world's oppressed to rise up and overthrow the capitalist system was proving to be false. There would be no revolution precisely because capitalism has been able to (re)organize itself to prevent the threat of one.[15]

But in what ways has capitalism been able to neutralize the threat of opposition? As just one example, Marcuse asks his readers to consider trends in the labor force and between the social classes. Once thought to be at the forefront of social change in orthodox Marxist doctrine, workers today are hardly a revolutionary force. In fact, with regard to any burgeoning antiwar campaign, the labor movement has become increasingly quiet. That is because in the post–World War II political climate, the economy has been marked by what President Dwight D. Eisenhower famously called a "military-industrial complex," in which people on the assembly line now benefit from a war economy. Today, both the unions *and* their corporate bosses lobby for bigger military contracts. According to the World Policy Institute, weapons manufacturing has become big business for workers and corporate executives alike, with fiscal year 2006 Pentagon contracts totaling nearly $300 billion.[16]

Not only have unions become pacified, but the masses have as well. For all practical purposes, "poverty" in the United States no longer exists; what we once called poverty is now called "debt." With the expansion of a credit-based economy, inequality is masked by a perceived equalization of class distinctions. Although the poor are mired in debt, Marcuse points out that they can now shop at the same stores as the wealthy, creating the appearance of a system predicated on equal opportunity. And as long as there is an appearance of class equalization, there will arise no sustainable countervailing force from the bottom of the economic ladder questioning or even challenging the Establishment. Marcuse therefore predicts that if current socioeconomic trends continue, society will be plagued by one-dimensional, uncritical thinking, and so long as superficial needs are fulfilled, politics as usual will remain. Under such a prevailing climate, opposition will not be possible because alternatives to the status quo (as well as strategies to realize those alternatives) will no longer be imagined, let alone demanded.

Extending Marcuse's argument, history professor Theodore Roszak describes contemporary society as one that has reached "the peak of its organizational integration," which is marked by a highly structured division of labor with each sector of society working with, while being wholly dependent on, the other. So complex is this highly specialized technical system that people feeling bewildered or disenfranchised have little recourse but to defer to the so-called experts, who—as we are so often told—know better than we do. Calling this complex system a "technocracy," Roszak notes that its constituents continue to place their faith in it, "despite its most appalling failures and criminalities," because their imaginations fail to see beyond a set of limited and acceptable options. Those rare few who refuse to abide by the system become the makings of a *counterculture*, yet this counterculture is one that is more likely to get turned on by psychedelics and to drop out of the mainstream altogether than it is to pose a meaningful or threatening political challenge.[17] Counterculture has simply become something that is measured by differences in persona or identity than by differences in politics or political ideology. Attire, hairstyle, and music have somehow become the chief means of distancing oneself from the body politic, yet the acquisition of the accoutrements to communicate a countercultural lifestyle merely feed back into the capitalist system. It simply creates a new culture, though one that is hardly oppositional.[18]

To be sure, this ability of capitalism either to incorporate or to pacify discontent is one about which contemporary activists are increasingly—though not entirely—cognizant. When the editors of *The Baffler* published their critique of corporate America under the title *Commodify Your Dissent*, they were acknowledging capitalism's ability to co-opt rebellion, and they warned readers that there was very little they could do to protest society that would not ultimately result in profit for big business. That is because the very idea of a counterculture has become a "capitalist orthodoxy."[19] Simply put, if respect for the status quo requires cultural conformity, then dissent naturally requires a distinction from the masses not only in politics but also in physical appearance, in attire, and in artistic preferences. The result of this line of thinking is twofold. First, the desire for counterculture has brought new opportunities for corporate America. In no time, identities have become a source of capitalist profit. In other words, counterculture has inevitably become a part of consumer culture, where merely shopping for the appropriate (e.g., humane, environmentally friendly, or merely different) product while boycotting mainstream trends has suddenly become a (life)stylized means of communicating dissent.[20]

The second result arising from the emergence of a counterculture is far more threatening to people truly concerned about the realization of social justice. Stated simply, the logic of counterculture is anathema to radical politics. That is because progressive change is dependent on the *unification* of the people to form a critical mass working toward a revolutionary goal. But counterculture eschews entirely the idea of the masses (i.e., its art, literature, and politics). Professors Joseph Heath and Andrew Potter argue in their book *Nation of Rebels* that during the second half of the twentieth century, radical politics took a dangerous turn. "Instead of treating the masses as an ally, the people began to be regarded, to an ever-increasing degree, as an object of suspicion."[21] The reasons for this turn are obvious. As Heath and Potter point out, for many people the rise of fascism in Nazi Germany most readily illustrated the trappings of conformity and collectivity. Years later, a series of studies on obedience to authority conducted by Yale University professor Stanley Milgram negated the argument that there was something unique to the psyche of the Third Reich; Milgram was able get everyday citizens to administer what they were told to be potentially lethal shocks to research subjects.[22] Before long, Heath and Potter argue, people already discontented with the conditions of modern civilization came to see the proverbial masses as the source of, rather than the solution to, all society's ills. What developed, then, was a deep distrust toward collective political action. In its place emerged a premium on individualism and a near complete withdrawal from politics altogether.

Beyond Autonomy: The Future of Dissent

It is easy to get carried away with the notion of individualism when what the political mainstream has to offer merely increases social injustice. The individualistic lifestyle also has a quixotic appeal. If Thoreau appeared alone in his refusal to pay the poll tax, then surely he appeared as a downright loner in *Walden,* in which he chronicled his days of solitude with nature. And he certainly had a point when he argued that we are often lonelier in a crowd of strangers than we are when alone in our surroundings. There is also an abundance of evidence pointing to the irrationality of groupthink, with Nazi Germany being the most obvious example. In short, if the twentieth century has taught us anything, it has taught us that the choreographed efforts of a collective can be far more destructive than the actions of lone individuals. Perhaps that lesson explains the writings of Theodore Kaczynski, a.k.a. the Unabomber. Writing from a secluded shack in the woods, Kaczynski suggested that since people have become increasingly dependent on large organizations such as government bureaucracies and corporations, and since we have been mainstreamed in our mental capacities through media, pharmaceuticals, and the like, it might be wise for us simply to "dump the whole stinking system." Today, his words (rather than his deeds) offer an important critique of contemporary social living, and they have even achieved cult status in such underground publications as John Zerzan's *Against Civilization.*[23]

Even if we acknowledge the appeal of solitude and the allure of nonconformist living, the fact remains that a strategy of isolation and counterculture only distances activists from the very injustices they seek to eradicate; it does little to obliterate them. This is a point that has been made rather aggressively by the late anarchist and social ecologist Murray Bookchin in his much-debated treatise *Social Anarchism or Lifestyle Anarchism.* Bookchin's main assertion is that much of what has been called anarchism during the twentieth century (or what I call anarchist activism) has been little more than "a minimalist credo of opposition to the State" rather than an articulation of the types of communities that should replace the State.[24] To be sure, this criticism of contemporary activism and of anarchism has itself been criticized (perhaps deservedly) for being too overreaching; after all, there has been a blossoming of radical and anarchist theory in recent years that has outlined everything from participatory economics to worker councils to green living. Still, where Bookchin's words are most relevant and most deserving of introspection is his call for anarchists to move beyond *lifestyle anarchism* and toward *social anarchism*. Such a move requires a move beyond autonomy as a political goal and toward collective, *cooperative* dissent.

As has been discussed throughout the book, autonomy is the practice of personal (rather than political) conscience; it is a rejection of State power and the expectation of obedience to policies not reflective of individual morality. But autonomy can become personally alienating. As Bookchin points out, the etymology of the word *autonomy* is linked to *independence* and connotes "sovereignty," "liberty," and even "ego." When taken to the extreme, concern for autonomy can foster a distrust of the *social*, rather than a distrust of the State. What materializes from this distrust is the formation of an individualistic or lifestyle anarchism, which Bookchin defines as "the tendency of many anarchists to root the ills of society in 'civilization' rather than in capital and hierarchy." In other words, activism/anarchism has become synonymous with difference. It has developed as its preoccupation what Bookchin called "'style' rather than society" and a near obsession about whether people eat the right diet and shop (or not) at the right stores and even about whether people "Kill Your Television," as the popular slogan goes, and avoid media altogether.[25] Yet as Marcuse, *The Baffler*, and others have pointed out, the very pursuit of the counterculture lifestyle, the very attempt to create a new civilization, merely feeds into the capitalist culture.

Although Bookchin has been condemned for the boldness with which he critiqued various strains of progressive radicalism, it is important to note that he is not alone in his analysis. Community organizer Mark Andersen has called for a much-needed "revolution without illusion." Like Bookchin, Andersen sees an obsession with lifestyle politics as potentially damaging to meaningful social change. To be sure, neither author sees anything inherently wrong with making politics personal. The problem arises when lifestyle politics all but replaces social politics and serves to divide the masses into various subcultures: those who shop at multinational clothing chains and those who do not; those who ride a bicycle to work and those who do not; those who eat organic foods and those who do not. As Andersen writes, this lifestyle approach to activism "may be best at simply dividing us." He continues, noting that "no one is going to be able to meet all the possible criteria involved" and that lifestyle activism is largely the privilege of the wealthy, who can afford to avoid discount retailers, who can afford to shop at organic groceries, and who can afford to purchase solar paneling for their homes.[26]

In place of autonomy, Bookchin recommends that activists move beyond concern for autonomy and toward a concern for freedom. More than just semantics, freedom acknowledges the interdependence of individuals; it "interweaves the individual with the collective." The point is that as stand-alone strategies, a rush toward individualism and a rejection of civilization outright does little to threaten the State. Moreover, the creation of a counterculture is not really countering anything; it merely substitutes one trend with another. If real change is going to take flight, it will require some level of a choreographed mobilization of the masses. Unfortunately, the idea of counterculture and the rejection of civilization "has almost completely replaced socialism as the basis of radical political thought." As a consequence, too often activist politics leaves society with much cynicism and with little vision for lasting and widespread social change.[27]

So what is to be done to salvage the future of dissent? Whether we view ourselves as anarchists or as socialists, as Marxists or merely as reformists, and even if we view ourselves as conservatives, it should be clear from the preceding discussion that for dissent to be meaningful, not only must it (on occasion) extend beyond the confines of the law, but it must also extend beyond the actions of the self. To that end, solidarity must arise *before* entering the jail cell. People discontented with politics as usual cannot retreat from society and from neighbors. Instead, they must reach out to them and appeal to their good judgment. Where there are no affinity groups, new ones must emerge. Activism must move beyond the isolationism of autonomy and connect with others.

But that is not all. For activism to have a future, for social justice (however defined) to be realized, people fretful about dissent must come to view an arrest (and a subsequent sentence) as a reward for the courage to dissent; arrest should not be viewed as punishment for wrongdoing. The suffragettes were jailed for having the courage to insist on the equality of women. Countless activists were imprisoned for having the courage to denounce racism and segregation. Perhaps most tellingly, Nelson Mandela spent most of his life behind bars for having the courage to challenge apartheid policies. After twenty-eight years of confinement, the one-time criminal became the president of South Africa. The point should be clear: as cultures change, yesterday's criminals can quickly become tomorrow's visionaries.

From Culture to Crime . . . and Back Again

And this book ends at the point where it began, with an acknowledgment of the intersection between cultural norms and criminal practices. Just as cultures seek to establish the demarcations of criminal behavior, some criminals in turn seek either to broaden or to narrow the scope of acceptable cultural practices. Collectively, crimes of dissent signify actions that attempt to negotiate accepted definitions of justice. Whether progressive or conservative, they are political expressions, to be sure, for in their staging they communicate deep-rooted commitments to values and practices that can serve as the cornerstones of a new or reaffirmed cultural climate. And that idea brings us back to an emphasis on cultural criminology, for crimes of dissent are seldom the acts of lone individuals. Rather, they are frequently staged collectively. They begin perhaps as marginal, subcultural, and even criminal behaviors carried out in small affinity groups, but they can quickly become the seeds of massive, widespread, and legitimized social movements.

One of the objectives of this book has been to describe how the justice system responds to acts of dissent and, in turn, to understand the impact of the system's responses on political actors. For some of them, the costs of dissent can be high. That is particularly true for activists in nondemocracies. For the activists featured in this book, a lifestyle of dissent has meant the (re)arrangement of lives to enable their activism to occur. It has meant days, weeks, or months in jail away from family and isolated from friends. And it has meant constant reflection and renewal of one's values in the face of State opposition. Yet cultural criminology reminds us that one can experience pleasure in even harsh circumstances. When it comes to confronting injustice, there are "criminal pleasures" to be derived when exposing "structures of political and economic power and inequality, especially when these injustices are confronted via participation in a larger affinity group." Call it the "politics of criminal pleasure," as Jeff Ferrell and Clinton R. Sanders have done, or perhaps call it the criminal pleasure *of* politics, as is the case when being arrested for acting on one's political views.[28] Either way, the study of cultural criminology is the study of transgressive pleasure, for it is not only a belief that another world is possible that sustains the activists featured in this book; it is also the friendship, camaraderie, and excitement that comes from dancing at the margins of society that keeps people fighting.

The theme of anarchy has also proved prominent throughout the pages of this book. Some readers may have objected to the characterization of dissent as anarchistic, viewing civil disobedience and nonviolent resistance instead as merely reformist strategies that ultimately fail to undermine political power. Other readers may have found the ideals of anarchism to be naive and idealistic. Hopefully, though, through a discussion of anarchy, readers have gained a sense of the extent to which we as a citizenry have become (too) dependent on government and the legal system to reverse the injustices that it originally set in motion. If this brief and admittedly incomplete introduction to anarchist thought has taught us anything, hopefully it has taught us to avoid being reliant on others to eradicate injustice. Instead, we must do it ourselves and trust that this anarchist spirit becomes contagious.

Finally, it has been my objective to frame dissent as criminal behavior. In doing so, my intent has not been to justify the criminalization of speech and of association that has periodically plagued the political landscape, whether during the Red Scare, during the era of COINTELPRO, or most recently in the post-9/11 political climate. Rather, my purpose has been to highlight the lesson that what society sometimes treats as criminal behaviors is later heralded as the starting points of justice. As unconventional as it may sound, it appears from the historical record that "crime" and other acts of legal transgression are sometimes necessary precursors to meaningful social change. Although the breaking of laws is certainly a problem to be prevented, the idea that civil disobedience, passive resistance, and direct action might sometimes be necessary to achieve political equality and social justice is one that until now has been too often overlooked by both mainstream and progressive criminological theorists. My hope, then, is that after reading this book, teachers of criminology, criminal justice, and justice studies will acknowledge that when properly understood, what we call crimes today are sometimes later recognized to be the antecedents to meaningful, progressive, and much-needed social change.

Appendix
Activist Profiles

Ellen Barfield was born in Macon, Georgia, in 1956 and grew up in Lubbock and Amarillo, Texas. She served in the U.S. Army from 1977 to 1981, stationed in Kitzingen, Germany; Fort Hood, Texas; Pyong-Taek, South Korea; and Fort Riley, Kansas. She earned a degree in animal science from West Texas State University and briefly attended veterinary school at Texas A&M University. Barfield left the army with an unfocused desire to do something about social ills. A peace camp at the Pantex nuclear weapons plant near Amarillo gave her the opportunity to learn about activism, and she has now been a full-time peace and justice activist for twenty years. Barfield serves on the national boards of Veterans for Peace, the War Resisters League, and the Legislative Working Group of School of the Americas Watch (SOAW), and she cochairs the national Disarmament Committee of the Women's International League for Peace and Freedom. She heads the local chapter of Veterans for Peace in her hometown of Baltimore, Maryland, and works with several other Baltimore peace and justice organizations, as well as with her church, First Unitarian Church of Baltimore.

Sanderson Beck was born March 5, 1947, in Los Angeles. He earned a B.A. in dramatic art from the University of California at Berkeley, an M.A. in religious studies from UC Santa Barbara, Ph.D. candidacy in the philosophy of education from UCLA, and a Ph.D. in philosophy from World University. Today a prolific writer, he was a conscientious objector during the Vietnam War. In 1982, Beck formulated "World Peace Movement Principles, Purposes, and Methods," and in 1987 he traveled to forty-seven states and met with six hundred peace groups to promote peace and disarmament. He has been arrested more than fifty times for nonviolently protesting nuclear weapons and military intervention. After challenging U.S. war crimes in court, he was imprisoned for six months in 1989 and for four months in 2003. Beck has taught philosophy and more than forty different college courses. He was a candidate for president of the United States in December 2002, and in May 2003 he endorsed Dennis Kucinich. He published the *Nonviolent Action Handbook* and *Guides to Peace and Justice* in 2003. To date he has written and published more than twenty books, including nine volumes in the ethics of civilization, through the nonprofit publisher World Peace Communications.

Flip Benham was born in 1948 in Syracuse, New York. He holds two bachelor's degrees from Florida State University (in political science and international relations) and a master of divinity from Asbury Theological Seminary. Appearing on numerous local and national television and radio programs, Rev. Benham is "a bold witness for the Lord Jesus Christ in the public arena." He has been interviewed by the *Washington Post, Washington Times, New York Times, Time, Newsweek, U.S. News and World Report, World Magazine*, and virtually every major newspaper in the country. Benham leads by example, having spent time in jail for the cause of Christ in Wichita, Baton Rouge, Birmingham, Chicago, Dallas, Houston, Orlando, Lynchburg, and Washington, D.C. Benham always preaches Jesus Christ as the answer to the multitude of sins presently savaging our nation. Married to his wife, Faye, for thirty-five years, Benham is the father of five wonderful children. The Benhams are also the proud grandparents of eight beautiful grandchildren.

Steve Clemens was born in 1950 and raised in southeastern Pennsylvania. After registering as a conscientious objector in 1968, he began his political activism against the Vietnam War in 1969. He burned his draft card in 1971. During a year of weekly Bible study and reflection with Phil Berrigan and Liz Macalister, he embraced nonviolent direct action. From 1975 to 1990, Clemens was resident partner at Koinonia Partners, an intentional Christian community in Georgia. Having been a member of the Pantex Six (1981), the White Train Five (1985), the SOAW Thirty-Seven (2005), and several dozen other nonviolent actions for peace and justice, Clemens remains active on a weekly basis with AlliantACTION. He was a member of the Iraq Peace Team in Baghdad in December 2002 and spoke at more than sixty events before the war began. He has been married thirty years to Christine Haas Clemens, and the couple has two grown sons. He is a member of the Community of St. Martin, an ecumenical faith community in Minneapolis committed to nonviolence, social justice, and inclusiveness. He also serves on the boards of Pax Christi Twin Cities and the Iraqi and American Reconciliation Project.

Marv Davidov has dedicated his life to the hope of creating a world of peace and justice. During more than fifty years of activism, Davidov has launched peace organizations, has performed countless acts of nonviolent civil disobedience, has been arrested fifty-one times, and has spent six months in jail. Raised in a working-class neighborhood of Detroit, in 1961 he joined the Freedom Rider Movement, which led to being jailed in the Mississippi State Prison. From 1963 to 1964, he was a team member of the Committee for Nonviolent Action Canada-to-Cuba Peace Walk, and he was a draft-resistance organizer between 1966 and 1968. Davidov is perhaps best known as the founder of the Honeywell Project, a nationally known peace organization considered the oldest project in the United States confronting war profiteering. When not protesting, Davidov serves as an adjunct professor within the Justice and Peace Studies program at the University of St. Thomas in St. Paul, Minnesota.

Sharon Delgado was born in 1948 and has lived all her life in Northern California. An ordained United Methodist minister, she is founder and executive director of Earth Justice Ministries. She is the author of *Shaking the Gates of Hell: Faith-Led Resistance to Corporate Globalization* (Fortress Press, 2007). Rev. Delgado leads seminars and workshops and speaks before both spiritual communities and secular audiences on issues related to war and peace, climate change, social and environmental justice, and corporate globalization and its alternatives. She has had many articles published on these themes. Rev. Delgado counters the views of the religious Right with an inclusive, progressive Christianity that links spirituality with social and ecological concern. Her analysis of the global economy is rooted in a vision of the sacredness of the earth, a radical critique of the institutions and systems the currently dominate the earth, and the hope of a spiritual renewal that mobilizes people to join in the global movement to create a peaceful, just, and sustainable world through nonviolent resistance and creative alternatives. She is married to poet Guarionex Delgado, has four grown children, and enjoys spending time with her grandchildren. To find out more go to www.shakingthegatesofhell.com or www.earth-justice.org.

Jeff Dietrich was born in 1946 in Newport News, Virginia, and raised in Fullerton, California. He is cofounder of the Los Angeles Catholic Worker and the editor of that community's publication, the *Catholic Agitator.* Dietrich's writing has appeared in the *Los Angeles Times, The Progressive, America,* and the *National Catholic Reporter.* He is also the author of *Reluctant Resister,* a collection of his prison letters. For the past thirty-eight years, he has worked with his wife, Catherine Morris, serving the poor of Skid Row. He has been arrested over forty times for acts of nonviolent civil disobedience in protest of war, economic injustice, and crimes against human dignity. Shortly after graduating from California State University at Fullerton in 1968, Dietrich refused induction into the U.S. Army. As a resister to the Vietnam War, he encountered the radical Catholic Worker Movement and after a brief period of time decided to make a lifetime commitment to its radical Christian vision of compassion and resistance. The Los Angeles Catholic Worker community is composed of ten full-time members and scores of volunteers. It operates a Skid Row soup kitchen serving over three thousand free meals a week, as well as providing a dental clinic, medical clinic, and a hospitality house, where community members live in voluntary simplicity with their poor and homeless guests.

David Gardner was born on September 25, 1977, in Sacramento, California, and was a member of the Los Angeles Catholic Worker community for four years (2002–2006), through which he became involved in civil disobedience actions centered on the start of the Iraq War. He currently works as a computer programmer.

Ed Hedemann was born in 1944 in San Francisco. He has a degree in astronomy from the University of California at Berkeley, and he spent four years working on a doctorate at the University of Texas at Austin before dropping out to organize against the Vietnam War. In 1969, Hedemann refused induction into the military and began resisting taxes for war in 1970. He was an organizer for the War Resisters League between 1973 and 1986, and he is the author of *War Tax Resistance* (2003) and the War Resisters League's *Organizers' Manual* (1986). In 1982, he cofounded of the National War Tax Resistance Coordinating Committee. In 1984, he created the first War Resisters League pie-chart flier, an analysis of the U.S. federal budget, now produced annually. In more than thirty-five years of refusing to send his income taxes to the IRS, Hedemann has instead redirected over seventy thousand dollars in taxes to community, national, and international aid and movement groups. In addition to routine contact from the IRS, in 1999 the Justice Department ordered him to federal district court in an unsuccessful attempt to get him to reveal the sources of his assets. Though he has been jailed in over forty acts of civil disobedience, he has yet to be imprisoned for his war tax resistance. Hedemann has appeared on a variety of radio and television talk shows, including *The Phil Donahue Show, CBS This Morning,* and Fox-TV's *Neil Cavuto Show,* to discuss his war tax resistance. He makes his living doing a variety of freelance jobs for individuals and nonprofit groups and has a passion for experiencing total solar eclipses. He currently lives in Brooklyn, New York.

Martha Lewis has been a mainstay of the Los Angeles Catholic Worker community for almost fifteen years. She is the coeditor of the community's newspaper, the *Catholic Agitator.* She has been arrested over a dozen times for nonviolent civil disobedience protests. Her most lengthy sentence was a nine-month jail term in 1998 for cutting the fence surrounding the Nevada Nuclear Test Site. Martha was born in 1956 and raised in Southern California's San Fernando Valley. Throughout the late 1960s, she distressed her parents by aspiring to be a hippie, which caused them to send her off to a church boarding school in Portland, Oregon. After high school, she returned to the San Fernando Valley and attended California State University at Northridge, where she became intrigued with radical Catholicism through a comparative religion class. After graduation from Cal State, she converted to Catholicism and subsequently took a job as a parish secretary at Our Lady of the Valley Catholic Church. Through friends at the parish, she was introduced to the Los Angeles Catholic Worker, and with the advent of the first Gulf War, she joined the group. She and her husband, Jesse Lewis, continue to work and live among the poor and homeless of Los Angeles.

Sharon Lungo was born in 1976 in Los Angeles, California—the daughter of Salvadoran immigrants. After completing high school, Lungo became active in the fight for open space in Los Angeles and the preservation of the Ballona Wetlands. She has been engaging in and training others for nonviolent direct action since the age of eighteen. In 2000, she learned about the Ruckus Society—which provides environmental, human rights, and social justice organizers with the tools, training, and support needed to achieve their goals—and in 2001 she joined the society's training network. She also became involved in the Global Women's Strike, an international network with presence in eighty countries. She has supported direct actions in issues ranging from environmental justice, indigenous rights, housing rights, social justice, and more. She currently works for the Ruckus Society and is based in Oakland, California.

Keith McHenry was born in Frankfurt, West Germany, in 1957 and moved with his family to Logan, Utah, in 1958. In 1974, McHenry began studying painting at Boston University and worked afternoons, weekends, and summers as a tour guide and museum curator at Old South Meeting House, where the Boston Tea Party began. In 1980, McHenry and seven friends created the all-volunteer group Food Not Bombs, which feeds the hungry in hundreds of communities in the Americas, Europe, Asia, and Africa. He also coauthored the book *Food Not Bombs: How to Feed the Hungry and Build Community,* which has sold more than ten thousand copies in four languages. His work with Food Not Bombs has appeared in Amnesty International's *Human Rights Report* in 1995 and in Howard Zinn's *A People's History of the United States.* He received the 1999 Local Hero Award from the *San Francisco Bay Guardian,* was Resister of the Year in 1995, and received the 2006 Advocate of the Year Award from the Arizona Coalition to End Homelessness. He has been maintaining the Food Not Bombs website since 1994, and he continues to revise its publications.

Catherine Morris was born in 1934 and grew up in Pasadena, California, where she attended parochial schools. After graduating from UCLA, she taught for a few years in a Los Angeles public school. Subsequently, she was associated with a religious community for fourteen years and taught in its elite schools. After a social justice conversion that was inspired by work with the United Farm Workers, she began her thirty-five years with the Catholic Worker Movement. She continues to work among the poor while advancing causes of peace and justice. This work has led to thirty arrests for civil disobedience and many short jail sentences. Her most noteworthy arrest was in 1973 with the United Farm Workers, when she was arrested on the picket line with Dorothy Day, the founder of the Catholic Worker Movement, and spent two weeks in jail with Day and hundreds of farmworker women.

By day, *Benjamin Shepard* works as an assistant professor of human services at New York City College of Technology, City University of New York. By night, he has battled to keep New York City from becoming a giant shopping mall. To that end, he has done organizing work with the AIDS Coalition to Unleash Power (ACT UP), SexPanic!, Reclaim the Streets New York, Time's Up, the Clandestine Rebel Clown Army, the Absurd Response Team, CitiWide Harm Reduction, Housing Works, the More Gardens Coalition, and the Time's Up Bike Lane Liberation Front and Garden Working Groups. He is also the author or editor of five books: *White Nights and Ascending Shadows: An Oral History of the San Francisco AIDS Epidemic* (Cassell, 1997), *From ACT UP to the WTO: Urban Protest and Community Building in the Era of Globalization* (Verso, 2002), *Queer Political Performance and Protest* (forthcoming, Routledge), *Play, Creativity, and Social Movements* (forthcoming, Routledge), and *Community Projects as Social Activism* (forthcoming, Sage).

James Tracy is a longtime antipoverty activist and organizer based in the San Francisco Bay Area. He cofounded the Eviction Defense Network and is a board member of the San Francisco Community Land Trust. His articles have appeared in *Race, Poverty and the Environment*, *Shelterforce*, *Contemporary Justice Review*, *Maximum Rock and Roll*, and *The Political Edge*. He has edited two activist handbooks for Manic D Press: *The Civil Disobedience Handbook: A Brief History and Practical Guide for the Politically Disenchanted* and *The Military Draft Handbook: A Brief History and Practical Guide for the Curious and Concerned*. When not organizing, he opens his big mouth as part of the Molotov Mouths Outspoken Word Troupe.

Freeman Wicklund was born in 1973 and raised in Eugene, Oregon. He has been active in the animal-protection community for more than two decades and has founded several university groups and community nonprofits. His efforts helped provide Lakeville High School students with alternatives to dissection, helped eliminate dog labs at the University of Minnesota, and generated a government report that details the harms caused to farmed animals, a report that will be used to shape the agricultural policy of Minnesota. He started the open rescue movement in the United States by organizing the first open rescue at an egg facility in 2001, and he has trained other groups to conduct their own rescues. Wicklund also has a diverse history of helping people. He has helped English language learners practice their English, tutored middle school students, promoted Habitat for Humanity, participated in peer mentoring, and lobbied his high school alma mater to start a gay-straight alliance. Wicklund currently lives in the Columbus, Ohio, area. He enjoys camping, the outdoors, triathlons, Toastmasters, reading, and dancing.

Notes

NOTES TO THE PREFACE

1. Alain Mabanckou, *African Psycho* (Brooklyn, NY: Soft Skull, 2003), 3, 29.

2. Rebecca Klatch, *A Generation Divided: The New Left, the New Right, and the 1960s* (Berkeley: University of California Press, 1999), 10–11.

3. Kathleen M. Blee and Verta Taylor, "Semi-Structured Interviewing in Social Movement Research," in *Methods of Social Movement Research,* ed. Bert Klandermans and Suzanne Staggenborg (Minneapolis: University of Minnesota Press, 2002), 92–117.

4. See, for example, Beverly Yuen Thompson, "The Global Justice Movement's Use of 'Jail Solidarity' as a Response to Police Repression and Arrest: An Ethnographic Study," *Qualitative Inquiry* 13 (2007): 141–159.

NOTES TO CHAPTER 1

1. Peter Singer, *Democracy and Disobedience* (Oxford, UK: Clarendon, 1973), v.

2. Howard Zinn, *Disobedience and Democracy: Nine Fallacies on Law and Order* (Cambridge, MA: South End, 2002), 3.

3. Louis Waldman, "Civil Rights—Yes: Civil Disobedience—No (A Reply to Dr. Martin Luther King)," in *Civil Disobedience: Theory and Practice,* ed. Hugo Adam Bedau (New York: Pegasus, 1969), 109.

4. Zinn, *Disobedience and Democracy,* 56–57.

5. Ibid., 60.

6. Ibid., 12.

7. Herbert J. Gans, "The Ghetto Rebellions and Urban Class Conflict," *Urban Riots: Violence and Social Change* (New York: Vintage, 1969), 45–54.

8. Gene Sharp, *The Politics of Nonviolent Action: Part One—Power and Struggle* (Boston: Porter Sargent, 1973), 183–214.

9. Peter Ackerman and Jack Duvall, *A Force More Powerful: A Century of Nonviolent Conflict* (New York: Palgrave, 2000), 2.

10. Donatella Della Porta and Mario Diani, *Social Movements: An Introduction* (New York: Blackwell, 2006), 166.

11. Eric Hoffer, *The True Believer* (New York: Harper & Row, 1989), 9.

12. Matthew Robinson, "Wither Criminal Justice? An Argument for a Reformed Discipline," *Critical Criminology* 10:2 (2001): 97–106.

13. Charles Tilly, Louise Tilly, and Richard Tilly, *The Rebellious Century, 1830–1930* (Cambridge, MA: Harvard University Press, 1975).

14. Frances Fox Piven and Richard A. Cloward, *Poor People's Movements: Why They Succeed, How They Fail* (New York: Vintage Books, 1979).

15. William A. Gamson, *The Strategy of Social Protest* (Homewood, IL: Dorsey, 1975), 28–37.

16. For a quick overview of the contributions of civil disobedience to democracy, see Kayla Starr, "The Role of Civil Disobedience in Democracy," adapted by Bonnie Blackberry, available online at www.civilliberties.org/sum98role.html (accessed February 28, 2007).

17. Christian Bay and Charles C. Walker, *Civil Disobedience: Theory and Practice* (Montreal: Black Rose Books, 1975), 13.

18. Zinn, *Disobedience and Democracy*, 22.

19. Crimethinc., "You May Already Be an Anarchist," *Fighting for Our Lives* (Atlanta: Crimethinc.), 2002. See also Crimethinc., *Days of War, Nights of Love: Crimethink for Beginners* (Atlanta: Crimethinc., 2001), 40.

20. Michael [Mikhail] Bakunin, *God and the State* (New York: Dover, 1970), 33.

21. Peter Kropotkin, *Mutual Aid: A Factor of Evolution* (Montreal: Black Rose Books, 1989), 229.

22. Bakunin, *God and the State*, 32, 35.

23. Emma Goldman, *Anarchism and Other Essays* (New York: Dover, 1969), 52.

24. Peter Kropotkin, *Act for Yourselves* (London: Freedom Press, 1998), 32.

25. Carl Nolte, "Homeless Shelters Fill Up Fast as Cold Snap Hits," *San Francisco Chronicle,* December 21, 1993, A1.

26. Crimethinc., "Glossary of Terms," *Rolling Thunder: An Anarchist Journal of Dangerous Living* 2 (Winter 2006): 4.

27. Crimethinc., *Recipes for Disaster: An Anarchist Cookbook* (Olympia, WA: Crimethinc., 2004), 22.

28. Henry David Thoreau, "On the Duty of Civil Disobedience," in *The Civil Disobedience Handbook,* ed. James Tracy (San Francisco: Manic D Press), 13.

29. Martin Luther King, Jr., "Letter from Birmingham City Jail," in *Revolution and the Rule of Law,* ed. Edward Kent (Englewood Cliffs, NJ: Prentice-Hall, 1971), 19.

30. Émile Durkheim, *Moral Education* (Mineola, NY: Dover, 1971), 53.

31. Ibid.

32. David F. Greenberg, *Crime and Capitalism: Readings in Marxist Criminology* (Philadelphia: Temple University Press, 1993), 666–671.

33. Richard Quinney, *Class, State, Crime* (New York: Longman, 1980), 104.

34. George Vold, *Theoretical Criminology* (New York: Oxford University Press, 1958), 203–219.

35. Donald Black, "Crime as Social Control," *American Sociological Review* 48:1 (February 1983): 41.

36. Ibid., 34, quoting Sally Falk Moore, "Legal Liability and Evolutionary Interpretation: Some Aspects of Strict Liability, Self Help and Collective Responsibility," in Max Gluckman, *The Allocation of Responsibility* (Manchester: Manchester University Press, 1972), 51–107.

37. Jeff Ferrell and Clinton Sanders, *Cultural Criminology* (Boston: Northeastern University Press, 1995), ix.

38. Ibid., 3–21.

39. Keith J. Hayward, *City Limits: Crime, Consumer Culture and the Urban Experience* (Portland, OR: Glasshouse, 2004), 9; emphasis added.

40. Mikhail Bakhtin, *Rabelais and His World* (Bloomington: Indiana University Press, 1984).

41. Emma Goldman, *Living My Life* (Bloomington: Indiana University Press, 1984), 56.

42. Ken Knabb, *Situationist International Anthology* (Berkeley, CA: Bureau of Public Secrets, 1995), 4.

43. Abbie Hoffman, *Revolution for the Hell of It!* (New York: Thunder's Mouth, 2005), 9.

44. Benjamin Shepard, "Absurd Responses vs. Earnest Politics," *Journal of Aesthetics and Protest* 1:2 (2003): 102.

45. Ibid., 97.

46. Mike Hudema, *An Action a Day Keeps Global Capitalism Away* (Toronto: Between the Lines, 2004), 8.

47. Stephen Duncombe, *Dream: Re-imagining Progressive Politics in an Age of Fantasy* (New York: New Press, 2007), 46.

48. Jack Katz, *Seductions of Crime* (New York: Basic Books, 1988), 311.

49. Jeff Ferrell, *Tearing Down the Streets: Adventures in Urban Anarchy* (New York: Palgrave, 2001), 136.

50. Mike Presdee, *Cultural Criminology and the Carnival of Crime* (New York: Routledge, 2002), 31–56.

51. Albert Cohen, *Delinquent Boys* (New York: Free Press, 1971), 59; emphasis in original.

52. Jeff Ferrell, *Empire of Scrounge* (New York: New York University Press, 2006), 170.

53. Kate Donnelly, *Handbook for Nonviolent Action* (New York: War Resisters League, 1995), 8.

54. Alexander Cockburn, Jeffrey St. Clair, and Allan Sekula, *Five Days That Shook the World: Seattle and Beyond* (New York: Verso, 2000), 52.

55. Hal Bernton, "Even Activists Surprised by Protest Success," *Oregonian,* December 12, 1999, A1.

56. Judd Slivka and Robert L. Jamieson, Jr., "Party Time for the Protesters: Buoyant Evening Isn't Shared by Somber Delegates," *Seattle Post-Intelligencer,* December 4, 1999, A6.

57. Cockburn, St. Clair, and Sekula, *Five Days That Shook the World,* 113.

58. Ibid., 67.

59. Nancy Chang and the Center for Constitutional Rights, *The Silencing of Political Dissent: How the USA Patriot Act Undermines the Constitution* (New York: Open Media Pamphlet Series, 2001), 3.

NOTES TO CHAPTER 2

1. C. Wright Mills, *The Power Elite* (New York: Oxford University Press, 1968), 170.

2. Edwin Sutherland, *White Collar Crime* (New York: Holt, Rinehart, and Winston, 1961), 46.

3. Herbert Schiller, *Culture, Inc.: The Corporate Takeover of Public Expression* (New York: Oxford University Press, 1989), 174.

4. Joseph E. Stiglitz, *Globalization and Its Discontents* (New York: Norton, 2003), 3–22.

5. Bill Bigelow and Bob Peterson, introduction to *Rethinking Globalization: Teaching for Justice in an Unjust World,* ed. Bill Bigelow and Bob Peterson (Milwaukee, WI: Rethinking Schools, 2002), 15.

6. Abigail Goldman and Nancy Cleeland, "The Wall-Mart Effect: An Empire Built on Bargains Remakes the Working World," *Los Angeles Times,* November 23, 2003, A1; David Moberg, "The Wal-Mart Effect: The Hows and Whys of Beating the Bentonville Behemoth," *In These Times,* June 10, 2004, www.inthesetimes.com/article/774/the_walmart_effect/.

7. Benjamin Shepard and Ronald Hayduk, *From ACT UP to the WTO* (New York: Verso, 2002), 197–201; Bill Bigelow and Bob Peterson, "Ten Arguments against the World Trade Organization," in *Rethinking Globalization* (see note 6), 105–107.

8. Bigelow and Peterson, "Ten Arguments," 105–107.

9. See Coleman McCarthy, *I'd Rather Teach Peace* (New York: Orbis Books, 2002).

10. Holly Sklar, Laryssa Mykyta, and Susan Wefald, *Raise the Floor: Wages and Policies That Work for All of Us* (Cambridge, MA: South End, 2002), 9.

11. Unless otherwise indicated, all statistics on poverty and wages are from *Income, Poverty, and Health Insurance Coverage in the United States: 2004* (Washington, DC: Government Printing Office, 2005).

12. Sklar, Mykyta, and Wefald, *Raise the Floor.*

13. The Sentencing Project, "Facts about Prisons and Prisoners," December 2006, www.sentencingproject.org.

14. All statistics on presidential elections and the makeup of Congress are from Charles Lewis and the Center for Public Integrity, *The Buying of the President 2004* (New York: HarperPerennial, 2004).

15. Lewis et al., *Buying of the President 2004*, 472.

16. David Croteau and William Hoynes, *The Business of Media* (Thousand Oaks, CA: Pine Forge, 2001).

17. Robert W. McChesney, "September 11 and the Structural Limitations of US Journalism," in *Journalism after September 11*, ed. Barrie Zelizer and Stuart Allan (New York: Routledge, 2002), 91–100.

18. Editorial, *Chicago Sun Times*, September 11, 2001, 30; W. J. Broad, "Protect Sharks? Attack Fuels Old Argument," *New York Times*, September 11, 2001, F1; Carla M. "Democrats Size Up 'Condit Country,'" *San Francisco Chronicle*, September 11, 2001, A3.

19. James Sullivan, "Radio Employee Circulates Don't Play List," *San Francisco Chronicle*, September 18, 2001, E1.

20. McChesney, "September 11 and the Structural Limitations," 94.

21. Herbert I. Schiller, *Culture Inc.: The Corporate Takeover of Public Space* (New York: Oxford University Press, 1991), 96.

22. John Delaney, "Art Wants Corporations: Corporations Want Art," and Richard Meyer, "After the Culture Wars," *Adbusters* 61 (September–October 2005).

23. For information on private contractors in Iraq, see www.corpwatch.org and Pratap Chatterjee, *Iraq Inc.: A Profitable Occupation* (New York: Seven Stories, 2004); for information about the privatization of prisons, see Nils Christie, *Crime Control as Industry* (New York: Routledge, 2000).

24. Thomas Frank and Matt Weiland, *Commodify Your Dissent* (New York: Norton, 1997), 31.

25. Sigmund Freud, *Civilization and Its Discontents* (New York: Norton, 1989), 49–50.

26. Ibid.

27. My discussion of such concepts as *authority, autonomy,* and *power,* as well as my discussion of the limitations of democracy, borrows generously from Robert Paul Wolff's *In Defense of Anarchism* (Berkeley: University of California Press, 1998). Wolff's book constitutes a major influence on my political thinking and thus forms a theoretical underpinning of this text.

28. Wolff, *In Defense of Anarchism*, 4.

29. Ibid., 4.

30. Ibid., 23.

31. Sanderson Beck, *Nonviolent Action Handbook* (Ojai, CA: World Peace Communications, 2003), 48.

32. Wolff, *In Defense of Anarchism*, 42.

33. Jean-Jacques Rousseau, *The Social Contract* (New York: Penguin, 1968), 141.

34. Robert Cover, "Violence and the Word," in *Narrative, Violence and the Law: The Essays of Robert Cover,* ed. Martha Minow, Michael Ryan, and Austin Sarat (Ann Arbor: University of Michigan Press, 1992), 203, 224.

35. Austin Sarat, *Law, Violence, and the Possibility of Justice* (Princeton, NJ: Princeton University Press, 2001), 3.

36. Crimethinc., *Days of War, Nights of Love: Crimethink for Beginners* (Atlanta: Crimethinc., 2001), 34.

37. For a typology of anarchist thought, see Paul Avrich, *The Anarchists in the Russian Revolution* (Ithaca, NY: Cornell University Press, 1973). For a discussion of libertarian anarchism, see Richard Kostelanetz, *Political Essays* (Brooklyn, NY: Autonomedia, 1999).

38. Jeffrey H. Reiman, *In Defense of Political Philosophy: A Reply to Robert Paul Wolff's "In Defense of Anarchism"* (New York: Harper & Row, 1972), xxxii.

39. Robert A. Dahl, *Democracy and Its Critics* (New Haven, CT: Yale University Press, 1989), 50.

40. David Graeber, *Fragments of an Anarchist Anthropology* (Chicago: Prickly Paradigm, 2004), 39.

41. Chris Crass, "Beyond Voting: Anarchist Organizing, Electoral Politics and Developing Strategy for Liberation," *Clamor Communique* 42, available online at http://clamormagazine.org/communique/.

42. Henry David Thoreau, "On the Duty of Civil Disobedience," in *The Civil Disobedience Handbook,* ed. James Tracy (San Francisco: Manic D Press), 13.

43. Gene Sharp, *The Politics of Nonviolent Action: Part One—Power and Struggle* (Boston: Porter Sargent, 2000); see also Erich Fromm, *Escape from Freedom* (New York: Avon Books, 1969).

44. Albert Camus, *The Rebel* (New York: Vintage, 1991), 16.

45. Alain Touraine, *The Voice and the Eye: An Analysis of Social Movements* (New York: Cambridge University Press, 1980), 61.

46. Eric Hoffer, *The True Believer* (New York: Harper & Row, 1989), 7–9.

47. Hans Toch, *The Social Psychology of Social Movements* (Indianapolis: Bobbs-Merrill, 1965), 26.

48. Donatella Della Porta and Mario Diani, *Social Movements* (New York: Blackwell, 2006), 119.

NOTES TO CHAPTER 3

1. Sophocles, *Antigone* (New York: Oxford University Press, 1998), 18.

2. Ibid., 5.

3. Plato, "The Apology of Socrates," in *Civil Disobedience: A Casebook,* ed. Curtis Crawford (New York: Thomas Y. Crowell, 1973), 8.

4. Ibid., 31.

5. "The Gospel According to Mark," in *Civil Disobedience* (see note 3), 47.

6. Curtis Crawford, ed., *Civil Disobedience* (see note 3), 36.

7. The debate over whether such tactics as sabotage, vandalism, property destruction, and self-defense qualify as nonviolent actions is one that is seemingly never ending. For a defense of property crime as nonviolent action, see Gene Sharp, *The Politics of Nonviolent Action—Part Three: The Dynamics of Nonviolent Action* (Boston: Porter Sargent, 1973), 608–611; for a justification of property crime and self-defense as nonviolent actions, see Amory Starr, "'. . . (Excepting Barricades Erected to Prevent Us from Peacefully Assembling)': So-Called 'Violence' in the Global North Alterglobalization Movement," *Social Movement Studies* 5:1 (May 2006): 61–81; see also David and X of the Green Mountain Anarchist Collective, *The Black Bloc Papers* (Baltimore: Black Clover, 2002), 16, 47–53.

8. Richard B. Gregg, *The Power of Nonviolence* (London: James Clarke, 1960), 43–51.

9. Sophocles, *Antigone*, 17.

10. Saul D. Alinsky, *Rules for Radicals* (New York: Vintage, 1989), 128.

11. Crawford, *Civil Disobedience*, 36–37.

12. Ibid., 37.

13. Gene Sharp, *The Politics of Nonviolent Action: Part One—Power and Struggle* (Boston: Porter Sargent, 1973), 7.

14. Quoted in ibid., 11.

15. Michael Foucault, *Power: Essential Works of Foucault, 1954–1984*, ed. James D. Faubion, trans. Robert Hurley et al. (New York: New Press, 2000), 317.

16. Ibid., 326–348.

17. Stanley Milgram, *Obedience and Authority* (New York: Harper & Row, 1974), 124.

18. Erich Fromm, *Escape from Freedom* (New York: Avon, 1969), 18, 157–230.

19. Mahatma Gandhi, *All Men Are Brothers* (New York: Continuum, 2002), 132.

20. Gregg, *Power of Nonviolence*, 43–51.

21. Eric Hoffer, *The True Believer* (New York: Harper & Row, 1989), 11.

22. Crawford, *Civil Disobedience*, 37.

23. Elliot M. Zashin, *Civil Disobedience and Democracy* (New York: Free Press, 1972), 105–148.

24. Ibid.

25. Ibid.

26. Christian Bay and Charles C. Walker, *Civil Disobedience: Theory and Practice* (Montreal: Black Rose Books, 1975), 16.

27. Zashin, *Civil Disobedience and Democracy*, 105–148. See also Bay and Walker, *Civil Disobedience*, 16.

28. Howard Zinn, *Disobedience and Democracy: Nine Fallacies on Law and Order* (Cambridge, MA: South End, 2002), 46.

29. Medea Benjamin, "Window-Smashing Hurt Our Cause," *San Francisco Bay Guardian*, December 15, 1999, www.sfbayguardian.com/news/34/11/ogtomb.html.

30. Francis A. Schaeffer, *A Christian Manifesto* (Westchester, IL: Crossway Books, 1982), 74, 118, 120.

31. Michelle Goldberg, *Kingdom Coming: The Rise of Christian Nationalism* (New York: Norton, 2007), 39–40.

32. Laurence H. Tribe, *Abortion: The Clash of Absolutes* (New York: Norton, 1992), 139–160.

33. Leonardo Boff and Clodovis Boff, *Salvation and Liberation* (Maryknoll, NY: Orbis Books, 1984), 4.

34. Leonardo Boff and Clodovis Boff, *Introducing Liberation Theology* (Maryknoll, NY: Orbis Books, 1987), 28.

35. Gustavo Gutierrez, quoted in Christopher Rowland, *The Cambridge Companion to Liberation Theology* (New York: Cambridge University Press, 1999), 2.

36. Roger Haight, S.J., *An Alternate Vision: An Interpretation of Liberation Theology* (New York: Paulist Press, 1985), 19.

37. Jeff Dietrich, "Biblical Anarchism and the Catholic Worker," *Catholic Agitator* (April 2007): 1–2.

38. Gary Blasi and the UCLA School of Law Fact Investigation Clinic, *Policing Our Way Out of Homelessness? The First Year of the Safer Cities Initiative on Skid Row* (Los Angeles: UCLA School of Law Fact Investigation Clinic, 2007).

39. Boff and Boff, *Introducing Liberation Theology*, 49–50.

40. Murray Edelman, *The Symbolic Use of Politics* (Urbana: University of Illinois Press, 1972), 5. See also Stephen Duncombe, *Dream: Re-imagining Progressive Politics in an Age of Fantasy* (New York: New Press, 2007), 28–50.

41. Peter Marshall, *Demanding the Impossible: A History of Anarchism* (London: Fontana, 1992), 551–553; Raoul Vaneigem, *The Revolution of Everyday Life* (London: Rebel, 2003), 185.

42. Images of the work of the Billboard Liberation Front can be accessed at www.billboardliberation.com.

43. Crimethinc., *Recipes for Disaster: An Anarchist Cookbook* (Olympia, WA: Crimethinc., 2004), 42.

44. War Resisters League, "History of War Tax Resistance" and "How to Resist War Taxes," www.warresisters.org.

45. Willard Gaylin, *In the Service of Their Country: War Resisters in Prison* (New York: Universal Library, 1970), 3.

46. Crimethinc., *Recipes for Disaster*, 162–177.

47. Peter Ackerman and Jack Duvall, *A Force More Powerful: A Century of Nonviolent Conflict* (New York: Palgrave, 2000), 311.

48. Ibid., 357.

49. Gene Sharp, *The Politics of Nonviolent Action: Part Two—The Methods of Nonviolent Action* (Boston: Porter Sargent, 1973), 228.

50. Critical Art Ensemble, Internet homepage, www.critical-art.net. See also Critical Art Ensemble, *Electronic Civil Disobedience* (New York: Autonomedia, 1996).

51. Michael Albert, *The Trajectory of Change: Activist Strategies for Social Transformation* (Cambridge, MA: South End, 2002), x.

52. Ibid., 9.

53. Ibid.

NOTES TO CHAPTER 4

1. Stefan C. Friedman, "'RAD' Alert at Convention," *New York Post*, April 9, 2004, 2.

2. Patrice O'Shaughnessy, "Fury at Anarchist Convention Threat," *New York Daily News*, July 12, 2004, 6.

3. Michael Wilson, "Police Show They're Ready for Convention Disorder," *New York Times*, August 20, 2004, B1; Philip Messing, "Cops Drill to Rein in Rally Rowdies," *New York Post*, August 20, 2004, 8.

4. Michele McPhee, "Finest Get RNC-Ready," *New York Daily News*, August 20, 2004, 25.

5. New York Civil Liberties Union, *Rights and Wrongs at the RNC* (New York: NYCLU, 2005).

6. Alex S. Vitale, "From Negotiated Management to Command and Control: How the New York Police Department Polices Protests," *Policing & Society* 15:3 (2005): 283–304.

7. New York Civil Liberties Union, *Rights and Wrongs at the RNC*, 17.

8. Ibid., 19–20.

9. Ibid., 22.

10. Clark McPhail, David Schweingruber, and John McCarthy, "Policing Protest in the United States: 1960–1995," in *Policing Protest*, ed. Donatella Della Porta and Herbert Reiter (Minneapolis: University of Minnesota Press, 1998), 49–69; Kristian Williams, *Our Enemies in Blue* (Brooklyn, NY: Soft Skull, 2004), 220.

11. Center for Research on Criminal Justice, *The Iron Fist and the Velvet Glove: An Analysis of the U.S. Police* (Berkeley, CA: Center for Research on Criminal Justice, 1975), 17.

12. Howard Zinn, *A People's History of the United States* (New York: Harper Perennial, 1995), 239.

13. Eugene E. Leach, "The Literature of Riot Duty: Managing Class Conflict in the Streets, 1877–1927," *Radical History Review* 56 (1993): 24.

14. Ibid., 24.

15. Zinn, *A People's History*, 244.

16. Quoted in Leach, "Literature of Riot Duty," 39.

17. Ibid., 30

18. Robert J. Donovan and Ray Scherer, *Unsilent Revolution: Television News and American Public Life, 1948–1991* (New York: Cambridge University Press, 1992), 16.

19. National Commission on the Causes and Prevention of Violence—Jerome Skolnick, *The Politics of Protest: Violent Aspects of Protest and Confrontation* (Washington, DC: Government Printing Office, 1969), xix.

20. The Walker Report, National Commission on the Causes and Prevention of Violence, *Rights in Conflict: Chicago's 7 Brutal Days* (New York: Grosset & Dunlap, 1968), vii.

21. The President's Commission on Campus Unrest—William W. Scranton, *Campus Unrest* (Washington, DC: Government Printing Office, 1970), 11.

22. Michel Foucault, *Discipline and Punish: The Birth of the Prison* (New York: Pantheon, 1977), 75.

23. Ibid., 75, 141–146.

24. McPhail, Schweingruber, and McCarthy, "Policing Protest in the United States."

25. Ibid., 52; emphasis added.

26. Foucault, *Discipline and Punish*, 183.

27. Phillipa Strum, *When the Nazis Came to Skokie: Freedom for Speech We Hate* (Lawrence: University Press of Kansas, 1999).

28. Ward Churchill, *Pacifism as Pathology* (Oakland, CA: AK Press, 2007), 62–63; see also Peter Gelderloos, *How Nonviolence Protects the State* (Harrisonburg, VA: Signalfire, 2005).

29. Churchill, *Pacifism as Pathology*, 63.

30. Kristian Williams, *Our Enemies in Blue* (Brooklyn, NY: Soft Skull, 2004), 222.

31. Ibid., 223.

32. Benjamin Shepard and Ronald Hayduk, *From ACT UP to the WTO* (New York: Verso, 2002), 38.

33. Associated Press, "AIDS Protesters-as-Santas at Macy's," *New York Times*, November 30, 1991, A22.

34. Martin Crutsinger, "WTO Struggles for Compromise," Associated Press Online, December 2, 1999.

35. American Civil Liberties Union, *Out of Control: Seattle's Flawed Response to Protests against the World Trade Organization* (Seattle: American Civil Liberties Union of Washington, June 2000).

36. Nils Christie, *Crime Control as Industry* (New York: Routledge 2000), 124.

37. John A. Noakes, Brian V. Klocke, and Patrick F. Gillham, "Whose Streets? Police and Protester Struggles over Space in Washington, DC, 29–30 September 2001," *Policing & Society* 15:3 (September 2005): 235–254.

38. Cheryl Simrell King and Camilla Stivers, "Citizens and Administrators: Roles and Relationships," in *Public Administration and Society*, ed. Richard C. Box (New York: M. E. Sharpe, 2004), 280.

39. Quoted in Philip S. Foner, *Fellow Workers and Friends: I.W.W. Free-Speech Fights as Told by Participants* (Westport, CT: Greenwood, 1981), 125.

40. Alfred Tucker, as quoted in Foner, *Fellow Workers and Friends*, 141.

41. Quoted in ibid., 125.

42. Quoted in ibid., 17.

43. Paul Buhle and Nicole Schulman, *Wobblies: A Graphic History of the Industrial Workers of the World* (New York: Verso, 2005), 120.

44. Ron Kurtus, "When Cops Were Pigs," School for Champions website, February 10, 2006, www.school-for-champions.com/history/cops_pigs.htm.

45. Anarchist Action Collective, *Bring the War Home! Volume 1: Forgotten Heros [sic]—The Black Liberation Army and the Weather Underground* (Eugene, OR: Anarchist Action Collective), 10.

46. Robert Amsel, "A Walk on the Wild Side of Stonewall," *Advocate*, September 15, 1987, http://www-2.cs.cmu.edu/afs/cs/user/scotts/ftp/bulgarians/stonewall.txt.

47. Green Mountain Anarchist Collective, *The Black Bloc Papers* (Baltimore: Black Clover, 2002), 16.

48. "Punch Cops in the Face . . . and Get Away with It," *Rolling Thunder: An Anarchist Journal of Dangerous Living* (Summer 2005): back cover.

49. Max Weber, *From Max Weber: Essays in Sociology* (New York: Oxford University Press, 1946), 228.

50. The Seattle Police Department, *The Seattle Police Department After Action Report: World Trade Organization Ministerial Conference*, April 4, 2000, 7–8.

51. Eric Hoffer, *The True Believer* (New York: Harper & Row, 1989), 26.

52. Kenneth Keniston, *Young Radicals: Notes on Committed Youth* (New York: Harcourt, Brace & World, 1968).

53. Irving Louis Horowitz and William H. Friedland, *The Knowledge Factory: Student Power and Academic Politics in America* (Carbondale: Southern Illinois University Press, 1972), 8.

54. Russell J. Dalton, *Citizen Politics: Public Opinion and Political Parties in Advanced Industrial Democracies* (Washington, DC: CQ Press, 2006), 71.

55. For example, for an early study on minority status and attitudes toward police, see David H. Bayley and Harold Mendelsohn, *Minorities and the Police: Confrontation in America* (New York: Free Press, 1969). For a more recent study that examines the interaction between race and neighborhood status, see Ronald Weitzer, "Citizens' Perceptions of Police Misconduct: Race and Neighborhood Context," *Justice Quarterly* 16:4 (1999): 819–846.

56. Harold D. Laswell, *National Security and Individual Freedom* (1950; New York: Da Capo, 1971), 23.

57. Ibid., 27–31.

58. David Cole, "The Course of Least Resistance: Repeating History in the War on Terrorism," in *Lost Liberties: Ashcroft and the Assault on Personal Freedom*, ed. Cynthia Brown (New York: New Press, 2003), 15.

59. Howard Zinn, *Declarations of Independence* (New York: HarperCollins, 1990), 206.

60. "Summary of H.R. 3162, the USA PATRIOT Act," in *The Civil Disobedience Handbook*, ed. James Tracy (San Francisco: Manic D Press, 2002), 63–64.

61. Nancy Chang, "How Democracy Dies: The War on Our Civil Liberties," in *Lost Liberties: Ashcroft and the Assault on Personal Freedom*, ed. Cynthia Brown (New York: New Press, 2003), 40.

62. Quoted in Patty Reinert, "Experts Fear Net Ensnarls Liberties: Privacy at Stake as Proposal Faces a Vote This Week," *Houston Chronicle*, October 7, 2001, A1.

63. "A Nation Challenged: The Immigrants: As Dragnet Continues, Citizenship Filings Rise," *New York Times*, January 1, 2002, A14.

64. "Fight to Retain Our Rights," *Oakland Tribune*, January 4, 2002, editorial.

65. Tim McGlone, "FBI Tried to Link PETA to Terror Groups," *Virginian Pilot*, December 22, 2005, B1.

66. Ryan J. Foley, "University and Four Peace Activists Subpoenaed over Anti-war Demonstration," Associated Press, February 7, 2004.

67. Ted Bridis, "ACLU Says FBI Misuses Terror Powers to Track Political Groups," Associated Press, December 20, 2005.

68. U.S. Senate, Committee on the Judiciary, *Misuse of Patriot Act Powers: The Inspector General's Findings of Improper Use of the National Security Letters by the FBI* (Washington, DC: Government Printing Office, 2007), 2.

NOTES TO CHAPTER 5

1. Liz Highleyman, "Scenes from the Battle of Seattle," posted online at www.black-rose.com, November 30, 1999; see also "world trade organization protests rock seattle! First-Hand Report from the Battle Lines From Combined shadow Sources," posted online at www.morc.info/MORC_Seattle.html, December 1999.

2. Susan Saulny, "Lawyers Flood the Courts, but Demonstrators Trickle In," *New York Times*, September 2, 2004, 10.

3. Robert D. McFadden, "Vast Anti-Bush Rally Greets Republicans in New York," *New York Times*, August 30, 2004, 1; Patrick Healy and Susan Saulny, "Demonstrators Held at Pier 57 Complain of Conditions and Long Waits," *New York Times*, August 31, 2004, 12.

4. Saulny, "Lawyers Flood the Courts."

5. Julia Preston, "Judge Keeps City on Notice over Convention Protest Arrests," *New York Times*, September 10, 2004, B3.

6. New York Civil Liberties Union, *Rights and Wrongs at the RNC: A Special Report about Police and Protest at the Republican National Convention* (New York: NYCLU, 2005), 7.

7. Fyodor Dostoevsky, *Memoirs from the House of the Dead* (New York: Oxford University Press, 2001), 16.

8. Eugene V. Debs, *Walls and Bars: Prisons and Prison Life in the "Land of the Free"* (Chicago: Charles H. Kerr, 2000), 132.

9. Eldridge Cleaver, *Soul on Ice* (New York: Dell, 1968), 43.

10. Mumia Abu-Jamal, *Live from Death Row* (New York: Avon Books, 1996), 53-54.

11. Gregory J. McMaster, "Maximum Ink," in *Writing as Resistance: The Journal of Prisoners on Prisons Anthology (1988–2002)*, ed. Bob Gauche (Toronto: Canadian Scholars Press, 2002), 64.

12. Commission on Safety and Abuse in America's Prisons, *Confronting Confinement: Summary Findings and Recommendations* (New York: Vera Institute of Justice, 2006), 1–2.

13. Eugene Tong and Charles F. Bostwick, "Inmate Killed in Pitchess Riot: Violence Occurs along Racial Lines," *Daily News of Los Angeles,* February 6, 2006, N3.

14. Daniel B. Wood, "Behind L.A. Jail Clashes: Rising Pressures," *Christian Science Monitor,* February 15, 2006, 3.

15. William J. Sabol, Todd D. Minton, and Paige M. Harrison, "Prison and Jail Inmates at Midyear 2006," *Bureau of Justice Statistic Bulletin* (Washington, DC: Government Printing Office, June 2007), 7.

16. Commission on Safety and Abuse in America's Prisons, *Confronting Confinement*, 29.

17. Kate Donnelly, *Handbook for Nonviolent Action* (New York: War Resisters League, 1995), 12.

18. Starhawk, "Coming Out of Jail Stronger," available online at www.starhawk.org/activism/trainer-resources/comingoutofjail2.html; Starhawk, "Organizing in Jail," available online at www.starhawk.org/activism/trainer-resources/organizinginjail.html.

19. Sanderson Beck, *Nonviolent Action Handbook* (Ojai, CA: World Peace Communications, 2003), 81.

20. Sharif Durhams, "Horowitz Placing New Ads; 'Anti-war' Demonstrations Sabotage Nation's Defense, Commentator Suggests," *Milwaukee Journal Sentinel,* September 29, 2001, 2B.

21. H. Bruce Franklin, *Prison Literature in America: The Victim as Criminal and Artist* (New York: Oxford University Press, 1989), 242.

22. Raymond Arsenault, *Freedom Riders: 1961 and the Struggle for Racial Justice* (New York: Oxford University Press, 2006), 140–176.

23. Donnelly, *Handbook for Nonviolent Action*, 16.

24. Beck, *Nonviolent Action Handbook*, 74.

25. Frances Olsen, "Legal Responses to Mass Protest Actions: The Dramatic Role of Solidarity in Obtaining Generous Plea Bargains," *Osgoode Hall Law Journal* 41:2–3 (2003): 363–369.

26. Ibid.

27. John Wiener, *Conspiracy in the Streets: The Extraordinary Trial of the Chicago Eight* (New York: New Press, 2006), 1–41.

28. Ibid., 24.

29. Elliot M. Zashin, *Civil Disobedience and Democracy* (New York: Free Press, 1971), 110.

30. Dana Priest, "U.S. Instructed Latins on Executions, Torture: Manuals Used 1982–91, Pentagon Reveals," *Washington Post*, September 21, 1996, A1.

31. Barrie Paskins, "Nuremberg Principles," in *World Encyclopedia of Peace*, ed. Ervin Laszlo and Jong Youl Yoo (New York: Pergamon, 1986), 117.

32. "Principle IV," General Assembly Resolution 177, United Nations, November 21, 1947.

33. Beck, *Nonviolent Action Handbook*, 83.

34. Ibid., 84.

35. International Committee of the Red Cross, "Landmines and International Humanitarian Law," http://www.icrc.org/web/eng/siteengo.nsf/htmlall/section_ihl_landmines.

36. Mark Lanier and Stuart Henry, *Essential Criminology* (Boulder, CO: Westview, 2004), 317–321.

37. National Lawyers Guild—Los Angeles, "Questions and Answers about Civil Disobedience and the Legal Process," available online at www.nlg-la.org/cd_questions.pdf.

38. Ibid., 1.

NOTES TO CHAPTER 6

1. Marco Giugni, Doug McAdam, and Charles Tilly, preface to *How Social Movements Matter*, ed. Marco Giugni, Doug McAdam, and Charles Tilly (Minneapolis: University of Minnesota Press, 1999), xi.

2. Bert Klandermans and Suzanne Staggenborg, preface to *Methods of Social Movement Research*, ed. Bert Klandermans and Suzanne Staggenborg (Minneapolis: University of Minnesota Press, 2002), ix.

3. William A. Gamson, *The Strategy of Social Protest* (Homewood, IL: Dorsey, 1975), 28.

4. Gene Sharp, *The Politics of Nonviolent Action: Part Two—The Methods of Nonviolent Action* (Boston: Porter Sargent, 1973), 705; Kate Donnelly, *Handbook for Nonviolent Action* (New York: War Resisters League, 1995), 29.

5. Carol Weiss, *Evaluation: Methods for Studying Programs and Policies* (Upper Saddle River, NJ: Prentice Hall, 1998), 24.

6. Ibid., 25.

7. Guy Debord, "For a Revolutionary Judgment of Art," in *Situationist International Anthology*, ed. Ken Knabb (Berkeley, CA: Bureau of Public Secrets, 2006), 396.

8. Jeff Ferrell, *Tearing Down the Streets: Adventures in Urban Anarchy* (New York: Palgrave, 2001).

9. Howard Becker, *Outsiders: Studies in the Sociology of Deviance* (New York: Free Press, 1991), 34.

10. Donatella Della Porta and Mario Diani, *Social Movements: An Introduction* (New York: Blackwell, 2006), 114–134.

11. Crimethinc., *Recipes for Disaster: An Anarchist Cookbook* (Olympia, WA: Crimethinc., 2004), 15.

12. "War against Eco-Terrorists," *Washington Times*, October 7, 2001, B2; Cesar G. Soriano, "Animal Activists Tone It Down," *USA Today*, October 3, 2001, 1D; Paul Tolme, "Real Patriots Don't Go on Witch Hunts," *Denver Post*, November 25, 2001, E4.

13. Joseph Hart, "Protest Is Dead. Long Live Protest. Dump Your Signs and Slogans—It's Time to Make Change," *Utne Reader* (June 2007): 39.

14. Critical Art Ensemble, *Electronic Civil Disobedience and Other Unpopular Ideas* (New York: Autonomedia, 1996), 10.

15. Herbert Marcuse, *One-Dimensional Man* (Boston: Beacon, 1964); *Counter-Revolution and Revolt* (Boston: Beacon, 1972).

16. William D. Hartung and Frida Berrigan, "Top Pentagon Contractors, FY 2006: Major Beneficiaries of the Bush Administration's Military Buildup," (New York: World Policy Institute, 2007), 1.

17. Theodore Roszak, *The Making of a Counter Culture* (Berkeley: University of California Press, 1995), 8.

18. Joseph Heath and Andrew Potter, *Nation of Rebels: Why Counterculture Became Consumer Culture* (New York: HarperBusiness, 2004), 13–35.

19. Thomas Frank, "Why Johnny Can't Dissent," in *Commodify Your Dissent: The Business of Culture in the New Gilded Age*, ed. Thomas Frank and Matt Weiland (New York: Norton, 1997), 34.

20. Heath and Potter, *Nation of Rebels*, 13–35; Frank, "Why Johnny Can't Dissent," 31–45.

21. Heath and Potter, *Nation of Rebels*, 19.

22. Stanley Milgram, Obedience to Authority (New York: Harper & Row, 1974), 178.

23. Unabomber (a.k.a. FC), "Industrial Society and Its Future," in *Against Civilization*, ed. John Zerzan (Eugene, OR: Uncivilized Books, 1999), 118–119.

24. Murray Bookchin, *Social Anarchism or Lifestyle Anarchism: An Unbridge-able Chasm* (San Francisco: AK Press, 1995), 4.

25. Ibid., 2, 34.

26. Mark Andersen, *All the Power: Revolution without Illusion* (Chicago: Punk Planet Books, 2004), 73–93.

27. Bookchin, *Social Anarchism*, 12.

28. Jeff Ferrell and Clinton R. Sanders, *Cultural Criminology* (Boston: Northeastern University Press, 1995), 313.

Index

Abu-Jamal, Mumia, 143–44
Ackerman, Peter, 6,
affinity groups, 27, 34, 55
affordable housing activism, 62, 126, 184, 193–95
AIDS Coalition to Unleash Power (ACT UP), 116–17
Albert, Michael, 102
Alinsky, Saul, 68
Alliance for Better Campaigns, 36
AlliantACTION, 22, 180, *181*
Alliant Techsystems, 22, 165–66, 170, 193
American-Arab Anti-Discrimination Committee, 135
American Civil Liberties Union (ACLU), 134–35; and the New York Civil Liberties Union, 107, 142
anarchism/anarchy, 10–16, 48–50, 52–53, 63, 81–82; biblical, 81–82; social versus lifestyle, 202–4
Andersen, Mark, 203–4
animal rights activism, 2, 55–58, 150, 164, 198
anti-abortion activism: as biblical obedience 77, 79–80; as direct action, 74; and effecting change, 192, 194; and the Hyde Amendment, 96; and police, 125; as a religious issue, 50–52, 58–60; as spectacle, 91; and stigmatization of dissenters, 187; as

tax resistance 41–43. *See also* pro-life "rescues"
Antigone, 65–69, 71–73, 75
apartheid (South Africa), 100
arrest, 67, 74–75, 90, 92, 106, 108; impact on families, 188; mass arrests, 114; at the Republican National Convention (2004), 104, 139–42; and social support, 189–90; and stigmatization of dissenters, 187–88; as a strategy for media attention, 183–185; at the World Trade Organization (1999) protests, 118
Artaud, Antonin, 24
authority, 43–48
autonomy, 43–53, 202–3
Avrich, Paul, 49

bail, 75, 171
Bakhtin, Mikhail, 23
Bakunin, Mikhail, 12, 68, 186
banner drops, 91–92
Barfield, Ellen, 98, 123, 139, 173, 179, 185
bearing witness, 74–75, 111
Beck, Sanderson, 60, 76–77, 98, *100*, 158, 163–64, *167*, 192
Becker, Howard, 187
Benham, Flip, *50*, 50–51, 77–80, 98, 148–49, 151, 187, 192, 194
Benjamin, Medea, 76
Billboard Liberation Front, *91*, 91–92

Billionaires for Bush, 25

Black, Donald, 18–19

Black Bloc anarchists, 10, 76, 117, 122, 126, 183

Black Liberation Army, 121

Black Panther Party, 122

blockades: and animal rights activism, 56, 164; and anti-abortion activism, 50–52, 74–75, 98, 125; and military recruitment centers, 98; 164; and munitions delivery, 98, 167; at the World Trade Organization (1999), 28–29, 34

Bly, Robert, 176

"Bob," 41–43, 45, 63, 96–97, 194–95

Boff, Leonardo and Clodovis, 80

Bookchin, Murray, 202–4

Boston Tea Party, 10, 73

boycotts, 99–102

"broken windows theory," 13, 82

Camus, Albert, 54–58

carnival, 2, 23–26, 68, 92

Catholic Worker Movement, 59, 81, 97, 135, 171, 193. *See also* Los Angeles Catholic Worker

Center for Public Integrity, 36–37

charges: as felonies, 170; as infractions or violations, 142, 157, 170; as misdemeanors, 170

Chicago Eight, 159–61, 167

Christ, Jesus, 6, 16, 66–69, 71–73

Christianity, 33, 59, 78–81, 192

Christie, Nils, 118

Churchill, Ward, 115

civil disobedience, viii; as blockades, 98; as contempt of court, 92–93; defined, 72–78, 83–85; as direct actions, 93–94; as draft resistance, 97–98; as economic noncooperation, 98–101; objections to, 2–7; as sit-ins, 88–90; as symbolic actions, 85–86;

as tax resistance, 94–97; as trespassing, 86–88. *See also* crimes of dissent

civil liberties, 111, 131–37, 140

Civil Rights Movement, 9, 54; and bearing witness, 111; and civil disobedience, 64; and effecting change, 192; and the Freedom Rider Movement, 152; and nonviolence, 68; and participant demographics, 129; and police use of force, 111

Cleaver, Eldridge, 143–44

Clemens, Steve, 75, 78, 150–51, 161–163, 165–66, 168, 190

Cloward, Richard, 8

Coalition on Revival, 79

Cockburn, Alexander, 29–30

Code Pink for Peace, 76, 91–92

Cohen, Albert, 26

Cold War, 118–19, 131

Commission on Safety and Abuse in America's Prisons, 144–45

consensus decision-making, 44–45

contempt of court. *See* civil disobedience

corporations, vii, 31–32, 35–38

Counter-Intelligence Program, FBI (COINTELPRO), 106, 132, 206

Cover, Robert, 47–48

Crass, Chris, 49–50

crime/criminal behavior, 3, 5–6, 17–20, 25–26, 39, 48, 54, 60, 205

crimes of dissent, 2, 65; and anarchism, 14; and collective behavior, 27; as culture and counterculture, 198–202; and humor, 102; post September 11, 24; as pure crime, 65–69; and social change, 8–9; as spectacle, 90–92, 102; and violence, 6; and virtue, 65, 67–69. *See also* civil disobedience

criminology/criminal justice, viii, 7, 25, 206; conflict, 17–18;

critical/radical, 17–18; cultural, 19–28, 43, 52, 205–6
Critical Art Ensemble, 101–2, 199
Critical Mass Movement, 21, 26, 92
crowd control strategies, 30; militarized policing, 115–20; negotiated management, 112–116; plainclothes police officers, 106; police display of force, 111; police use of force, 109–12, 117; provocateurs, 106; protest marshals (peacekeepers), 113, 115; protest zones (metal barricade "pens"), 104–8, 112, 114, 117–18; surveillance, 106, 112, 114, 118–119; visible police presence, 109

Dahl, Robert, 49
Dalton, Russell J., 129
Davidov, Marv, 151–53, *178*, 177–80
Davis, Rennie. *See* Chicago Eight
Day, Dorothy, 6, 81, 193
Debord, Guy, 182
Debs, Eugene V., 143
Declaration of Independence, 63–64
Delgado, Sharon, 33–35, 60, 94, 108, 127, 129–30, 145
Della Porta, Donatella, 6
Dellinger, Dave. *See* Chicago Eight
democracy, 3–5, 17; as majority rule, 45–48; representative, 46–47; unanimous direct, 44–46
detournement, 90–91
Diani, Mario, 6
Dietrich, Jeff, 1, 59–60, *60*, *61*, 82, *84*, 97, 169, 196–98
direct action, viii, 2, 6, 47, 62, 74, 93–101; and policing strategies, 115–16
Donnelly, Kate, 175
Dostoevsky, Fyodor, 143
draft resistance, 17, 41, 62–63, 97–98
Drake University, 135

Durkheim, Emile, 16–17
Duvall, Jack, 6

economic noncooperation, 98–101
Edelman, Murray, 85
elections, 36–37, 40, 47, 52. *See also* voting
Engels, Friedrich, 17
environmental activism, 2, 31, 33–34, 56, 116, 195, 198

fear, 71–72
Federal Bureau of Investigation (FBI), 132, 135, 195
Ferrell, Jeff, 19, 25–26, 205
fines, 157
First Amendment rights, 30, 38, 47, 86–88, 111–15, 120–21, 134, 171. *See also* civil liberties; permits
Food Not Bombs, 12–15, 93, 195
Foucault, Michel, 70–71, 112–13, 118, 146
Frank, Thomas, 39
Franklin, H. Bruce, 151
Freedom Rider Movement, 151–53, 177
free trade, 28, 33–34
Freud, Sigmund, 39–43
Froines, John. *See* Chicago Eight
Fromm, Erich, 71

Gamson, William, 8, 178
Gandhi, Mohandas, 6, 9, 68, 71, 166, 193
Gardner, David, 158, 188
Gaylin, Willard, 97
gender, 7, 54
Giuliani, Rudolph, 88
globalization, 28, 30–31, 33–36, 116–17, 195
Goldman, Emma, 12, 24
Gospel According to Mark, 66–69, 75

Graeber, David, 49
graffiti, 25
Gregg, Richard, 68
Greenpeace, 135, 198
Guerilla Theater, 24, 101

Harris v. McRae, 96
Hayden, Tom. *See* Chicago Eight
Heath, Joseph, 201
Hedemann, Ed, 40–41, 45, 62–64,
    94–96, 108, 126, 153, 191, 194–95
Hennacy, Ammon, 15
Hoffer, Eric, 7, 58, 128
Hoffman, Abbie, 24, 159, 169. *See also*
    Chicago Eight; Youth International
    Party (Yippies)
Hoffman, Julius, 160
homelessness, 1, 12–14, 19, 83, 171–72
Honeywell Project, 175–77, 193
hunger strikes, 9; while incarcerated,
    157–58
Hyde Amendment, 96

incarceration rates, 36, 39, 72
individualism, 10–12, 39–40, 71,
    202–4
Industrial Workers of the World
    (IWW), 8–9, 120–21
International Monetary Fund (IMF),
    32
Iraq War, viii, ix, 5, 21, 23, 35, 38, 77,
    89–90, 182

jail/prison, 129; and differential treat-
    ment, 149–50; and harm to the
    human spirit, 143–44; physical
    violence and overcrowding, 144–45;
    protesters' assessment of guards,
    148–49, 153; psychological control
    and humiliation, 146–50, 153–54; as
    a transformative experience, 151–53
jail solidarity, 142, 154–58

Jim Crow laws, 9, 15, 74, 151–52, 192
judges, 168–69, 172
jury nullification, 165

Kaczynski, Theodore (Unabomber),
    202
Katz, Jack, 25
Keniston, Kenneth, 128
King Jr., Martin Luther, 6, 15, 111
Kostelanetz, Richard, 49
Kropotkin, Peter, 11–12
Kunstler, William, 160

La Boetie, Etienne de, 70
labor struggle/workers' rights, 8, 17,
    33, 35, 101, 195, 199–200; and po-
    lice, 109–10, 117, 120–21
Lacassagne, Alexandre, 31
Lasswell, Harold, 131
law, interpretation of, 47–48, 52
law enforcement. *See* police
legal defenses. *See* necessity defense;
    Nuremberg Principles
Lewis, John, 9
Lewis, Martha, 82, *89*
liberation theology, 78–83
lockboxes, 98
Los Angeles Catholic Worker, 1,
    59–60, 82–83, *84*, 129, 156, 184–85,
    187–88, 193, 196. *See also* Catholic
    Worker Movement
Los Angeles Police Department
    (LAPD), 82–83, 155–56
Lungo, Sharon, 21, 130–31, 198

Mabanckou, Alain, viii
Mandela, Nelson, 204–5
marches and rallies, 9, 94; non-permit-
    ted/illegal, 21, 25, 74, 86–88, 104,
    107, 141
Marcuse, Herbert, 199–200, 203
martyrdom, 48, 69, 75, 83, 111

Marx, Karl/Marxism, 17, 80, 199
mass media, 31, 37–38, 85–86, 89–90,
    92, 111; and coverage of dissent,
    182–86, 196–97
Maurin, Peter, 81
McHenry, Keith, 12–15, *15*
Milgram, Stanley, 71, 201
military spending, 13, 35, 95
Miller, Judith, 93
Mills, C. Wright, 31–32
Montgomery bus boycott (Alabama),
    99–100
moral jiu-jitsu, 68
Morris, Catherine, 148–49

Nash, Diane, 152
National Guard, 110, 117
National Lawyers Guild, 169
National Socialist Party of America,
    114–15
necessity defense, 77, 161–67
Nevada Nuclear Test Site, ix, 21, 86,
    87, *147*
New York Police Department
    (NYPD), 103–8, *105*, *107*, 111, *119*,
    122–123, *136*, 140
New York Times Square, 88
noncooperation, 6–7, 73–74, 92–94,
    97, 154–58. *See also* economic
    noncooperation
nonviolence, 6, 67–68, 124
North American Free Trade Agree-
    ment (NAFTA), 29, 116
nuclear disarmament, 20–21, 56, 58,
    86, 165, 179–80, 192
Nuremberg Principles, 161–67

obedience, 71–72; and biblical obedi-
    ence, 77–83
O'Brien, David, 76
Operation Rescue, 79, 96
Operation Save America, 50, *51*, 125

Parks, Rosa, 99
People for the Ethical Treatment of
    Animals (PETA), 135
permits, 74, 86–88, 104, 113–14
picket lines, 9, 109, 176, 195. *See also*
    marches and rallies
Pier 57, 139–42, *140*, 144
Piven, Francis Fox, 8,
Plato: *Apology*, 66–67, 72, 75; *Crito*,
    72–73
plea bargaining, 75, 168, 170
pleas: as "guilty," 170; as "not guilty,"
    163–64, 168–70
pleasure of resistance, 20–26, 146–47,
    173, 198, 205–6
Ploughshare's Movement, 76
police, 17, 47–48, 75–76, 82; and crowd
    incitement, 111; and police violence,
    119, 126–27; and protester opinions,
    120–127, 129; and protest-policing
    reform, 111–13; and training for
    nonviolent direct action, 127. *See
    also* crowd control strategies
political campaign contributions,
    31–32, 36–37, 39
Potter, Andrew, 201
poverty, 6, 10, 35–36, 55, 80, 151, 200
power, political, 43–44, 53, 67, 69–72, 113
Presdee, Mike, 26
prisoners, 70
privatization, 31, 33, 38–39
probation. *See* punishment
pro-life "rescues," 51; during the
    1980s,79–80; and effecting change,
    192, 194; and police, 125; and stig-
    matization of dissenters 187
property destruction, 8, 10, 17–18,
    28–29, 73, 76; at the World Trade
    Organization (1999), 117, 122, 183
prosecution, 18, 170–73
protesters, characteristics of, viii, xi,
    53–64, 127–31, 187–89, 198

protest zones, 30
public opinion, 102, 193
punishment: as community service,
    157–58; as fines, 156–57, 170–71;
    as jail, 171–72; as probation, 157,
    171–72; as work camp, 158. *See also*
    Appendix for descriptions of vari-
    ous punishments
"pure" crime, 65–69. *See also* crimes
    of dissent

race/ethnicity, 5, 18–19, 35–36, 54,
    127–31; and jail/prison, 149, 172;
    and jail solidarity, 154–56; and
    justice, 172–73. *See also* protesters,
    characteristics of
Radical Cheerleaders, 24–25
Raging Grannies, 1, 89–90, *90*, 182–
    83, 185
Railroad Strikes of 1877, 9, 109–10
raising social cost, 101–2
Reclaim the Streets, 26, 92, 137
Reiman, Jeffrey, 49
rent-withholding (rent strikes), 8,
    100–101
Republican National Convention
    (2004), ix, 21, 103–8, 122–23, ar-
    rests at, 104–8, 139–42
Reverend Billy and the Church of Stop
    Shopping, 101
riots, 5, 54–55
Robinson, Matthew, 7
Roszak, Theodore, 199–200
Rousseau, Jean Jacques, 45–47
Rubin, Jerry, 176. *See also* Chicago Eight

Sanders, Clinton, 19, 205
Schaeffer, Francis, *A Christian Mani-
    festo*, 78–79
Schiller, Herbert, 32
School of the Americas (SOA), viii, 75,
    149–50, 161–62; SOA Watch, 189

Seale, Bobby. *See* Chicago Eight
Seattle protests. *See* World Trade Orga-
    nization Seattle protests
Seattle Police Department (SPD), 116,
    118, 127
segregation, 99, 151, 177, 192. *See also*
    apartheid (South Africa); Jim Crow
    laws
Sekula, Allan, 29–30
self-representation (pro se), 168
Sentencing Project, 36
September 11, 2001, 24, 37–38, 118,
    132, 136–37, 149, 188, 198, 206
sexual orientation, 7, 54
Sharp, Gene, 6
Shepard, Benjamin, 24, 55, 87–89, 103,
    122–23, 137, 170
Shepard, Matthew, 87–88
sick-outs, 101
sit-ins, 6, 28–29, 74–75, 88–92, 184
Situationist International (Situation-
    ists), 24, 90–91, 102
Skid Row (Los Angeles), 82–84
slavery, 4, 8, 14–15, 70, 95, 120
slowdown strikes, 101
social change, 3, 6–7, 69; and struc-
    tural resistance, 199–201
social justice, 7, 16
socioeconomic status, 5, 17–19, 54,
    127–31; and jail/prison, 149, 171–72;
    and jail solidarity, 154–56; and jus-
    tice, 172–73; and prosecution, 172.
    See also protesters, characteristics of
Socrates, 16, 66–69, 71–73
Sophocles, 65, 75
spectacle, 90–92, 102, 182
squatting, 25
Starhawk, 146–47
St. Clair, Jeffrey, 29–30
Stonewall Riots, 122
strikes, 8–9, 17, 101, 109–10
Strossen, Nadine, 135

subculture, 19, 26–27
"success" of protests, 8, 10, 29–30, 102;
  as community-building, 186–91;
  difficulties in assessment, 178–81;
  as effecting change, 191–198; as
  media publicity, 182–86
surveillance. *See* crowd control strategies; USA Patriot Act
Sutherland, Edwin, 32

tax resistance, 1, 94–97; and Thoreau,
  14–15, 74; as an anti-abortion
  strategy, 43; as an anti-war strategy,
  40–41; as domestic terrorism, 134;
  and effecting change, 194; and raising social cost, 102
terrorism, 104, 118–19; domestic,
  132–34, 198
Thoreau, Henry David, 14–15, 40, 52,
  74, 95, 171, 191, 202
Tilly, Charles, 7–8
Toch, Hans, 59
Touraine, Alain, 54–55
Tracy, James, 61–62, 126–27, 184, 193, 195
trespassing, 21, 86–88, 176
trials, 77, 158, 159–61; as public fo-
  rums, 161, 163–64, 169

UCLA School of Law Fact Investiga-
  tion Clinic, 82–83
Universal Declaration of Human
  Rights, 162
USA Patriot Act, 30, 132–137
U.S. Supreme Court, 51, 86, 96, 100,
  115, 143, 194

vandalism. *See* property destruction
Vaneigem, Raoul, 90
"Veronica," 20, 56–58, 124, 149, 151,
  156–57, 171, 193
Vietnam War, 41, 54, 60, 62–63, 76,
  96–97

Villaraigosa, Antonio, 82, *84*
violence, 6–7, 47–48, 67–68, 71–72, 76
Vold, George, 17
voting, 3–5, 7–8, 36–37, 40, 47, 52,
  63, 78

war/anti-war activism, 5–6, 12–14, 20,
  30, 51
War on Terror, 30. *See also* September
  11, 2001
War Resisters League (WRL), 42, 95,
  106–8, 139
Weathermen/Weather Underground,
  121
Weber, Max, 124
Weiner, Lee. *See* Chicago Eight
Weiss, Carol, 180–81
Western Hemisphere Institute for Se-
  curity Cooperation (WHINSEC).
  See School of the Americas (SOA)
Wicklund, Freeman, 56, *57*, 150, 157–
  58, 164, 168, 171–72
Williams, Kristian, 116
Wobblies. *See* Industrial Workers of
  the World (IWW)
Wolf, Josh, 93
Wolff, Robert Paul, 43–47
women's suffrage, 4, 9, 64, 180
World Economic Forum, 183–84
World Trade Organization Seattle
  protests, viii, 10, 28–35, 98, 116–18;
  arrests, 139, 157; critiques of police
  response, 126–27; and jail solidarity, 157; and media coverage, 117,
  183

Yes Men, 101
Youth International Party (Yippies),
  24, 91, 102, 121, 159, 169

Zerzan, John, 202
Zinn, Howard, 5, 10, 19, 76

About the Author

JARRET S. LOVELL is Associate Professor of Politics, Administration, and Justice at California State University, Fullerton, and author of *Good Cop/Bad Cop: Mass Media and the Cycle of Police Reform*.